D1570585

Whistleblowers

Founded in 1807, John Wiley & Sons is the oldest independent publishing company in the United States. With offices in North America, Europe, Asia, and Australia, Wiley is globally committed to developing and marketing print and electronic products and services for our customers' professional and personal knowledge and understanding.

The Wiley Corporate F&A series provides information, tools, and insights to corporate professionals responsible for issues affecting the profitability of their companies, from accounting and finance to internal controls and performance management.

Whistleblowers

Incentives, Disincentives, and Protection Strategies

FREDERICK D. LIPMAN

WILEY

John Wiley & Sons, Inc.

Published by John Wiley & Sons, Inc., Hoboken, New Jersey.
Published simultaneously in Canada.

For general information on our other products and services or for technical support, please contact our Customer Care Department within the United States at (800) 762-2974, outside the United States at (317) 572-3993 or fax (317) 572-4002.

Wiley also publishes its books in a variety of electronic formats. Some content that appears in print may not be available in electronic books. For more information about Wiley products, visit our web site at www.wiley.com.

Library of Congress Cataloging-in-Publication Data:

Lipman, Frederick D.
  Whistleblowers : incentives, disincentives, and protection strategies / Frederick D. Lipman.
    p. cm. — (Wiley corporate F&A series)
  Includes index.
  ISBN 978-1-118-09403-7 (hardback); ISBN 978-1-118-16848-6 (ebk);
  ISBN 978-1-118-16857-8 (ebk); ISBN 978-1-118-16858-5 (ebk)
  1. Whistle blowing—United States. 2. Business ethics—United States.
  3. Whistle blowing—Law and legislation—United States. 4. Whistle blowing—
Case studies. I. Title.
  HD60.5.U5L57 2012
  344.7301′2598—dc23

                                                                      2011029141

Printed in the United States of America

10 9 8 7 6 5 4 3 2 1

To my grandchildren,
Tyler Keith Lipman and Jordan Sienna Lipman

Other Works by Frederick D. Lipman

Contents

PART IV: STATUTORY INCENTIVES AND SEC AWARD REGULATIONS

Foreword

by Dr. Gaytri D. Kachroo, Esq.

A FEW YEARS AGO, the term "whistleblower" called to mind odd and sporadic anecdotes about one or two courageous individuals who dared confront and expose wrongdoing within political and corporate halls. However, two events over the last few years have overhauled whistleblowing into an industry, capable of diverse creative frameworks and modeling of the kind I am engaged in with my plethora of whistleblowing clients and incentivized by a burgeoning regulation encouraging reform and a new form of internal audit that is discussed in detail in the pages you are about to turn. These two events are the exposure of the Madoff fraud by Harry Markopolos and Julian Assange's WikiLeaks. Markopolos's testimony before the House Finance Committee in large part fueled the new whistleblower legislation, part of the Dodd-Frank Reform Act, analyzed in this book, and WikiLeaks is touted by many to have catalyzed the popular political uprisings throughout the Middle East. Each event marks major changes in the global transition to greater transparency and accountability of financial and political institutions.

When Madoff gave up his immense fraudulent endeavor on December 11, 2008, he sealed not only his own fate but also that of Harry Markopolos, the shadow that had chased him for almost a decade alongside his stellar team of fraud fighting detectives, Frank Casey, Neil Chelo, and Michael Ocrant, and persisted in blowing the whistle about Madoff to the U.S. Securities and Exchange Commission. I was privileged to join that team in 2005 as the attorney for Harry's new business, when he decided that fraud fighting through whistleblowers would become his life's work. It is therefore fitting and a great honor to introduce this text by Fred Lipman to the world, as it becomes clearer than ever before that rules and regulations relating to whistleblowing are changing, becoming ever-pervasive and affecting a multitude of industries. Without doubt, there is an added need to consult texts that simply and clearly explicate these reforms and also the background for these changes.

Fred Lipman in this text claims that had the independent directors of Enron, WorldCom, and Lehman "established a robust whistleblower mechanism . . . they might have been able to obtain the information necessary to prevent these scandals." (See Chapter 7.) Too often, senior management and boards in public and private companies insulate themselves from information to their own detriment. In addition to the risks and exposure to shock, scandal, illegal activity, and the liability inherent in such endeavors underscored by Lipman, these directors may find corporate misdealing exposed on sites such as WikiLeaks now, if greater internal transparency and compliance measures supporting whistleblowers are not adopted.

Step by step, as a wise and learned guide, Mr. Lipman takes us through the legislation and institutional frameworks allowing whistleblowers a voice. He asserts and attempts to change the current notion in corporate boardrooms that the whistleblower is the company's enemy and not a best friend. In his systematic approach, Mr. Lipman demonstrates the possibility of an aligned company policy to reward and successfully protect corporate interests through public and private schemes incentivizing whistleblowers. He highlights the large penalties paid by such pharmaceutical companies as GlaxoSmithKline to the U.S. government on the basis of a whistleblower complaint triggered to protect the public. He also summarizes, in an easy-to-read fashion for attorneys, corporate compliance officers, and whistleblowers alike, whistleblower protections, incentives, and complaint submission procedures of the Dodd-Frank Reform Act of July 2010 as well as other statutes. Combining policy and regulatory analysis in this one text provides a powerful message to U.S. corporations to seriously overhaul their compliance measures and use the best practices necessary to create internal informants protected by management, who can in turn advise management of internal wrongdoing and oust perpetrators.

I encourage you to begin this journey into whistleblowing law. From stories of outstanding whistleblowers, analysis of the Dodd-Frank reforms, and other whistleblowing statutes including those relating to the Internal Revenue Service, to best practices in dealing with whistleblowers, to providing whistleblowers with appropriate forms to submit information to the SEC, Fred Lipman leaves no stone unturned in his A-to-Z account of whistleblower law in the United States.

Dr. Kachroo is a contributing author of No One Would Listen, *by Harry Markopolos.*

Acknowledgments

THE AUTHOR wishes to acknowledge the assistance of these attorneys at Blank Rome LLP in preparing this book: Jennifer L. Bell, Esq.; Jeanne M. Grasso, Esq.; Joseph Gulant, Esq.; Anthony B. Haller, Esq.; Joseph G. Poluka, Esq.; and W. Scott Simmer, Esq. Several of my partners, including Richard H. McMahon, Esq., and David Gitlin, Esq., properly challenged me on some of the recommendations made in this book and helped me to sharpen my own thinking. My partners do not necessarily agree with all of the statements contained in this book, and I absolve them of any errors that I committed.

Jeffrey M. Taylor, Esq., is the coauthor of Chapter 11 of this book. Jane K. Storero, Esq., was helpful in reviewing Chapter 1.

I want to thank Eugene C. Fazzie for explaining to me the nature of an effective internal audit process that some public companies have.

Dr. Gaytri D. Kachroo, Esq., a contributor to *No One Would Listen* (John Wiley & Sons, Inc., 2010), who represents Harry Markopolos (the Madoff whistleblower) and other whistleblowers, was kind enough to write a foreword to this book.

The author would also like to thank Kathleen Kirchner, Lynn Bogina, June Polito, and Rosemarie Rao for their help with proofreading the manuscript.

Finally, the author would like to acknowledge the excellent and invaluable service of Barbara Helverson, who served as typist and an editor of this book. Her suggestions and comments were very useful and helpful in the preparation of the book.

Introduction

I once asked a room full of compliance officers if
their company had ever made an internal whistleblower "employee of the month" or given them a
raise. The room burst out laughing.

—Patrick Burns, Director of Communications of
Taxpayers Against Fraud Education Fund

B OTH THE FEDERAL GOVERNMENT and many states have statutes
reflecting a public policy that rewards and protects whistleblowers.[1]
None of these statutes requires employee whistleblowers to abide by
internal corporate compliance policies as a condition for receiving the reward,
including the Dodd-Frank Wall Street Reform and Consumer Protection Act
(Dodd-Frank), which became effective in July 2010. Despite these new public
incentives for employee whistleblowing, few companies have reexamined the
effectiveness of their current compliance policies.

Although the Sarbanes-Oxley Act of 2002 mandated that listed public companies establish an anonymous whistleblower policy, some companies have
established good whistleblower policies while many others have created only

1

ineffective paper policies. These public companies have done just the minimum amount required to comply with the law, partly because although some complaints by whistleblowers are legitimate, many are spurious. Many public company whistleblower policies are largely unpublicized, do not provide adequate protection for internal whistleblowers, and afford no meaningful reward or recognition for them. Even the supposedly "good" whistleblower policies provide no meaningful reward or recognition for legitimate employee whistleblowers and use internal auditors or compliance officers to investigate complaints, even though these persons may not be viewed as independent and are not experienced forensic investigators.

Potential internal legitimate whistleblowers face daunting cultural disincentives from their fellow workers, supervisors, and management who ostracize so-called snitches. Most potential internal whistleblowers, including executive-level ones, will not jeopardize their careers without an absolute guarantee of anonymity, a meaningful reward, and an independent investigation of their allegations.

The scandals and financial disasters of the twenty-first century have one thing in common: The independent members of the boards of directors of Enron, WorldCom, and Lehman Brothers Holdings, Inc., among others, were completely surprised by the impending scandal. The primary reason that the board was clueless was because it relied solely on information supplied by top management and incorrectly assumed that the independent or internal auditors would detect illegal activity or major risk exposure. Every scandal, starting with Enron, resulted in a claim that the board was duped by management.[2] Even the most recent disaster involving Lehman resulted in a claim that management withheld key information from the board until immediately before its bankruptcy filing.[3] Had the independent directors of these companies established a robust whistleblower mechanism, as described in this book, they might have been able to obtain the critical information necessary to prevent these scandals.

Whistleblowing works. Indeed, according to the Association of Certified Fraud Examiners (ACFE), tips were the source of information for more than 40 percent of reported instances of occupational fraud.[4] Figure I.1 reflects the fact that tips are more effective in detecting occupational fraud than the collective total of management review, internal audit, and external audit.

Figure I.2 shows that organizations without employee hotlines receive substantially fewer tips.

Unfortunately, most organizations have ineffective hotlines and policies that do not encourage legitimate whistleblowers. Directors and senior executives tend to greatly underestimate the disincentives to the disclosure

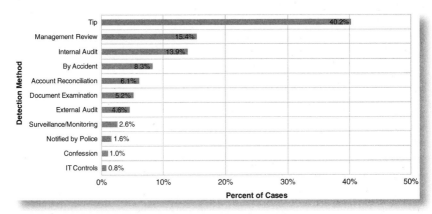

FIGURE I.1 Initial Detection of Occupational Frauds

Source: ACFE, 2010 Global Fraud Study, "Report to the Nations on Occupational Fraud and Abuse," www.acfe.com/rttn/rttn-2010.pdf.

of wrongdoing and have not provided sufficient protection to whistleblowers and adequate rewards for what may be a career-ending decision. Directors and management may incorrectly assume that the lack of hotline reports of illegal activity means that nothing illegal is happening, never appreciating that there is no incentive for employees to use the hotline.

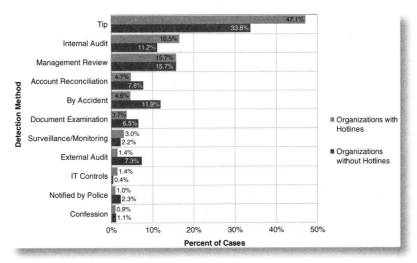

FIGURE I.2 Impact of Hotlines

Source: ACFE, 2010 Global Fraud Study, "Report to the Nations on Occupational Fraud and Abuse," www.acfe.com/rttn/2010-conclusions.asp.

Conscientious directors and CEOs who value their business reputations should insist on an effective whistleblower system, administered by independent counsel or another independent party (an ombudsman)[5] who reports directly to the independent directors. It is time for every organization to stop treating legitimate whistleblowers as pariahs rather than heroes. Good corporate governance practices require a robust, proactive approach by the independent directors to encourage legitimate internal whistleblowing. The system, which is an important internal control, should include meaningful rewards for internal whistleblowers, provide for anonymous reports of both potential law violations and significant risk exposures of the organization, and mandate that independent counsel investigate such reports while providing complete anonymity for whistleblowers to avoid retaliation. An effective whistleblower system would have the internal auditor or director of corporate compliance report directly to the independent directors and become the eyes and ears of those directors within the organization.

Recent media publicity concerning large bounty payments to whistleblowers in the pharmaceutical industry, using private qui tam actions (suits on behalf of the government under the False Claims Act), has heightened the interest in this topic. A few examples are presented next.

In October 2010, Cheryl Eckard, a former GlaxoSmithKline employee, won $96 million, which is believed to be the largest reward ever given to an individual U.S. whistleblower. The award is part of a $750 million settlement the pharmaceutical company paid to settle U.S. government fraud charges over its manufacturing practices in Puerto Rico. Eckard's $96 million may well be increased by bounties paid by various states.

In September 2009, John Kopchinski, a former Pfizer sales representative, earned more than $51 million as a result of a whistleblower lawsuit against Pfizer relating to the company's sales tactics in marketing the pain drug Bextra. Including a criminal fine, Pfizer's settlement in the case totaled $2.3 billion. Five other whistleblowers will earn an aggregate total of over $50 million as their rewards. Kopchinski, a Gulf War veteran who was dismissed by Pfizer after raising his concern in this case, stated: "In the Army I was expected to protect people at all costs. At Pfizer I was expected to increase profits at all costs, even when sales meant endangering lives."[6] The large fines, penalties, and other payments paid by these and other corporations may well have been averted by using best practices described in this book in dealing with the whistleblowers.

In April 2011, the Internal Revenue Service paid a $4.5 million bounty to an anonymous accountant who blew the whistle on his employer, a financial services firm.

These huge awards are not typical. According to the Taxpayers Against Fraud, a nonprofit organization, the median average reward for a whistleblower is about $150,000.[7] In return, these whistleblowers may be socially ostracized, their employment may be terminated, and they will have a hard time getting another job in the same industry. Who wants to hire a snitch? Is it any wonder that no whistleblower system can be effective unless the identity of whistleblowers is fully protected from disclosure?

Incentives to whistleblowers have been increased dramatically as a result of Dodd-Frank and the changes to the Internal Revenue Code in December 2006 mandating whistleblower rewards. Dodd-Frank provides rewards to whistleblowers with respect to violations of the federal securities laws (including the Foreign Corrupt Practices Act), without regard to whether there was any false claim made against the government, and requires the Securities and Exchange Commission (SEC) to create whistleblower rewards, without the necessity of a private qui tam action permitted under the False Claims Act. Dodd-Frank incorporates whistleblower incentives for violations of securities laws by private companies as well as public companies since capital raising by private companies is subject to various provisions of securities laws. The law has expanded the potential for whistleblower bounties enormously.

Many whistleblower complaints are without merit. Some employees blow the whistle on perfectly legal company activities because of a misunderstanding of the facts or the law. Other employees, in an attempt to manipulate the system, decide to blow the whistle when they believe that their employment is about to be terminated. Doing so gives employees the protections of whistleblowers and typically prevents or delays the employment termination. Discovering who is a legitimate whistleblower and who is not is one of the most difficult tasks facing businesses today.

 ## CLASSIFICATION OF WHISTLEBLOWERS

Whistleblowers may be classified in various ways. In this book, the term "internal whistleblower" refers to an employee of an organization who provides information to the organization. If the information is provided to governmental authorities or publicly, the internal whistleblower is regarded as having made a public disclosure. An "external whistleblower" is a nonemployee or ex-employee of the organization who may provide information either to authorities or publicly or to the organization itself.

ORGANIZATION OF BOOK

This book is organized into four parts. Part I (Chapters 1 through 3) discusses identified whistleblowers and the rewards they receive and reviews in detail the dramatic expansion of whistleblower rewards under Dodd-Frank. Part II (Chapters 4 and 5) discusses the disincentives to internal whistleblowing and the factors that motivate public disclosure by whistleblowers. Part III (Chapters 6 and 7) describes the reasons why boards of directors should adopt robust whistleblower systems and a description of such a system. This is the heart of the book. Part IV (Chapters 8 through 11) contains a review of other statutory incentives to whistleblowing, including Internal Revenue Service (IRS) and state awards and contains a detailed step-by-step guide to SEC whistleblowing awards under Dodd-Frank.

A brief description of the chapters of this book follows.

Chapter 1 discusses the $1 million reward made to Glen and Karen Kaiser by the SEC for providing information on insider trading by Karen's ex-husband. This chapter also provides an introduction to the enormous scope of the new statutory incentives to whistleblowing under Dodd-Frank that were effective in July 2010.

The remarkable story of Cheryl Eckard, the $96 million bounty winner, is detailed in Chapter 2.

Chapter 3 contains the story of the Pfizer whistleblowers who received collectively over $100 million in bounties, out of which John Kopchinski personally received more than $51 million.

The payments to Cheryl Eckard and the Pfizer whistleblowers are all based on provisions of the False Claims Act, a statute that became law in 1863 during the American Civil War and is known as Lincoln's Law. The False Claims Act authorized the U.S. Justice Department to pay awards to those who report fraud against the federal government in an amount ranging from 15 to 30 percent of what is recovered based on the whistleblower's report, subject to certain exceptions.

Chapter 4 analyzes the disincentives to whistleblowers and contains an empirical study of retaliation against whistleblowers.

Chapter 5 discusses why so many women are whistleblowers and the factors motivating employees to make public disclosure to regulators.

Chapter 6 explains why every organization should adopt a more robust whistleblower system. This chapter contains an empirical study of the adverse long-term financial consequences of illegal corporate behavior. A robust whistleblower system will permit the independent directors of a company to obtain information from lower-level executives and employees. This will better enable the directors to detect and prevent corporate wrongdoing and major risk exposures, thereby enabling them to better perform their fiduciary duties. The chapter contains the story of Eugene Park, an AIG executive who, in March 2005, discovered the huge AIG exposure on credit default swaps and whose warning was dismissed by the chief deputy to Joseph Cassano (AIG's executive in charge of swaps). This chapter also reviews the potential civil and criminal liability of the organization and its CEO and directors.

Chapter 7 gives a blow-by-blow account of exactly how an organization can establish a robust whistleblower policy. The chapter begins with an analysis of the deficiencies in the current whistleblower systems established under the Sarbanes-Oxley Act of 2002 (SOX). The chapter also includes a list of major "Dos and Don'ts" for CEOs. This is the most important chapter in the book.

Chapter 8 contains a history of the False Claims Act and the actions that may be brought under that Act, which are called qui tam suits. This chapter also contains a memorandum from the U.S. Department of Justice that provides a brief, general overview of qui tam litigation under the False Claims Act.

Chapter 9 reviews the current IRS bounty program. Unlike the False Claims Act, private litigation is not permitted under this statute. Appendix 1 of this book contains the form (Form 211) for applying for an IRS whistleblower bounty.

Chapter 10 discusses other federal and state statutory incentives and protections for whistleblowers. The state statutory incentives are generally based on provisions similar to the False Claims Act of the federal government. The statutory incentives in certain major states are covered in this chapter.

Chapter 11 contains a detailed review of the SEC's new whistleblower rules proposed under Dodd-Frank. Proposed forms for making SEC whistleblower claims are also discussed in this chapter and are contained in Appendixes 2 and 3 of this book. Appendix 4 contains the SEC's whistleblower rules.

 NOTES

1. Anthony Heyes and Sandeep Kapur, "An Economic Model of Whistle-Blower Policy," *Journal of Law, Economics, & Organization* 25, no. 1; doi:10,1093/jeo/ewim049, advance access publication January 3, 2008; Robert Howse and Ronald J. Daniels, "Rewarding Whistleblowers: The Costs and Benefits of an Incentive-Based Compliance Strategy," University of Pennsylvania, Scholarly Commons, Departmental Papers (School of Law), January 1, 1995.

2. Andrea Redmond and Patricia Crisafulli, *Comebacks: Powerful Lessons from Leaders Who Endured Setbacks and Recaptured Success on Their Terms* (San Francisco: Jossey-Bass, 2010). See also Benson Smith and Tony Rutigliano, "Enron and You—A Lesson for Sales Execs: You Don't Have the Luxury of Invoking the Fifth," *Gallup Management Journal*, February 25, 2011. http://gmj .gallup.com.

3. See "Report of Anton R. Valukas, Examiner," March 11, 2010, pp. 1460–1465.

4. Association of Certified Fraud Examiners, 2010 Global Fraud Study, "Report to the Nations on Occupational Fraud and Abuse." http://www.acfe.com/rttn/ rttn-2010.pdf.

5. The use of an organizational ombudsman was suggested by Francis J. Milliken, Elizabeth W. Morrison, and Patricia F. Hewlin in "An Exploratory Study of Employee Silence: Issues that Employees Don't Communicate Upward and Why," November 4, 2003. http://w4.stern.nyu.edu/emplibrary/Milliken .Frances.pdf.

6. Bill Berkrot, "Pfizer Whistleblower's Ordeal Reaps Big Rewards," Reuters, September 2, 2009.

7. Conversation with Patrick Burns, Director of Communications, Taxpayers Against Fraud Education Fund, based on a review of whistleblower claims on the website: www.taf.org/abouttaf.htm.

PART ONE

The Whistleblowers and the Dodd-Frank Incentives

CHAPTER ONE

The Dramatic Expansion of Whistleblower Awards under Dodd-Frank

O N JULY 23, 2010, the Securities and Exchange Commission (SEC) announced an award of $1 million to Glen Kaiser and Karen Kaiser (formerly Karen Zilkha) of Southbury, CT, for providing information on alleged illegal insider trading in Microsoft Corp. by a hedge fund advisor (Pequot Capital Management, Inc.); its chief executive, Arthur J. Sanberg; and David E. Zilkha. Mr. Zilkha was previously a Microsoft employee who was married to Karen and who accepted an employment offer at Pequot. Karen subsequently married Glen Kaiser, an anesthesiologist. While Pequot was in the process of hiring him, Mr. Zilkha allegedly tipped Pequot and Sanberg about an upcoming earnings report from Microsoft that indicated that the company would beat its earnings target. Sanberg allegedly traded on this inside information, reaping $14.8 million in profits, and the SEC won a judgment (including interest) against Pequot and Sanberg for $17,938,468. Documents in the Zilkhas' divorce proceedings revealed that Pequot agreed to make a $2.1 million payment to David Zilkha several years after his departure from Pequot in November 2001.[1]

How did Karen Kaiser uncover the specific evidence that resulted in her $1 million award? When Karen and David Zilkha divorced, Karen had kept the hard drive from the family's computer because it contained family photos.

During the divorce and child support proceedings, David Zilkha listed a $2.1 million settlement that had never appeared before in any of his affidavits to the court. Karen's attorney searched the hard drive to try to find the origin of the $2.1 million and discovered that the payment came from Pequot. Also on the hard drive were the e-mails from a Microsoft employee to Mr. Zilkha, which indicated that he had advance notice that Microsoft would beat its earnings target. These e-mails were turned over to the SEC, which earlier had closed its investigation of Pequot. On the basis of these e-mails, the SEC decided to reopen the investigation.[2]

The reward to the Kaisers preceded the passage of the Dodd-Frank Wall Street Reform and Consumer Protection Act (Dodd-Frank). Under Dodd-Frank, Glen Kaiser and Karen Kaiser would have received a minimum of 10 percent of the recovery or $1,793,847 to a maximum of 30 percent of the recovery, or $5,381,540. Congress decided that the SEC was not being generous enough to whistleblowers and "mandated" much higher rewards and extended the bounty program beyond illegal insider trading violations to any violation of the federal securities laws. This decision was influenced by the failure of the SEC to uncover the Madoff Ponzi scheme for more than 20 years after investors had been bilked of approximately $65 billion. Dodd-Frank also mandated the payment of such bounties that were "discretionary" prior to its enactment.

The theory for the bounties is that people will not reveal frauds unless there is something in it for them. Laura Goldman, a money manager who claims to have figured out the Madoff fraud in about 45 minutes, justified her not blowing the whistle in this way: "People on Wall Street are not Mother Teresas. They are not going to the S.E.C. unless there is something in it for them."[3]

Harry Markopolos, a quantitative financial analyst, first blew the whistle on Bernard Madoff's multibillion-dollar Ponzi scheme in 2000 and, over the ensuing eight years preceding Madoff's arrest, sent detailed accusations to various SEC offices. Each report met with a thundering silence. Markopolos's investigation started when his bosses at the money management firm he worked for wanted him to design a financial product that was as consistently profitable and low risk as the one offered by Madoff. It took Markopolos only a few minutes to study Madoff's supernaturally consistent rate of return and "investment strategy" to realize it was most likely a fraud.

To get his bosses off his back about creating a similar product, Markopolos had to get the SEC to put Madoff out of business. It is not surprising that the SEC ascribed Markopolos's initial and subsequent accusations to that of a jealous competitor trying to tear down a more successful rival, one who had formerly headed the Nasdaq Stock Market. Markopolos's utterly tone-deaf and repeated requests to be paid a bounty if Madoff's fraud qualified under whistle-blower statutes didn't help his credibility either. Markopolos never received a bounty from the SEC, but he did get a book deal after the Madoff scandal was publicized.[4]

 ## WHISTLEBLOWER PROVISIONS OF DODD-FRANK

Prior to Dodd-Frank and the 2006 amendments to the Internal Revenue Code, whistleblower rewards were pretty much limited to the violations of the False Claims Act, similar state statutes, and miscellaneous other laws described in Chapter 10. The False Claims Act basically required that there be a false claim against a government, such as Medicare or Medicaid fraud.

Dodd-Frank greatly expands the violations for which a whistleblower bounty may be awarded. This chapter reviews the broad scope of Dodd-Frank. The last chapter of this book and Appendixes 2 through 4 describe, in detail, how whistleblowers can obtain rewards under the SEC bounty program man-dated by Dodd-Frank.

Under Dodd-Frank, whistleblowers who provide "original information" (discussed later) leading to a successful enforcement action by a judicial or administrative body under the securities and commodities laws receive not less than 10 percent or more than 30 percent of the total recovery "ordered to be paid" if it is greater than $1 million, including penalties, disgorgement,[5] and interest. The SEC was required to implement whistleblower provisions by rules and regulations described in detail in Chapter 11 of this book.

Thus, the minimum bounty a whistleblower can receive is effectively $100,000. However, the maximum jackpot is enormous. For example, Sie-mens paid $800 million for violation of the Foreign Corrupt Practices Act (FCPA), which is part of the securities laws. Had original information been given to the SEC that led to the recovery from Siemens, the whistleblower could have collected a minimum of $80 million and a maximum of $240 million. That amount is a lot higher than any state lottery normally provides, and the odds are a lot better than the state lottery. Other groundbreaking settlements for violation of the FCPA include a $579 million sanction and disgorgement against Kellogg Brown & Root LLC (part of which was paid by Halliburton Co.), a $365 million payment by Snamprogetti Netherlands B.V. and its parent, and a $185 million payment by Daimler AG.

The drafters of Dodd-Frank believe that the SEC had not been sufficiently generous in the past to whistleblowers. Indeed, it had paid less than $160,000

TABLE 1.1 Bounty Payments to Whistleblowers

Bounty Claimant	Year	Bounty Amount
Claimant 1	1989	$ 3,500
Claimant 2	2001	$ 18,152
Claimant 3	2002	$ 29,079
Claimant 4	2005	$ 17,500
Claimant 4	2006	$ 29,920
Claimant 4	2009	$ 55,220
Claimant 5	2007	$ 6,166
Total		$159,537

Source: Generated by the Office of the Inspector General.

in total since 1989, excluding the $1 million payment to the Kaisers. This poor bounty payment history is illustrated in Table 1.1.[6]

 WHAT IS "ORIGINAL INFORMATION"?

To hit the jackpot under Dodd-Frank, the whistleblower must provide what is called "original information." This means information that:

- Is derived from the independent knowledge or analysis of a whistleblower;
- Is not known to the SEC from any other source, unless the whistleblower is the original source of the information; and
- Is not exclusively derived from an allegation made in a judicial or administrative hearing, in a governmental report, hearing, audit, or investigation, or from the news media, unless the whistleblower is a source of the information.[7]

A potential whistleblower will likely need the assistance of an attorney, preferably one specializing in securities law, to identify what is original information and then submit the information to the SEC. In the Karen Kaiser case, it was an attorney working on her divorce and property settlement who discovered the damaging information.

A whistleblower is not entitled to an award if the whistleblower knowingly and willfully makes any false, fictitious, or fraudulent statement or representation or uses any false writing or document knowing the writing or document contains any false, fictitious, or fraudulent statement or entry. Likewise certain compliance personnel are not eligible, as described more fully in Chapter 11.

WHAT ARE VIOLATIONS OF THE FEDERAL SECURITIES LAWS?

The federal securities laws contain numerous provisions that can be violated and can result in monetary sanctions[8] exceeding $1 million. Keep in mind when reading this chapter that any violation of these provisions resulting in monetary sanctions exceeding $1 million can produce a reward for a whistleblower who provides the SEC with "original information."

Some of the more important provisions and examples of how they have been violated in the past are discussed next.

FCPA Violations

Generally speaking, the Securities Exchange Act of 1934 (1934 Act) makes it illegal for any public company, as well as any officer, director, employee, or stockholder acting on behalf of the company, to pay, promise to pay, or authorize the payment of money or anything of value to:

- Any official of a foreign government or instrumentality of a foreign government;
- Any foreign political party;
- Any candidate for foreign political office; or
- Any person whom the company knows or has reason to know will make a proscribed payment or will promise to make or authorize payment of a proscribed payment

if the purpose is to induce the recipient to: (a) use his or her influence with the foreign government or instrumentality; (b) influence the enactment of legislation or regulation by that foreign government or instrumentality; or (c) refrain from performing any official responsibility, in each case, for the purpose of obtaining or retaining business for or with, or directing business to any person.[9]

In order to fall within the 1934 Act's proscriptions, the payment, or promise or authorization of payment, must be "corrupt"; that is, whether it is legal under the laws of the foreign jurisdiction or not, it must be intended to induce the recipient to use his or her official position for the benefit of the person offering the payment or his client. The 1934 Act prohibits not only the payment of, but also the promise or authorization of, a corrupt foreign payment. Therefore, the law can be violated even if the payment is never in fact made. Since a corrupt payment that is requested by the foreign official (rather than offered to him or her) involves a decision to accede to the request, it is not a defense that the payment was requested. However, payments that are extorted and are made to protect physical assets from capricious destruction are not within the ambit of the 1934 Act. In addition, so-called grease payments (e.g., payments to ministerial or clerical employees of foreign government or agencies, to speed them in the performance of or encourage them to in fact perform their duties) are not prohibited by the 1934 Act.

It is clear that, if authorized, the making of a foreign corrupt payment by a foreign subsidiary of a U.S. company is prohibited by the 1934 Act. Also prohibited are payments to an agent (even one who is not him- or herself subject to the 1934 Act) when it is known or should be known that they will be used to make corrupt payments.

Violations of the corrupt payment provisions of the 1934 Act are punishable by fines and civil penalties against corporations or business entities of up to $2 million ($10,000 civil penalty in an action brought by the SEC). In addition, officers, directors, employees, agents, and shareholders can be fined up to $100,000 (plus a $10,000 civil penalty in an action brought by the SEC) or imprisoned for not more than five years, or both, for violations of the corrupt payment provisions of the 1934 Act. The 1934 Act further provides that fines imposed on an individual violator cannot be paid, directly or indirectly, by the company for whose benefit the bribe was paid or promised.

The FCPA applies to bribes of "any official of a foreign government or instrumentality of a foreign government." In a number of countries, the government is an owner or partial owner of all sorts of ventures. In China, the government is an owner or government officials are owners of what appear to be commercial ventures, and that government ownership creates major issues from an FCPA perspective. For example, in May 2005, a wholly owned Chinese subsidiary of Diagnostic Products Corp. (DPC), a U.S.-based medical equipment firm, pled guilty to criminal charges arising out of approximately $1.6 million in sales "commissions" made by DPC, through its subsidiary, to doctors and laboratory staff employed by state-owned hospitals in China in order to generate business. The doctors and laboratory staff were considered officials of a foreign government or its instrumentality.[10]

The broad scope of the foreign bribe provisions of the FCPA is best illustrated by the next case dealing with travel and entertainment expenses for Chinese foreign officials:

> In *SEC v. Lucent Technologies, Inc.*,[11] the Commission's complaint alleged that over a three year period Lucent, through a subsidiary, paid over $10 million for about 1,000 Chinese foreign officials to travel to the U.S. The SEC concluded that about 315 of the trips had a disproportionate amount of sightseeing, entertainment and leisure. Some of the trips were, in fact, vacations to places such as Hawaii, Las Vegas, the Grand Canyon, Disney World and similar venues. These expenses, for officials Lucent was either doing business with or attempting to do business with, were booked to a factory inspection account. The company failed over the years to provide adequate FCPA training.
>
> To resolve the SEC's case, Lucent consented to an injunction prohibiting future violations of the FCPA books and records provisions. In addition, the company agreed to pay a $1.5 million civil penalty.[12]

Theoretically, an FCPA violation consisting of a significant bribe to a foreign official can produce a double-dip reward for the whistleblower. The whistleblower could receive one reward from the SEC and a second bounty from the Internal Revenue Service if the company improperly deducted the bribe payment for federal income tax purposes. (See Chapter 9.)

Ponzi Schemes

As the SEC defines it, a Ponzi scheme is:

> an investment fraud that involves the payment of purported returns to existing investors from funds contributed by new investors. Ponzi scheme organizers often solicit new investors by promising to invest funds in opportunities claimed to generate high returns with little or no risk. In many Ponzi schemes, the fraudsters focus on attracting new money to make promised payments to earlier-stage investors and to use for personal expenses, instead of engaging in any legitimate investment activity.[13]

Ponzi schemes require a consistent flow of funds from new investors to continue and usually collapse when it becomes difficult to recruit new investors or when old investors want to cash out.

Ponzi schemes are named after Charles Ponzi. In the 1920s, Ponzi convinced thousands of New England residents to invest in a postage-stamp speculation scheme. He promised investors that he could provide a 50 percent return in just 90 days and initially purchased a small number of international mail coupons in support of his scheme. However, Ponzi soon switched to using new funds to pay off earlier investors.[14]

Ponzi schemes can involve substantial amounts of money, as in the case of Madoff, which involved approximately $65 billion. Unfortunately, the fraudster typically cannot pay any significant part of the monetary sanctions imposed by the SEC as a result of the whistleblower's actions. However, as in the Madoff Ponzi scheme, usually other persons who are involved can pay monetary sanctions.

Illegal Insider Trading

The term "illegal insider trading" refers generally to purchasing or selling a security in breach of a fiduciary duty or other relationship of trust and confidence while in possession of material, nonpublic information about the security. Insider trading violations may also include "tipping" such information to third persons, securities trading by the person tipped, and securities trading by those who misappropriate such information.

Examples of insider trading cases that have been brought by the SEC are cases against:

- Corporate officers, directors, and employees who traded the corporation's securities after learning of significant, confidential corporate developments;
- Friends, business associates, family members, and other "tippees" of such officers, directors, and employees, who traded the securities after receiving such information;
- Employees of law, banking, brokerage and printing firms who were given such information to provide services to the corporation whose securities they traded;
- Government employees who learned of such information because of their employment by the government; and
- Other persons who misappropriated, and took advantage of, confidential information from their employers.[15]

It is the SEC's position that the insider trading "undermines investor confidence in the fairness and integrity of the securities markets." Accordingly, the SEC has treated the detection and prosecution of insider trading violations as one of its enforcement priorities.[16]

The Kaisers received their $1 million bounty because Pequot and Sanberg allegedly received and traded on confidential information belonging to Microsoft that was revealed to them by David Zilkha in breach of his fiduciary duty to Microsoft.

RULE 10b-5: MARKET MANIPULATION

Section 10(b) of the 1934 Act and Rule 10b-5 thereunder protect against a wide variety of securities fraud and manipulation. They are the most important provisions of all of the federal securities laws. Ponzi schemes and illegal insider trading, previously discussed, violate these antifraud rules.

However, Rule 10b-5 has a much broader scope and covers the sale or purchase of securities by any persons, whether those securities are publicly traded or not and whether the companies involved are public or private. Hedge funds are increasingly being targeted by the SEC for violating Rule 10b-5 as well as comparable provisions of the Investment Advisors Act of 1940, another securities law subject to bounties under Dodd-Frank.

Rule 10b-5 also covers various forms of market manipulation. For example, in May 2009, the SEC filed securities fraud charges against Pegasus Wireless Corporation and two Pegasus officers who allegedly illegally sold hundreds of millions of Pegasus shares they secretly controlled and lied about the transactions in company filings. The SEC alleged that former CEO Jasper Knabb and former chief financial officer Stephen Durland reaped more than $30 million in illicit profits and used these profits to support their extravagant lifestyles, including the purchase of homes, boats, and sports cars. According to the complaint, Knabb and Durland created Pegasus from a dormant shell company around 2005. They then touted several acquisitions in a series of press releases, causing Pegasus's stock price to soar and briefly giving the company a market capitalization of more than $1.4 billion. Unbeknownst to investors, however, Knabb and Durland are alleged to have secretly controlled through nominees hundreds of millions of Pegasus shares, which they sold to individual investors and dumped on the open market through 2008. Pegasus saw its share price steadily decline to less than a penny.

VIOLATING THE ACCOUNTING STANDARDS

A public company is required by the 1934 Act to:

- make and keep books, records and accounts, which, in reasonable detail, accurately and fairly reflect the transactions and dispositions of the assets of the company; and
- devise and maintain a system of internal accounting controls sufficient to provide reasonable assurance that:
  - transactions are executed in accordance with management's general or specific authorization;
  - transactions are recorded as necessary (a) to permit preparation of financial statements in conformity with generally accepted accounting principles or any other criteria applicable to such statements, and (b) to maintain accountability for assets;
  - access to assets is permitted only in accordance with management's general or specific authorization; and
  - the recorded accountability for assets is compared with the existing assets at reasonable intervals and appropriate action is taken with respect to any differences.[17]

The 1934 Act's requirements with regard to the maintenance of books and records and a system of internal control were enacted largely in response to disclosures that many U.S. corporations had established so-called off-the-book accounts and slush funds. However, they are applicable to all U.S. public companies, whether or not they engage in foreign business or employ slush funds.

It must be borne in mind that the accounting standards imposed by the 1934 Act are directed at the accuracy of the company's books, records, and accounts, not its financial statements. Thus, even though the company has not paid foreign bribes and even though its published financial statements may be accurate in all respects, it could nonetheless be in violation of the 1934 Act if, for example, its books and records improperly characterized the nature of a perfectly legitimate item of expense.

FALSE FINANCIAL STATEMENTS BY PUBLIC COMPANIES

If a public company knowingly provides the public with false financial statements, or files such knowingly false financial statements with the SEC, this violates the 1934 Act, whether or not the company is in compliance with the accounting standards recited above. For example, if an employee or other person, whether employed by the company or not, knows that the company is materially overstating its income and provides original information to the SEC about this practice, and that information ultimately leads to a judicial or administrative order to have the company or its insiders pay more than $1 million, that whistleblower may be entitled to the bounty.

State and Municipal Financings

States and municipalities issue debt securities to finance their operations. These debt securities are accompanied by offering circulars, prospectuses, or other marketing materials that are subject to the antifraud provisions of federal securities laws. For example, the SEC charged the State of New Jersey with securities fraud for misrepresenting and failing to disclose to investors in billions of dollars' worth of municipal bond offerings that it was underfunding the state's two largest pension plans, the Teachers' Pension and Annuity Fund and the Public Employees' Retirement System.[18]

Private Company Violations

The antifraud provisions of the 1934 Act apply to the issuance of stock or other securities by private companies. For example, if a private company raises $10 million in private equity and it can be proven that the company knowingly made material misstatements, that is a violation of the 1934 Act and is subject to the bounty provision.

Private companies can also violate the FCPA either directly or by assisting a public company to do so. Although the U.S. Department of Justice can enforce the FCPA against a private company, the SEC could have jurisdiction to name the private company as an aider and abettor of the violation of the FCPA by the public company. Technically, Dodd-Frank applies its bounty provisions only to judicial or administrative actions by the SEC. However, the U.S. Department of Justice also has its own bounty program.

Broker-Dealer Violations

The 1934 Act requires broker-dealers to be registered with the SEC, subject to certain exemptions, and vigorously enforces this registration provision. For example, in February 2009, the SEC brought action against UBS AG, a Swiss investment bank. The complaint alleged that UBS's conduct facilitated the ability of certain U.S. clients to maintain undisclosed accounts in Switzerland and other foreign countries, which enabled those clients to avoid paying taxes related to the assets in those accounts. UBS agreed to settle the SEC's charges by consenting to the issuance of a final judgment that permanently enjoins UBS and orders it to disgorge $200 million. As alleged in the SEC's complaint, from at least 1999 through 2008, UBS acted as an unregistered broker-dealer and investment advisor to thousands of U.S. persons and offshore entities with U.S. citizens as beneficial owners. UBS had at least 11,000 to 14,000 such clients and held billions of dollars of assets for them. The U.S. cross-border business provided UBS with revenues of $120 to $140 million per year.

Cases are also brought by the SEC for violation of the duty of broker-dealer firms to supervise registered representatives. However, these cases typically are settled for amounts less than $1 million.

 ## OTHER SECURITIES LAWS

Other securities law statutes include the Trust Indenture Act of 1939, the Investment Advisors Act of 1940, and the Investment Company Act of 1940. The Trust Indenture Act regulates, among other things, indenture trustees (typically banks) for large bond and other debt issues. The Investment Advisors Act covers, among others, persons who provide advice on investing in securities. The Investment Company Act regulates all mutual funds as well as other types of funds.

For example, in May 2009, the SEC filed a civil action charging the persons who operate the Reserve Primary Fund (a money market mutual fund) with fraud for failing to provide key material facts to investors and trustees about the fund's vulnerability as Lehman Brothers sought bankruptcy protection. The Reserve Primary Fund "broke the buck" on September 16, 2008, when its net asset value fell below $1.00 per share, meaning investors in the fund would lose money. According to the complaint, defendants failed to provide key material information to the Reserve Primary Fund's investors, board of trustees, and ratings agencies after Lehman filed for bankruptcy protection on September 15, 2008. The fund, which held $785 million in Lehman-issued securities, became illiquid on that day when the fund was unable to meet investor requests for redemptions. According to the complaint, the defendants misrepresented that the investment advisor to the fund would provide the credit support necessary to protect the $1 net asset value of the Reserve Primary Fund.

If a whistleblower provided the "original information" to the SEC with respect to principals of the Reserve Primary Fund and if fines and penalties collected by the SEC exceeded $1 million, the whistleblower could be entitled to a bounty.

PROTECTIONS FOR WHISTLEBLOWERS

Dodd-Frank contains the following protections for whistleblowers:

- A whistleblower may make a claim anonymously. However, the anonymous whistleblower must be represented by counsel when claiming the award and, prior to payment, the identity of the whistleblower must be disclosed together with any other information that the SEC requires.
- Dodd-Frank extends the protection against retaliation to include employees of consolidated subsidiaries and affiliates of public companies, thereby removing limitations imposed by prior U.S. Department of Labor decisions.
- Whistleblowers who allege that they were discharged or discriminated against in violation of the anti-retaliation provisions can bring a cause of action in federal court and, if they prevail, the court is required to order reinstatement, double back pay with interest, and compensation for litigation costs, expert witness fees, and reasonable attorney's fees. (See Chapter 10 for more information.)
- Subject to exceptions, the SEC is prohibited from disclosing information that could reasonably be expected to reveal the identity of the whistleblower.

The SEC whistleblower rules are extremely detailed and complex. Accordingly, we have devoted a full chapter, Chapter 11, to a detailed review of these rules. It is clear that potential whistleblowers will need the help of a securities attorney to guide them through these complex rules.

COMMODITY EXCHANGE ACT

Dodd-Frank not only mandated whistleblower bounties be paid by the SEC but also mandated that the Commodity Futures Trading Commission (CFTC) pay similar bounties. Dodd-Frank amended the Commodity Exchange Act by adding Section 23, "Commodity Whistleblower Incentives and Protection."[19] Section 23 directs that the CFTC must pay awards, subject to certain limitations and conditions (similar to the SEC conditions cited in Chapter 11 of this book), to whistleblowers who voluntarily provide the CFTC with original information about a violation of the Commodity Exchange Act that leads to successful enforcement of an action brought by the CFTC that results in monetary sanctions exceeding $1 million and of certain related actions.

Many of the definitions and requirements for an award under the Commodity Exchange Act are similar to those under the securities laws, which are discussed in Chapter 11. However, there are a few differences, and it should not be assumed automatically that the CFTC rules are identical to the SEC rules. For example, the statute of limitations for retaliation claims by employee whistleblowers under the Commodity Exchange Act is only 2 years after the retaliation. In contrast, the statute of limitations for retaliation claims by employee whistleblowers with respect to the securities laws is the lesser of (1) 6 years after the date of the retaliation or (2) 3 years after the date when facts material to the retaliation claim are known or should have been reasonably known by the employee whistleblower, but not more than 10 years after the violation.

The Commodity Exchange Act covers the sale of commodities—the futures trading of fungible goods and assets, such as agricultural products (grain, animal products, fruits, coffee, sugar), energy (crude oil, coal electricity), natural resources (gold, precious gems, plutonium, water), commoditized goods (generic pharmaceuticals), and financial commodities (foreign currencies and securities). The stated mission of the CFTC is to protect market users and the public from fraud, manipulation, and abusive practices related to the sale of commodity and financial futures and options and to foster open, competitive, and financially sound futures and option markets.

Chapter 2 of this book is devoted to the $96 million payment to Cheryl Eckard that was paid on the False Claims Act, which is much older than the Dodd-Frank statute. In fact, the False Claims Act was passed by Congress on March 2, 1863, in the middle of the Civil War.

The bounty payments under the False Claims Act typically are based on so-called qui tam actions (private lawsuits to enforce the right of government), which are discussed in detail in Chapter 8. In contrast to the False Claims Act, Dodd-Frank does not permit qui tam actions. Instead, the SEC is required to make the necessary bounty payments without the necessity of a private lawsuit.

The story of Cheryl Eckard's whistleblower reward is followed, in Chapter 3, by the story of the Pfizer whistleblower rewards, which totaled over $100 million.

NOTES

1. SEC Litigation Release No. 21540, May 28, 2010.
2. D. Malan, "Messy Divorce Leads to Whistleblower Bounty in Pequot Capital Case," Law.com, August 12, 2010. www.law.com/jsp/law/LawArticleFriendly .jsp?id=1202464787161.
3. S. Dugner, "Would a Fraud Bounty Have Exposed Madoff Years Ago?" *Freakonomics*, February 26, 2009. www.freakonomics.com/2009/02/26/ would-a-fraud-bounty-have-exposed-madoff-years-ago.
4. K. Frieswick, "Madoff Whistle-Blower Offers His Account," *Boston Globe*, March 2, 2010. See also H. Markopolos, *No One Would Listen* (Hoboken, NJ: John Wiley & Sons, 2010).
5. Limited to the extent deposited into a disgorgement fund or other fund pursuant to Section 308(b) of the Sarbanes-Oxley Act of 2002. See SEC Rule 21F-4(e).
6. Assessment of the SEC's Bounty Program, Report No. 474, March 29, 2010. www.sec-oig.gov/Reports/AuditsInspections/2010/474.pdf.
7. www.sec.gov/comments/s7-33-10/s73310-166.pdf. See Chapter 11 for more detailed information.
8. SEC Rule 21F-4(e) defines "monetary sanctions" to mean any money, including penalties, disgorgement, and interest, ordered to be paid and any money deposited into a disgorgement fund or other fund pursuant to Section 308(b) of the Sarbanes-Oxley Act of 2002 as a result of a commission action or a related action.
9. Section 30A of 1934 Act.
10. Securities Exchange Act of 1934 Release No. 51724, May 20, 2005.
11. *SEC v. Lucent Technologies, Inc.*, Civil Action No. 07-092301 (D.D.C. Filed December 21, 2007).
12. Frederick Lipman, *International and U.S. IPO Planning: A Business Strategy Guide* (Hoboken, NJ: John Wiley & Sons, 2009), pp. 90–91.
13. www.sec.gov/answers/ponzi.htm.
14. Ibid.
15. www.sec.gov/answers/insider.htm.
16. Ibid.
17. Section 13(b)(2) of 1934 Act.
18. "SEC Charges State of New Jersey for Fraudulent Municipal Bond Offerings," SEC Press Release 2010-152, August 18, 2010. www.sec.gov/news/ press/2010/2010-152.htm.
19. Section 748 of Dodd-Frank.

The Remarkable Story of Cheryl Eckard and the $96 Million Bounty under the False Claims Act

O N OCTOBER 26, 2010, GlaxoSmithKline (Glaxo) issued a press release disclosing a settlement with the U.S. Department of Justice with respect to the investigation of the company's former manufacturing facility in Cidra, Puerto Rico. Glaxo had issued a press release on July 15, 2010, disclosing a $750 million charge to its second-quarter 2010 earnings in connection with an agreement in principle with the U.S. Department of Justice.

Neither press release revealed a $96 million bounty payment to Cheryl Eckard that was paid in connection with the settlement, equal to 22 percent of the federal settlement. Eckard was also entitled to an additional bounty payment from the settlement with the Medicaid participating states as well as a percentage of the interest paid by Glaxo on both the federal and state settlements.

WHO IS CHERYL ECKARD?

Cheryl Eckard worked for SmithKlineBeecham Corporation d/b/a GlaxoSmith-Kline from 1992 through May 2003, when her employment was terminated after she had repeatedly expressed to her superiors serious concerns about quality assurance and compliance problems at the Cidra plant in Puerto Rico.

The complaint, filed by Eckard in February 2004 and (as amended) more than 130 pages long, stated that Eckard was the manager of global quality assurance for Glaxo. Much of the information in this chapter is based on allegations contained in the complaint against Glaxo filed by Eckard under the False Claims Act. Glaxo likely would dispute most of the material allegations. The author has afforded Glaxo an opportunity to tell its side of the story and received no response. No negative inference should be drawn by the reader from Glaxo's silence because the matter has been settled, and Glaxo may not wish to revisit it. A Glaxo spokesman did state to a media source on January 7, 2011, that the Puerto Rican plant is closed, that "no drugs made there are on the market today" and "there is no evidence that anyone was hurt by the defective medications."[1]

In early May 2003, Eckard received a phone call from the Glaxo human resources (HR) department advising her that she was being offered a redundancy package. Eckard stated that she was not interested in a package and was told that she had no choice. She was advised to take a couple of weeks off with pay. In late May, the HR department asked her to attend a meeting at which the vice president of HR for global operations formally presented the redundancy package to her, took her security badge, and escorted her from the premises. Glaxo stated that "the company strongly rejects any claim of retaliation for whistleblowing."[2]

Eckard, 51, who grew up near Raleigh, North Carolina, spoke to reporters after federal officials announced the $750 million penalty and the $96 million bounty for Eckard. "I'm a little emotional, so you'll have to forgive me for that." She further stated, "This is not something I ever wanted to do. . . . It's difficult to survive this financially, emotionally, you lose all your friends, because all your friends are people you have at work."[3]

 ## ECKARD'S POST-TERMINATION ACTIVITIES

Even after her termination, Eckard allegedly continued her efforts to have Glaxo address Cidra's quality and compliance problems. According to the complaint, in or about July 2003, she allegedly called Glaxo's general counsel and chief executive officer in the United Kingdom, who declined to speak with her. Glaxo denied this allegation, although the company admitted that Eckard sought to communicate with certain Glaxo personnel.

The complaint alleges that Eckard then called Glaxo's general counsel in the United States and explained the general nature of her concerns to his secretary. According to the complaint, the secretary referred Eckard to the vice president for compliance, whom Eckard phoned on or about July 14, 2003. Eckard allegedly detailed the serious quality assurance and compliance problems at Cidra, including diversion of products to the "black markets." Glaxo denied these allegations but did admit that Eckard participated in a July 14, 2003, teleconference with certain Glaxo personnel, communicated with a Glaxo vice president and compliance officer, and raised concerns about quality assurance and compliance at Cidra.

According to the complaint, on or about August 27, 2003, Eckard participated in a teleconference with other Glaxo compliance personnel in which she again detailed her concerns. As a result of this call, the complaint alleges that she formed the view that the compliance department lacked authority internally and that regardless of the outcome of its investigation, if any, Glaxo was unlikely to take any corrective action. On the same day, she allegedly called the San Juan District Office of the U.S. Food and Drug Administration (FDA), where she spoke with Compliance Officer Carmelo Rosa. Over two to three hours, she detailed all of the serious quality assurance and compliance problems at Cidra, including the alleged product diversion. Glaxo admitted that Eckard participated in a teleconference about Cidra with Glaxo personnel on August 27, 2003, but denied the remaining allegations or denied knowledge or information sufficient to form a belief as to their truth or falsity.

According to the complaint, on or about October 3, 2003, following a phone conversation with the Compliance Department, Eckard called Rosa at the San Juan District Office of the FDA and informed him that Glaxo did not intend to take any corrective actions as a result of her report.

On or about October 22, 2003, Glaxo announced in a Securities and Exchange Commission filing that in October 2003 the FDA had begun an investigation of its manufacturing facility in Cidra, Puerto Rico.

 ## ECKARD'S SUPERIORS

An article dated October 28, 2010, in the London *Guardian,* stated that five of the six senior Glaxo executives cited by Eckard as part of a cover-up of contamination problems at the Cidra plant are understood to still be employed by Glaxo and named the six executives.[4] According to the same article, Eckard believed that "these executives were unwilling to acknowledge the gravity of the violations at the Cidra plant and to take the action that Eckard had recommended in part because the FDA had indicated that it would not consider approvals for [Glaxo drugs] Avandamet and Factive until [a previous FDA warning was] resolved."

BACKGROUND ALLEGATIONS

The complaint contains the following background allegations. Glaxo denied some of these allegations in its answer or denied knowledge or information sufficient to form a belief as to the truth or falsity.

The complaint states that the U.S. government endeavors to ensure the safety and efficacy of drug products consumed by Americans through a combination of approvals, inspections, enforcement, and self-regulation by drug manufacturers. The current Good Manufacturing Practices (cGMPs) contain the minimum requirements that pharmaceutical companies must satisfy in manufacturing, processing, packing, and holding drugs to ensure that they meet the safety, identity, strength, quality, and purity characteristics that they purport to possess. Manufacturers demonstrate compliance with cGMPs through written documentation of procedures and practices. The complaint alleged that Eckard was an expert on the technical, legal, regulatory, and compliance aspects of the pharmaceutical cGMPs and quality systems regulations relating to the development, manufacture, packaging, testing, holding, and distribution of drug products. Eckard performed compliance functions that included quality management of multiple manufacturing sites and preparing manufacturing sites for FDA preapproval and cGMPs profile inspections. She managed international commercial investigation teams, technical working parties, and "Warning Letter Recovery" teams, and worked closely with the FDA and other regulatory bodies in developing implementation plans to respond to regulatory sanctions. Eckard had a B.A. in chemistry.

Drugs are considered to be adulterated if they are not manufactured in compliance with the cGMPs or if they are contaminated. The FDA is authorized to conduct inspections of drug manufacturing facilities, including inspections of records, files, papers, processes, controls, and facilities. After an inspection, the FDA provides the pharmaceutical company with a Form FD483 (FDA-483) or a list of "observations" representing violations the FDA believes the manufacturer has committed. The pharmaceutical company is expected to respond in writing to each observation, stating its position and any corrective action it proposes to take. The FDA takes this response into account in deciding whether further enforcement action is warranted.

Under FDA procedures, following an inspection or discovery of a violation, the FDA may issue a warning letter to the manufacturer representing its official findings of violations. The warning letter is the FDA's primary means of notifying pharmaceutical companies of violations and of achieving prompt corrective action. The FDA rules require the manufacturing company to respond in writing to the warning letter within 15 days, stating what action is being taken to correct the violations, what action will be taken to prevent similar violations, and the time frame for such action. The FDA also operates a Drug Quality Reporting System, which includes the MedWatch reporting program designed to quickly identify significant health hazards associated with the manufacturing and packaging of drugs and to establish a central reporting system for detecting problem areas or trends requiring regulatory action.

According to the complaint, manufacturers are required to notify the FDA by filing a "field alert" within three working days of the receipt, via the Medwatch system or otherwise, of:

(i) information concerning any incident that causes the drug product or its labeling to be mistaken for, or applied to, another article;

(ii) information concerning any bacteriological contamination, or any significant chemical, physical, or other change or deterioration in the distributed drug product, or any failure of one or more distributed batches of the drug product to meet the specifications established for it in the new drug application.[5]

The complaint describes a July 2, 2002, meeting with the FDA as follows:

On or about July 2, 2002, Glaxo met with the FDA to discuss issues arising from the FDA-483 and the Warning Letter. Glaxo's representatives at that meeting included Janice Whitaker ("Whitaker"), Senior Vice President for Global Quality, Steve Plating ("Plating"), Vice President for Quality North America, Jose Luis Rosado ("Rosado"), the President and General Manager of Cidra, and Adalberto Ramirez ("Ramirez"), Director of Solid Manufacturing and Packaging at Cidra. At that meeting, the FDA informed Glaxo that pending approvals for Glaxo's new diabetes drug, Avandamet, and a new antibiotic, Factive, would not proceed until Glaxo's response to the Warning Letter was deemed adequate by the FDA and the FDA had reinspected the Cidra plant. Avandamet and Factive are manufactured at the Cidra plant.[6]

 ALLEGED VIOLATIONS

The complaint contains these allegations as to the violations of law, all or substantially all of which were denied by Glaxo:

■ Glaxo and the other defendants made false claims for payment for prescription drugs covered by Medicare, State Medicaid programs, the Department of Veterans Affairs, the Public Health Service and other federal, state and city purchasers of prescription drugs. The false claims were allegedly made to the United States, the fifty state governments and the District of Columbia.

■ The claims were allegedly false and fraudulent because the drugs, which were manufactured at the Glaxo plant in Cidra, Puerto Rico, were defective, misidentified as a result of product mix-ups, not manufactured in accordance with FDA approved processes, and/or did not come with the assurance of identity, strength, quality and purity required for distribution to patients; and/or approvals for the drugs were obtained through false representations to the FDA. The false claims arose out of chronic, serious deficiencies in the quality assurance function at the Cidra plant and the defendants' ongoing serious violations of the laws and regulations designed to ensure the fitness of drug products for use, including the Federal Food, Drug and Cosmetics Act.[7]

The complaint identified the affected drugs in this way:

■ The drugs involved include Paxil, Paxil CR, Avandia, Avandamet, Coreg, Bactroban, Abreva, Cimetidine, Compazine, Denavir, Dyazide, Thorazine, Stelazine, Ecotrin, Tagament, Relafen, Kytril, Factive, Dyrenium, and Albenza.

■ Paxil and Avandia were among the world's 50 top-selling drug products. Other drugs affected included the chest infection treatment Factive; Bactroban ointment, an antibiotic used to treat skin infections in babies; Kytril, an antinausea injection for cancer patients; and Tagamet, for heartburn and peptic ulcers. Drugs of different types and strengths were found in the same bottle; Avandamet was shipped in tablets of the wrong strength; and Bactroban was "contaminated with a micro-organism associated with bacteranemia, urinary tract infections, meningitis, wound infection, and peritonitis," court documents show.[8]

The complaint also provides these comments on the affected or misidentified drugs:

Examples of the defective and/or misidentified products that Glaxo allegedly released to the United States market from the Cidra plant were:

- Drug product that was mixed up with drug product of a different type or strength, e.g., 30 mg and 10 mg tablets of an anti-depressant mixed in the same bottle, and 12.5 and 6.25 mg tablets of a heart medication mixed in the same bottle.
- A diabetes medication that was sub-potent and/or super-potent.
- An antibiotic ointment used to treat a skin infection common to small children that was contaminated with a micro-organism associated with bacteranemia, urinary tract infections, meningitis, wound infection and peritonitis.
- An injectable drug used to treat nausea and vomiting in patients undergoing chemotherapy that was contaminated with micro-organisms.
- Employees of the defendants allegedly diverted reject drug product from the Cidra plant to black markets in Latin America.[9]

The complaint alleged that these acts constitute violations of the federal False Claims Act and numerous equivalent state and city statutes.[10]

 ## TIMELINE OF ECKARD'S ALLEGED ACTIVITIES

The complaint alleges the events as described next. Glaxo denied many of these allegations and denied knowledge or information sufficient to form a belief as to the truth or falsity of the others:

> In early July 2002, Eckard traveled to Cidra in order to assist in the preparation of Cidra's preliminary response to the Warning Letter, which was delivered to the FDA on or about July 17, 2002. At approximately that time, Glaxo undertook to immediately notify the FDA if any problems were found that could present a public health risk.
>
> On or about July 17, 2002, Glaxo made the following specific commitments to the FDA in response to the Warning Letter received on July 1, 2002, and the FDA-483 received on April 10, 2002 including:

- Reviewing all investigation reports from 2000 to date and prepare a summary of findings, this review to be conducted by consultants.
- Defining an action plan for corrective actions.
- Evaluating the adequacy of current SOPs [standard operating procedures] for handling [out-of-specifications] investigation results.
- Determining the adequacy of corrective actions taken.

On or about August 7, 2002, Eckard was assigned by Glaxo headquarters in Research Triangle Park, NC, . . . to lead the Warning Letter Recovery Team in Cidra.

Eckard's role was to coordinate and oversee the work of Compliance Action Plan Team Leaders who were assigned to each functional area, including Materials, Equipment, Facilities/Utilities, Validation, Laboratory, Computer Validation, Quality Assurance, Production, and Calibration. The Team Leaders were to work on their action plans on a fully dedicated basis for the seven weeks following August 7, 2002, and to communicate serious incidents to top management with the objective of resolving the Warning Letter issues and making the site ready for FDA reinspection, which was a precondition to obtaining FDA approval for Avandamet and Factive. The reinspection was scheduled to commence on or about October 9, 2002. There were over 100 people on the Warning Letter Recovery Team, approximately 75 of them from the Cidra Plant and 25 from Glaxo headquarters.

Shortly after her arrival at Cidra, Eckard asked Cidra's Quality Assurance and Regulatory Manager, Gloria Martinez ("Martinez"), to report on any compliance issues that the FDA had not identified in its recent inspections.

The complaint described the Martinez internal report as follows:

Martinez presented an internal report . . . on or about August 14, 2002, which was attended by Cidra senior managers including Rosado. Martinez outlined the following compliance issues:

- Product mix-ups: Cidra had filed at least 7 Field Alert reports with the FDA during 2002 due to complaints of product comingling from patients, pharmacies or physicians, i.e., tablets of a different type or strength were found in the same bottle. Martinez also stated that Cidra had internally identified nine similar (though distinct) product mix-ups at the plant. Eckard also learned that in the Field Alerts filed with the FDA arising from consumer complaints, Cidra had assured the FDA that, for a variety of reasons, the mix-ups could not have happened at the plant, despite the fact that nine separate and contemporaneous similar incidents had been identified inside the plant. Product mix-ups typically are treated in the industry as Class I or Class II recall events, and yet no recalls had been initiated. Cidra had made no attempt to correct the cause of the mix-ups and had lied to the FDA in its

Field Alert filings by stating that the mix-ups must have occurred outside of Cidra's control.

▪ Cidra did not have a calibration program for the laboratory, and over 20,000 pieces of equipment were in urgent need of calibration in the manufacturing areas. As a result, the validity of data gathered during manufacture and testing to assure product quality could not be relied upon as accurate.

Immediately after the . . . meeting on or about August 14, 2002, Eckard phoned Plating at Glaxo's headquarters. . . . She gave him the information that she had received at the meeting. She recommended that Glaxo stop shipping all products from the Cidra plant, stop manufacturing product for two weeks in order to investigate and resolve the issues raised and the impact on released batches, and notify the FDA about the product mix-ups. Eckard faxed to Plating the overheads that Martinez had used in her presentation, consisting of approximately 13 pages ("the Martinez presentation").

On or about August 15, 2002, Eckard returned to Glaxo headquarters in Research Triangle Park, NC, where she immediately reported her concerns to Whitaker. Eckard reached Whitaker, who was out of the country, by phone. Eckard gave Whitaker the information that she had received at Cidra, including that Cidra had lied to the FDA. She recommended that Glaxo stop shipping all product from the Cidra plant, stop manufacturing product for two weeks in order to investigate and resolve the issues raised and the impact on released batches and notify the FDA about the product mix-ups. Eckard reminded Whitaker of Glaxo's promise to the FDA at the meeting on July 17, 2002, that Glaxo would immediately notify the FDA if any problems were found that could present a public health risk. Eckard told Whitaker that she believed the Cidra plant was headed for a Consent Decree if the problems were not handled with speed and integrity. Eckard left a copy of the Martinez presentation on Whitaker's desk.

On or about August 18, 2002, Eckard met with Plating to reiterate the concerns she had communicated to him by phone on August 14, 2002.

In September 2002, Eckard spoke by phone with David Pulman ("Pulman"), who was then Vice President of Manufacturing and Supply for North America. Pulman was promoted to President, Global Manufacturing and Supply in December 2002. Plating had provided Pulman with a copy of the Martinez presentation on or about August 15, 2002.

Pulman's overriding concern was to make the Cidra plant ready for the FDA reinspection to commence on or about October 9, 2002. As stated above, passing this inspection was a precondition to obtaining FDA approval for Avandamet and Factive. Pulman asked Eckard for specific examples of the quality problems at the plant. She gave him a few examples and later sent him, via email, a report prepared by the Director of Validation for the sterile facility at Glaxo's Barnard Castle plant in the United Kingdom, who had been brought in to review validation in the sterile suite in Cidra. His report was scathing. Eckard told Pulman that nothing had improved at the Cidra plant since her report to Plating on or about August 24, 2002.

If the allegations of the complaint are true, Eckard had done her job as a global quality assurance employee. Management's reactions to Eckard's efforts are described in the next allegations of the complaint:

Eckard did not have the authority to order recalls or suspension of manufacturing or shipment of product, or to report regulatory concerns to the FDA. Pulman and Whitaker had ultimate authority to order action of this kind. Throughout 2002 and into April 2003, Eckard continued to urge Glaxo managers to take the action that she had recommended and to correct the quality and compliance problems at the Cidra plant. They failed to do so.

According to the complaint, Eckard believed that Whitaker, Pulman and other Glaxo executives were unwilling to acknowledge the gravity of the cGMP violations at the Cidra plant and to take the action that Eckard had recommended in part because the FDA had indicated that it would not consider approvals for Avandamet and Factive until the Warning Letter issues were resolved. Such approvals were unlikely to be obtained if the FDA were aware of the gravity of the quality assurance deficiencies at the Cidra plant. Once the objective of approval for Avandamet was achieved, Glaxo and Cidra management alike lost interest in correcting the deficiencies at the Cidra site and resumed their focus on maximizing productivity at the plant. As stated above, the Cidra plant manufactured $5.5 billion of Glaxo's product and was the most important of all Glaxo's plants worldwide.

Assuming that the complaint allegations are true, the question arises as to whether named Glaxo executives were making the decisions or merely following orders from higher-up Glaxo executives. We will never know this.

The complaint then describes Eckard's actions in preparation for the reinspection of the Cidra plant:

> On or about August 20, 2002, Eckard returned to Cidra. The Compliance Action Teams continued to prepare for the Avandamet reinspection, which was held in October. The focus of the inspection was on the progress of the recovery effort. During the inspection, Cidra informed the FDA that it had begun to put together Corrective and Preventive Action Plans but had not yet fully implemented them. Avandamet was approved by the FDA on October 8, 2002. Factive was approved on April 4, 2003.
>
> Eckard left Cidra and returned to North Carolina immediately after the inspection, having been at the plant for a period of ten weeks. After three weeks, she returned to Cidra to resume work on Warning Letter recovery and the longer-term correction of Cidra's systemic quality assurance and compliance problems. However, Rosado and Ramirez stated that they wanted to take over the leadership of that effort, including leadership of the Compliance Action Teams. Following a meeting with Plating, it was agreed that Ramirez would lead the effort and Eckard would play an "oversight" role and report to Plating.
>
> Thereafter, Eckard visited Cidra periodically for 1–3 days at a time, on each occasion receiving a progress report from Ramirez and reporting to Plating almost on a daily basis.

The complaint then details what happened in 2003 with the Cidra plant reinspection:

> On or about January 24, 2003, Rosado, Plating, Ramirez and Edwin Lopez, Cidra's Director of Quality ("Lopez") met with the FDA to discuss the FDA-483 and Warning Letter Commitments set forth above. . . . Eckard attended that meeting, but was not on the agenda and did not present any items.
>
> In or about February 2003, Eckard learned that Ramirez had repeatedly lied to her about the status of work in the written and verbal progress reports he had provided to her since assuming control of Warning Letter recovery. She also learned that the Compliance Action Teams had been disbanded immediately after the FDA's October reinspection and the approval of Avandamet, and that Rosado, Ramirez and Lopez had misrepresented the true status of Warning Letter recovery to the FDA at the January 24, 2003 meeting. . . .

Eckard reported these concerns to Plating and to her immediate boss, Diane Sevigny ("Sevigny"), Director of Global Quality Assurance for North America Pharma.

From February 4 through 8, 2003, Eckard and two other . . . personnel, representing the Global Quality Assurance team, conducted an internal audit at Cidra. . . . That audit found continuing serious quality control problems and cGMP violations. The findings were communicated to Rosado, Ramirez, Lopez, and senior Glaxo managers Sevigny, Plating and Jonathon Box ("Box"), the Vice President of Manufacturing and Supply for North America who took Pulman's job when Pulman was promoted in December 2002. . . .

Following her findings in the . . . audit and her discovery that Ramirez had lied to her about the status of progress by the Compliance Action Teams, Eckard told Sevigny in substance that she would not participate in a cover-up of the quality assurance and compliance problems at Cidra and would not take part in any further meetings with the FDA about the Cidra plant. During this period and thereafter, Eckard and Sevigny were in frequent and increasing conflict about Glaxo's management of the quality and compliance problems at Cidra.

In or about March 2003, Glaxo made a general call to employees for volunteers to accept a redundancy package arising from the merger of Glaxo Welcome and SmithKlineBeecham, which took place in December 2000. Eckard was so demoralized that she initially expressed interest in this package. However, upon reflection and discussion with colleagues, she soon withdrew her expression of interest, believing that she should continue to seek to make things right from within Glaxo rather than simply resign.

This allegation presumably was designed to forestall an argument by Glaxo that Eckard's ultimate employment termination was voluntary. The complaint goes on to contain the next allegations, including the process of excluding Eckard from meetings on a Cidra issue and the completion of the internal investigation with no recommendation that the Cidra plant be closed:

Eckard continued to press Glaxo senior management for action. In or about March 2003, Eckard put together a binder of materials detailing the quality assurance and compliance problems at Cidra and presented it to Plating and Marion Lon ("Lon"), who was to become and became the site director of Cidra when Rosado retired on or about April 1, 2003. Eckard also asked to meet with Plating and Lon.

On or about April 2, 2003, Eckard delivered to Glaxo senior managers Box, Peter Savin (Vice President of Global Quality Assurance), Whitaker, Plating and Sevigny, and Cidra managers Lon and Ramirez, a non-routine detailed memorandum on Current Compliance Risks for Manufacturing and Supply of Drug Products at Cidra. . . . Eckard provided Ramirez with a copy. She detailed the following high risk compliance problems:

- Product mix-ups;
- Documentation quality;
- Computer validation;
- Sterile manufacturing facility activities and documentation, including Kytril injection;
- Quality and control of water systems; and
- [out-of-specifications] events for environmental monitoring of manufacturing areas and clean equipment.

Eckard called for increased monitoring by Glaxo management of compliance improvement initiatives at Cidra. However, she did not receive any response to her memorandum from any of the seven managers to whom she sent the report.

In or about early April 2003 Eckard learned of internal allegations that persons at the Cidra plant were skimming product during manufacture, including reject product, and diverting the product to Latin America.

Corporate Security and Glaxo senior manager Box were notified of these allegations in February 2003. The allegations were made by a current and a former Cidra employee, both unidentified. Background checks conducted by an outside private investigation company identified connections between a senior manager at Cidra, and companies alleged to distribute the "black market" product. One of these companies was identified as MOVA Pharmaceuticals, Inc. ("MOVA"), a contract manufacturer located in Caguas, Puerto Rico.

In or about the week beginning April 7, 2003, Sevigny took a team to Cidra to investigate these allegations, bypassing Eckard who would normally have been assigned leadership of the investigation. Sevigny took Eckard's employee, Kristal Adams, as part of the team. Although she had been told by Sevigny, in substance, to "stay out of it," Eckard nonetheless provided informal advice to Kristal Adams and received information from her about the investigation.

On or about April 27, 2003, following a consumer complaint, Cidra filed a Field Alert reporting that Avandamet 40 mg tablets had been found in the United States mixed up with unidentified tablets stamped "MOVA" or "MBO."

In or about April or May of 2003, Glaxo closed its internal investigation for lack of sufficient evidence.[11]

THE LESSONS OF GLAXO

We do not know Glaxo's version of the events. Glaxo expressly denied many of the allegations of the complaint or that it engaged in any wrongful conduct. However, a Glaxo subsidiary, SB Pharmco Puerto Rico, Inc., entered a plea in the related criminal case brought by the U.S. Department of Justice that stated:

> SB Pharmco expressly and unequivocally admits that it committed these offenses and further admits that it acted with the intent to defraud or mislead. Defendant expressly and unequivocally further admits that it is in fact guilty of this offense, and agrees that it will not make any statements inconsistent with this explicit admission.[12]

For purposes of this discussion, we will assume the truth of the complaint and subsequent statements. According to Eckard, Glaxo's management decided to cover up the problems at the Cidra plant in order to obtain FDA approval of two new products, the diabetes drug Avandamet and Factive, a drug used for chest infections. Thus, Glaxo's management allegedly made a business decision that the potential profits of obtaining quicker FDA approval for these two drugs outweighed the risk of civil or criminal penalties related to the Cidra plant.

A representative of the U.S. Department of Justice was asked by a reporter how the $750 million penalty compared to Glaxo's net income—in other words, could wrongdoing have turned out to be net profitable? The representative stated, "The fine is significantly higher than the profits that were made by the company."[13]

We do not know if Glaxo's management was aware of the total potential civil and criminal liability to which their business decision exposed the company. Nor do we know whether the Glaxo board of directors was aware of the business decision or the risks to which the company was exposed by virtue of the alleged management decision. There is no record of either the

Glaxo management or its board of directors employing independent counsel to investigate the Eckard complaints or advising them as to Glaxo's total potential exposure.

The lessons of Glaxo are:

- Corporate compliance policies must involve the board of directors in any significant whistleblower complaint. A committee of independent members of the board of directors must receive notice of legitimate whistleblower complaints.
- The independent board committee should employ independent counsel (or an ombudsman) to investigate any serious whistleblower complaints. An ombudsman is an independent party whom employees would feel comfortable speaking to with regard to potential problems or issues of significance to the organization.[14]
- The company's chief executive officer must set a tone at the top that encourages an ethical, law-abiding culture within the company. In this connection, it was reported that Eckard phoned J. P. Garnier, then Glaxo chief executive officer, who declined to take the call to speak to her about the findings and the cover-up.[15] Moreover, the fact that five of the six executives allegedly involved in the alleged cover-up remained employed by Glaxo raises serious issues as to the tone at the top.
- Risk/reward decisions that could materially affect the company must be made by the board of directors. The independent members of the Glaxo board would arguably be more dispassionate in deciding risk/reward issues because their compensation typically is not tied to the company's financial results.
- Executive compensation plans should punish management for poor risk decisions that affect the company in future years by providing long-term incentives that can be reduced for bad business decisions rather than using short-term rewards based on annual profits.
- Legitimate whistleblowers should be rewarded internally by the corporate compliance policy and should be treated as heroes rather than pariahs.
- Legitimate whistleblowers should not have their employment terminated without prior approval of the independent members of the board of directors. It is questionable whether independent directors would have approved the abrupt dismissal of Eckard under the circumstances of this case. It should be noted that Eckard reported Glaxo to the FDA in August 2003, approximately three months after she had been fired in May 2003.[16]

Perhaps Glaxo has learned its lesson. According to the *Wall Street Journal*, Deirdre Connelly, president of Glaxo's North American pharmaceuticals unit, said the company has stepped up its commitment to operate with integrity, to be more respectful of patients and more transparent in how it conducts business. She cited Glaxo's recent elimination of individual sales targets from the bonus criteria for sales representatives, a move aimed at reassuring doctors that Glaxo reps are not focused primarily on pushing pills.[17]

The next chapter deals with the payment of more than $100 million to six whistleblowers in connection with the $2.3 billion payment by Pfizer, Inc. and its subsidiary.

 NOTES

1. Daniel Schorn, "Glaxo Whistle-Blower Lawsuit: Bad Medicine," CBS News, January 7, 2011.
2. www.cbsnews.com/stories/2010/12/20/60minutes/main7195247.shtml.
3. See http://www.necn.com/pages/landing?blockID=339520.
4. See http://www.guardian.co.uk/business/2010/oct/28/glaxosmithkline -executives-allegedly-ignored-eckard.
5. www.taf.org/eckardcomplaint3.pdf.
6. Ibid.
7. Ibid.
8. See http://pharmagossip.blogspot.com/2010/10/gsk-cheryl-eckard-tried-to -warn-ceo-but.html.
9. www.taf.org/eckardcomplaint3.pdf.
10. The complaint alleged that the defendant's acts constituted violations of the California False Claims Act, Cal. Gov't Code §§ 12650–12655; the Delaware False Claims and Reporting Act, 6 Del. C. §§ 1201 *et seq.*; the District of Columbia Procurement Reform Amendment Act, D.C. Code Ann. §§ 2-308.13–21; the Florida False Claims Act, Fla. Stat. Ann. §§ 68.081–092; the Georgia State False Medicaid Claims Act, Ga. Code Ann. §§ 49-4-168 *et seq.*; the Hawaii False Claims Act, Haw. Rev. Stat. §§ 661-21–29; the Illinois Whistleblower Reward and Protection Act, 740 Ill. Comp. Stat. §§ 175/1–8; the Indiana False Claims and Whistleblower Protection Act, IC 5-115.5 *et seq.*; the Louisiana Medical Assistance Programs Integrity Law, La. Rev. Stat. 46:437.1–14; the Massachusetts False Claims Act, Mass. Gen. L. Ch. 12, §§ 5B *et seq.*; the Michigan Medicaid False Claims Act, MCL §§ 400.601 *et seq.*; the Nevada False Claims Act, Nev. Rev. Stat. §§ 357.010 *et seq.*; the New Hampshire Medicaid Fraud and False Claims Act, RSA §§ 167.58 *et seq.*; the New Mexico Medicaid False Claims Act, N.M. Stat. Ann. §§ 27-12-1 *et seq.*; the New York False Claims Act, N.Y.

State Fin. Law §§ 187–194; the Tennessee Medicaid False Claims Act, Tenn. Code Ann. §§ 71-5-182 *et seq.*; the Tennessee False Claims Act, Tenn. Code Ann. §§ 4-18-101 *et seq.*; the Texas Medicaid Fraud Prevention Law, Tex. Hum. Res. Code Ann. §§ 36.001 *et seq.*; the Virginia Fraud Against Taxpayers Act, Va. Code Ann. §§ 8.01-216.3 *et seq.*; the Chicago False Claims Act, Chicago Municipal Code Ch. 1-21 *et seq.*; and the New York City False Claims Act, Local Law 53 of 2005, Title 7, New York City Admin. Code §§ 7-801 *et seq.*

11. www.taf.org/eckardcomplaint3.pdf.
12. http://freepdfhosting.com/da79d56653.pdf.
13. Peter Howe, "Whistleblower Wins 96 Million in GlaxoSmithKline Case," NECH.com, October 26, 2010. http://www.necn.com/10/26/10/Whistleblower-wins-96-million-in-GlaxoSm/landing_business.html?blockID=339520&feedID=4209.
14. Francis J. Milliken, Elizabeth W. Morrison, and Patricia F. Hewlin, "An Exploratory Study of Employee Silence: Issues that Employees Don't Communicate Upward and Why," November 4, 2003. http://w4.stern.nyu.edu/emplibrary/Milliken.Frances.pdf.
15. See http://pharmagossip.blogspot.com/2010/10/gsk-cheryl-eckard-tried-to-warn-ceo-but.html.
16. Ibid.
17. Peter Loftus, "Glaxo Pulls Some Ads, Citing Image," *Wall Street Journal*, January 25, 2011, p. D4.

CHAPTER THREE

The Pfizer Whistleblowers Who Collected Over $100 Million under the False Claims Act

ON SEPTEMBER 2, 2009, the U.S. Department of Justice announced that American pharmaceutical giant Pfizer Inc. and its subsidiary Pharmacia & Upjohn Company, Inc. (hereafter together Pfizer) had agreed to pay $2.3 billion, the largest healthcare fraud settlement in the history of the Department of Justice, to resolve criminal and civil liability arising from the illegal promotion of certain pharmaceutical products. That same day, Pfizer issued a press release announcing the settlement of the investigation regarding past off-label promotional practices related to Bextra, which the company voluntarily withdrew from the market in 2005.

Like the Glaxo press release discussed in Chapter 2, the Pfizer press release omitted any reference to payments to whistleblowers. However, the settlement agreement signed by Pfizer provided for payments by the Department of Justice of the following amounts to the listed whistleblowers:

John Kopchinski: $51,500,999
Stefan Kruszewski: $29,013,420
Ronald Rainero: $9,321,369
Glenn DeMott: $7,431,505

Dana Spencer: $2,743,637
Blair Collins: $2,354,582

This chapter relies primarily on allegations contained in the whistle-blower complaint. Pfizer likely would deny most of the material allegations of the complaint even though it did not file an answer. The author has given Pfizer a chance to tell its own side of the story, and no response was received from Pfizer. No negative inference should be drawn by the reader from Pfizer's silence because the matter has been settled, and Pfizer may not wish to revisit it.

JOHN KOPCHINSKI

John Kopchinski is a 1989 graduate of the United States Military Academy (West Point) and a decorated veteran of the Gulf War. Prior to attending West Point, he served as an enlisted service member for three years as an air traffic controller. After West Point, he served for three years as an officer and was discharged honorably at the rank of first lieutenant.

During his military service, Kopchinski received the Meritorious Service Medal for his service during Operation Desert Shield (the first stage of the 1990–1991 Gulf War against Iraq); the Army Commendation Medal for his service during Operation Desert Storm (the second stage of the same war); an Army Achievement Medal for exemplary service while serving in Panama; the Southwest Asia Service Medal with two Bronze Stars for his service in the Gulf War; the Kuwaiti Liberation Medal; and numerous other awards and citations.

Kopchinski was hired directly out of the army in January 1992 by the then chief executive officer and chairman of Pfizer, Edward Pratt, to work as a Pfizer sales representative. During his employment with Pfizer, Kopchinski earned a master's in business administration in 1994 from Washburn University and Medical Representative Certification in 1997 from the Certified Medical Representative Institute.

According to the complaint, Kopchinski was continuously employed by Pfizer from January 1992 until his alleged retaliatory discharge on March 7, 2003. At the time of his employment discharge, Kopchinski was employed by Pfizer as a senior specialty representative in the fields of rheumatology, orthopedics, and neurology covering the territory of Broward County, Florida.

According to Reuters,[1] Kopchinski, appalled by Pfizer's tactics in selling the pain drug Bextra, filed a qui tam lawsuit in 2003, after his dismissal, sparking federal and state probes that led to the agreement by Pfizer to pay $2.3 billion in civil and criminal penalties and plead guilty to a felony charge for promoting Bextra and 12 other drugs for unapproved uses and doses.

"In the Army I was expected to protect people at all costs," Kopchinski said in a statement. "At Pfizer I was expected to increase profits at all costs, even when sales meant endangering lives."

"I couldn't do that," added Kopchinski, 45, who was fired by Pfizer in March 2003, two years before the company pulled Bextra from the market over concerns it raised the risk of heart attacks and strokes.

At the time of his dismissal after raising his concerns with the company, Kopchinski had a baby son and his wife was pregnant with twins. He went from earning about $125,000 a year to living off his retirement fund before landing a job with an insurance company for $40,000 a year.

"It was a lot of stress on the family. I pretty much depleted my entire 401(k)," he said.

"The last six years have been pretty hard, so going forward after the settlement it's going to be pretty much easier," said Kopchinski, noting that college for his young children "is taken care of."

Kopchinski's lead attorney stated that large rewards are justified because of what whistleblowers must endure, often for many years, after complaints within the company go unheeded.

Including Kopchinski, there were a total of ten whistleblowers who signed the settlement agreement, only six of whom were named as receiving awards. Stefan Kruszewski was a psychiatrist in Harrisburg, PA, and the rest of the whistleblowers worked in sales positions at Pfizer.

 BEXTRA

Bextra is Pfizer's trade name for the drug valdecoxib, which is a so-called COX-2 inhibitor. The COX-2 class of drugs, which is designed to relieve various forms of pain and inflammation, includes the previously released drug Celebrex, also marketed by Pfizer, and the competing drug Vioxx, manufactured by Merck.

In November 2001, Bextra was first approved by the U.S. Food and Drug Administration (FDA) for relief of the symptoms of osteoarthritis and adult rheumatoid arthritis and for treatment of primary dysmenorrhea. Significantly, Pfizer also had sought approval for several additional indications, including acute pain, preoperative dosing, and opioid sparing, but use for these indications was rejected by the FDA.

Since Bextra's initial FDA approval, Pfizer allegedly sought to expand its approved indication only once. On or about December 23, 2002, Pfizer submitted a supplemental new drug application to the FDA for approval to market Bextra for the treatment of adult migraines.

According to the complaint, Bextra's narrow FDA-approved indication limited the potential sales growth of the drug, particularly in view of the fact that numerous other approved pain medications are also available to the public. As alleged in the complaint filed by the whistleblowers, to grow drug sales in a constrained environment, Pfizer resorted to marketing strategies prohibited by federal law, including kickback schemes and off-label promotion.

 ## THE COMPLAINT

The complaint contains these additional allegations, which Pfizer denied:

- Pfizer and Pharmacia circumvented federally mandated FDA approval processes by aggressively marketing Bextra for numerous unapproved uses—including, but not limited to, treatment for general acute pain; chronic arthritis at doses greater than 1 mg/day; pre-surgical dosing; and post-surgical pain, among many others. Indeed, Pfizer's requests for approval for treatment for acute pain other than dysmenorrhea; chronic arthritis at doses greater than 10 mg/day; and dysmenorrhea at doses greater than two 20 mg doses/day, were specifically rejected by the FDA.
- Pfizer and Pharmacia have violated federal anti-kickback laws by paying and offering to pay financial inducements to physicians and other providers to influence their Bextra prescribing practices.
- Pfizer and Pharmacia utilized their substantial field sales force to improperly promote excessive dosages of Bextra for chronic arthritis. In particular, Pfizer and Pharmacia developed sales "scripts" and marketing materials for sales representatives to use to encourage doctors to prescribe Bextra for chronic arthritis at dosages above 10 mg/day, the dose approved by the FDA (either by prescribing 20 mg or more or by prescribing 10 mg twice a day rather than once a day). These scripts and marketing materials were designed to convey several false impressions: (1) that doses of Bextra above 10 mg/day were more effective for chronic arthritis than doses of 10 mg a day, (2) that doses of Bextra above 10 mg per day were safe for long-term use for chronic arthritis, and (3) that

Bextra was safer than Vioxx (its chief competitor), even though no head-to-head clinical trials had been conducted.[2]

The complaint alleged that Pfizer and Pharmacia used various illicit methods to circumvent FDA rules in promoting Bextra for nonapproved uses. These alleged methods included the use of unsolicited articles and "clinical seminars." The allegations are:

- Although federal regulations prohibit Pfizer and Pharmacia from promoting Bextra for non-FDA approved uses, it is permitted to distribute publications created by third parties that describe results of off-label use of Bextra, provided such material was only distributed in response to *non-solicited* requests from physicians. Pfizer and Pharmacia circumvented this narrow exception by encouraging sales representatives to solicit physicians to "request" medical information regarding Bextra, and then either leaving with physicians such medical articles, or having such medical articles mailed to the physician. In many instances these materials were mailed or delivered to physicians even without the pretext of a request from the physician. [emphasis in original]
- In Mr. Kopchinski's sales district, for example, there was an employee paid by Pfizer, as a so-called "meeting coordinator," who was responsible for sending one unsolicited article per month to 20 physicians, for each of the nine sales representatives in Mr. Kopchinski's district, for a total of 180 unsolicited articles per month. The sales representatives would be sent a copy of the article distributed so they would know what information had been disseminated to the doctors. While sometimes these articles would relate to approved usages of Bextra, more frequently than not they would relate to unapproved usages of the drug. In addition, Mr. Kopchinski and his fellow sales representatives were provided with article reprints about unapproved uses of Bextra and instructed to disseminate such articles, whether the physicians requested them or not.
- So-called "clinical seminars" were another essential component of Pfizer and Pharmacia's Bextra off-label marketing strategy. At these seminars, which were presented by doctors paid by Pfizer and Pharmacia as medical consultants, attending doctors (who were frequently paid money to attend on the pretense that they would provide "consulting" information to Pfizer and Pharmacia, or at the very least were provided with free meals, accommodations and/or travel expenses) . . . would be immersed in

information about Bextra's use for the management of post-surgical pain and other acute pain at doses above 10 mg/day. Such seminars would not disseminate information regarding the FDA medical review's findings that Bextra was neither safe nor more effective for chronic arthritis pain at doses above 10 mg/day.

■ Pfizer and Pharmacia typically paid the physician participants between $250 and $1,500 each to simply attend a single consultant meeting. The doctors also received travel expenses, accommodations at luxury hotels and meals. The "honorarium" payments did not reflect the value of services provided. The physician was not required to do anything but show up to receive his or her payment. In addition, Pfizer and Pharmacia had no legitimate business reason to hire hundreds, if not thousands, of "consultants"—who were also high or potentially high prescribers—to "consult" with Pfizer and Pharmacia about a single drug. Each of these payments constituted a reward or kickback for the purpose of influencing the prescribing practices.

■ Pfizer also offered physicians kickbacks in the form of payments for reviewing clinical papers selected by Pfizer. The clinical payer reviews were putatively for sales representatives' training and education. Providers were given reprints to review and discuss for 20 or 30 minutes with a sales representative. Although the training was supposedly for the Pfizer and Pharmacia sales representatives, in fact, the sales force was already familiar with the materials being reviewed.

■ Pfizer typically paid providers an average of $500 (usually from $250 to $1,000) to read and review the reprint material with a sales representative. That meeting usually took about half an hour or less to complete.[3]

The complaint also contained detailed allegations concerning the use of "journal clubs" and "speaker training programs" to circumvent FDA rules. These allegations are presented next.

■ Pfizer also paid $250 to $1,000 honoraria to physicians who attended and moderated "journal clubs." Typically, the "journal club" would involve 3 or 4 participants—usually rheumatologists—who once a month convened to discuss a clinical paper.

■ Each "club" meeting was moderated by a physician who was paid a generous honorarium by Pfizer. The moderator position rotated every month among the club members.

- The clinical paper discussed at the roundtable was selected by Pfizer—not the participants—on the basis of its promotional value.
- "High decile" physicians [highest frequency of prescription writing] targeted for Pfizer's various kickback programs also were invited to attend "speaker training" programs at luxury resort destinations, such as the Caribbean. In addition to airfare, luxury hotel accommodations and meals, invited physicians also received at least $1,000 to attend.[4]

 ## PFIZER LESSONS

As in the Glaxo whistleblower case, there is no record as to whether the Pfizer board of directors or any of its committees were made aware of the whistleblower complaints or were advised of the potential criminal and civil consequences of ignoring these complaints. Likewise, there is no record of an investigation by independent counsel, reporting to the board, of these whistleblower complaints.

Some whistleblower advocates have argued that Pfizer made more money from continuing the sale of off-label uses for Bextra and other drugs than from heeding the whistleblower complaints and stopping the sale. The Pfizer press release indicated that Pfizer had ceased selling Bextra in 2005 but does not indicate the motivation for so doing.

The settlement agreement with the U.S. Department of Justice required Pfizer to enter into a corporate integrity agreement (CIA). Some of the terms of this agreement are quite revealing and reflect internal controls that could have been adopted had the whistleblower complaints been taken seriously.

The following are a few highlights of the CIA that provided internal safeguards against repetition of the Bextra disaster:

- Throughout the term of this CIA, Pfizer shall also maintain a centralized, electronic system to be used by field sales representatives in connection with the detailing of HCPs [healthcare professionals] (detailing system). . . . The detailing system shall include a centralized mechanism through which sales representatives shall submit Inquiries to Pfizer's Medical Information Department, including a requirement that the requesting HCP sign the Inquiry prior to submission. With regard to the distribution of samples, the detailing system and its controls shall identify which HCPs are eligible to receive what type of sample based upon whether the HCP is likely to prescribe the product for a use consistent with the FDA-approved label for the product.

- To the extent not already accomplished, Pfizer shall institute a Speaker Monitoring Program under which Pfizer personnel or outside personnel acting on behalf of Pfizer shall attend 200 speaker programs during each Reporting Period and conduct live audits of the programs (Speaker Program Audits).

- As a component of the FFMP [Field Force Monitoring Program], Pfizer field-based attorneys or other compliance/legal personnel shall conduct observations of field sales representatives to assess whether the messages delivered and materials distributed to HCPs are consistent with applicable legal requirements and with Pfizer's Policies and Procedures. These observations shall be full day ride-alongs with field sales representatives (Observations) and each Observation shall consist of directly observing all meetings between a sales representative and HCPs during the workday. The Observations shall be scheduled throughout the year, judgmentally selected by Pfizer compliance personnel, include a review of each therapeutic area and actively promoted product, and be conducted across the United States. At the completion of each Observation, Pfizer compliance/legal personnel shall prepare a report which includes [various details].

- Pfizer represented that its sales and marketing departments have no involvement in, or influence over, the review and approval of medical education grants or healthcare related charitable contribution requests.[5]

The CIA also requires Pfizer to publicly identify physicians who receive certain payments by Pfizer. These agreements are detailed next.

- On or before March 31, 2010, Pfizer shall post in a prominent position on its website an easily accessible and readily searchable listing of all U.S.-based physicians, and Related Entities [any entity employing the physician or in which the physician has tenure or any ownership] . . . who or which received Payments . . . directly or indirectly from Pfizer between July 1, 2009 and December 31, 2009 and the aggregate value of such Payments.

- Each listing shall be arranged alphabetically according to the physicians' last name or the name of the Related Entity. The Payment amounts in the lists shall be reported in $10,000 increments (e.g., $0–$10,000; $10,001–$200,000; etc.) or in the actual amount paid. . . . The term "Payments" is defined to include all payments or transfers of value (whether in cash or in kind) made to physicians including all payments (including, for example, honoraria payments, other payments, and reimbursement for lodging, travel and other expenses) made in connection with physicians serving as speakers, participating in speaking, training, or serving as Consultants or Authors; payments or compensation for services rendered; grants, fees; payments relating to research; payments relating to education; and payment or reimbursement for food, entertainment, gifts, trips or travel, product(s)/items(s) provided for less than fair market value, or other economic benefit paid or transferred.

▪ Pfizer represents that it expects all Authors of biomedical manuscripts to fully comply with the International Committee of Medical Journal Editors . . . criteria regarding authorship and disclosure of their relationship with Pfizer.[6]

Part II of this book discusses the substantial disincentives to employee whistleblowers, the factors motivating employees to make public disclosure of wrongdoing, and the role of women as whistleblowers.

 NOTES

1. This discussion of Kopchinski is based on Bill Berkrot, "Pfizer Whistleblower's Ordeal Reaps Big Rewards," Reuters, September 2, 2009.
2. Third Amended Complaint, entitled *United States of America Ex Rel. John Kopchinski, Relators, v. Pfizer, Inc. and Pharmacia Corp., Defendants,* filed in the United States District Court for the District of Massachusetts, C.A. No. 05-CV-12115-RCL, and on file in the author's office.
3. Ibid.
4. Ibid.
5. Ibid.
6. Ibid.

PART TWO

Disincentives and Factors Motivating Public Disclosure

CHAPTER FOUR

Disincentives to Internal Whistleblowers

It is said that nobody likes a snitch.[1]

THERE ARE SERIOUS DISINCENTIVES to internal whistleblowing. The phrase "internal whistleblowing" refers to employees of an organization providing information about its illegal or unethical conduct. External whistleblowers, such as Harry Markopolos, the Madoff whistleblower, do not suffer these same disincentives.

According to the former general counsel of the Securities and Exchange Commission (SEC):

> [Whistleblower advocates] would tell you that it takes extraordinary courage to be a whistleblower, because blowing the whistle on corporate misconduct invariably means, at a minimum, ostracism in the workplace. Often it means the loss of one's job, or at the very least the loss of one's ability to do one's job, and it may also mean the loss of one's friends. There is only a small prospect of vindication; or if it comes, it comes only after many years.[2]

Organizations that wish to have an effective whistleblower policy, such as the one described in this book, must devise a system that either eliminates or at least ameliorates these disincentives. Other chapters of this book discuss the huge potential statutory bounties available to whistleblowers, but it should be remembered that these people have to endure many years of litigation to obtain these awards and that the median whistleblower award is only approximately $150,000 after legal fees.[3]

Disincentives to internal whistleblowing can be divided into two categories: financial and nonfinancial.

FINANCIAL DISINCENTIVES

The financial disincentives to internal whistleblowers include:

- Poor performance reports by the whistleblower supervisors
- Disqualification from incentive bonuses
- Destruction of potential for career advancement
- Being fired, as happened to Cheryl Eckard
- Inability to obtain new employment because of poor recommendations or no recommendations from prior employer

Whistleblowing negatively affects the reputation of the whistleblowers, who rarely get reemployed in the same industry.[4] Their careers are over, at least in their industry, and sometimes in other industries as well.

One academic study has stated:

> The phenomenon that potential future employers will refuse a whistle-blower is called blacklisting, the whistleblower is put on the "black list" of the "not to be employed." Although he has done the right thing, he is considered to be a disloyal employee and a potential liability for future employers. Who would want to have the whistle blown on his own company? Partly this fear and partly the informal boycott by the "old boys" network of the industry make a further career in this field almost impossible. . . . This means his career is virtually dead.[5]

Does anyone really believe that it would have been easy for Cheryl Eckard to obtain a full-time job in the pharmaceutical industry after 2004 when she blew the whistle on Glaxo?

James F. Bingham, an assistant treasurer at Xerox, was terminated by Xerox in 2000 and alleged in his subsequent lawsuit that he was fired for reporting accounting irregularities in the company's Mexican business. Xerox claimed that Bingham's allegations were presented to directors and auditors and found to be "without merit."[6] The SEC began an investigation, after which Xerox restated its earnings for four years and paid a fine of $10 million.[7] The lawyer for James Bingham summed up Bingham's situation in this way: "Jim had a great career, but he'll never get a job in Corporate America again." Unfortunately, the lawyer's prediction was true not only of Bingham but of many other whistleblowers.[8]

 ## NONFINANCIAL DISINCENTIVES

The predominant nonfinancial disincentive is psychological pressure.

The psychological pressure on the whistleblower typically starts immediately after fellow employees find out about the whistleblowing and increases quickly thereafter. This building up of "psychological pressure might even be as subtle as silent social ostracism,[9] excluding the employee in question from any social gatherings, e-mails, carpools and giving him 'the silent treatment.'"[10]

One source of psychological pain from the disclosure of wrongdoing is that it requires deviation from a group. A whistleblower may have to self-identify as different from his or her fellow workers in order to make such a disclosure. The accusation by the whistleblower can undermine the employee's own identity within the group.[11]

Fear of social ostracism is a strong disincentive facing potential whistle-blowers.[12] William James, a psychologist and philosopher, wrote that "[n]o more fiendish punishment could be devised" than social ostracism.[13] Ostracism threatens a basic human motivation to avoid exclusion from important social groups.[14] It may be as simple as giving the cold shoulder or the silent treatment to a whistleblower, or it may evolve into full-blown social rejection.[15] It may also take more modern forms, such as cyber-ostracism, in which an employee no longer receives as many company e-mails.[16]

"Other nuisances might be transferring [the whistleblower] to other locations, giving him or her a closet for an office,[17] increased scrutiny, investigation of his personal background to detract from his statements, etc."[18]

The people denounced may be not only the whistleblower's employer, which is "the hand that feeds him," but also "colleagues and business relations, who have often become friends":

Retaliation by the organization and even fellow employees can be very indirect and subtle. For instance, workplace harassment and threats devised to make a potential whistleblower, or one in the process of blowing the whistle, lose faith in his or her whistleblowing and the possibility of bringing it to a good end.[19]

All these psychological harassments are very difficult to successfully prove and be protected against, as we can see in general harassment in the workplace lawsuits.

This altogether can have devastating effects on the whistleblower and those close to him or her.[20]

The psychological pressures on the whistleblowers have been described as follows:

Usually the whistleblower is not fired outright. The organization's goal is to disconnect the act of whistleblowing from the act of retaliation, which is why so much legislation to protect whistleblowers is practically irrelevant. The usual practice is to demoralize and humiliate the whistleblower, putting him or her under so much psychological stress that it becomes difficult to do a good job.[21]

The SEC's general counsel has stated:

Whistleblowers often have to go through a hellish ordeal for years. If rationality means the outcome of disinterested calculation, I'm not at all sure it's rational to be a whistleblower. But that hardly means that the claims made by whistleblowers are invariably untrue.[22]

 ## CONTRACTUAL COMMITMENTS AND FIDUCIARY DUTIES

Another disincentive arises if the whistleblower has an employment contract and can be sued for breaching confidentiality clauses. This threat of a breach-of-contract lawsuit is possible, as many contracts include confidentiality clauses and "all contracts of employment involve an implied 'duty of fidelity' which requires honest, loyal and faithful service and forbids competition with the employer."[23]

Employee confidentiality agreements are now standard practice.[24] Several employers have enforced confidentiality agreements in an effort to prevent whistleblowers from testifying about employer wrongdoing.[25]

In addition to contractual concerns, potential whistleblowers may be worried about possible liability for breach of a fiduciary duty—particularly if there is no solid proof of wrongdoing. According to one law professor, blowing the whistle to outsiders—including regulatory authorities—might even constitute conversion of corporate property, which could certainly be said to violate an employee's duty of loyalty.[26]

 ## ETHICS RESOURCE CENTER SURVEY

The Ethics Resource Center (ERC) conducted a survey in 2009[27] of retaliation rates and of employees who experience retaliation. These terms refer to those employees who observed some form of misconduct, reported their observation to an appropriate person within the company, and felt that they were punished as a result of their decision to report.

The ERC study noted that it was possible that employees felt that they were retaliated against when, in fact, they were not. However, in the ERC's view, retaliation is a case in which perception is reality, since an employee's perception of retaliation is sufficient to alter his or her opinion of the workplace.

In 2009, 15 percent of all those who observed and then reported misconduct felt that they were retaliated against as a result. However, this figure is misleading, since the actual percentage varies with the type of misconduct reported and the power position of the person reporting the misconduct within the organization. Furthermore, the 15 percent represents an average frequency of retaliation for both minor as well as major misconduct. The more serious the wrongdoing, the higher the probability of retaliation, particularly for women, who are usually in low-power positions within the corporate hierarchy.[28] Thus, a whistleblower who informs about serious misconduct is much more likely than 15 percent to be the victim of retaliation.

If a whistleblower who is an executive goes over the head of the CEO and reports a problem directly to the independent directors, the possibility of retaliation may be closer to 100 percent rather than 15 percent. For example, if an executive at Merrill Lynch in 2007 had gone over the head of Stan O'Neal, then its chief executive, to report directly to the independent directors the excessive accumulation of subprime mortgages in the company's portfolio, one would suspect that the risk of retaliation would have been quite high.

Moreover, the mere fact that there is a significant possibility of retaliation is sufficient to make potential whistleblowers seriously consider whether they will be retaliated against. Accordingly, the mere prospect of retaliation is sufficient to deter many whistleblowers.

The ERC survey indicated a wide range of retaliation, ranging from exclusion from work activity to actual physical harm. Participants reported 10

TABLE 4.1 Retaliation Experience by Whistleblowers

Forms of Retaliation	Percentage Who Experienced Retaliation
Supervisor or management excluded employee from decisions and work activity	62%
Other employees gave a cold shoulder	60%
Verbally abused by supervisor or someone else in management	55%
Almost lost job	48%
Not given promotions or raises	43%
Verbally abused by other employees	42%
Relocated or reassigned	27%
Other form of retaliation	20%
Demoted	18%
Experienced physical harm to person or property	4%

Source: © 2011, Ethics Resource Center. Used with permission of the Ethics Resource Center, 2345 Crystal Drive, Suite 201, Arlington, VA 22202, www.ethics.org.

different forms of retaliation. Table 4.1 shows the percentages of various forms of retaliation experienced by whistleblowers in the survey.[29]

Different groups of employees experience the various forms of retaliation at different rates (see Table 4.2). According to the survey:

> For example, overall, 18 percent of those who have been retaliated against were demoted, but only 9 percent of men cited such an experience compared with 26 percent of women. And 52 percent of workers in publicly-traded companies were denied promotions or raises, noticeably higher than employees of privately-held companies (36 percent) and workers overall (43 percent).[30]

REINSTATEMENT AS A REMEDY

Many statutes to protect whistleblowers contain provisions for the reinstatement of the whistleblower. That is true of the Dodd-Frank Act. Regaining employment at the whistleblower's former seniority level or protection from

TABLE 4.2 Forms and Rates of Retaliation for Different Groups

Form of Retaliation	Percentage of Reports Who Experienced Retaliation	Groups LESS Likely to Experience This Form of Retaliation	Groups MORE Likely to Experience This Form of Retaliation
Supervisor or management excluded employee from decisions and work activity	62%	Employees who do not supervise others (48%)	Employees who supervise others (72%)
		Workers in privately held companies (51%)	Workers in publicly traded companies (71%)
		3 to 5 years' tenure (52%)	1 to 2 years' tenure (71%)
		Members of unions (55%)	6 to 10 years' tenure (68%)
		18- to 29-year-olds (58%)	
		First-line supervisors (58%)	Top management (67%)
			11 or more years' tenure (66%)
Other employees gave a cold shoulder	60%	Middle management (35%)	6 to 10 years' tenure (72%)
		Top management (40%)	Members of unions (72%)
		1 to 2 years' tenure (44%)	18- to 29-year-olds (68%)
		Nonunion employees (55%)	First-line supervisors (67%)
			Nonmanagement employees (65%)
			Workers in publicly traded companies (65%)
			3 to 5 years' tenure (64%)
Verbally abused by supervisor or someone else in management	55%	Employees who do not supervise others (43%)	Workers in publicly traded companies (70%)
		Top management (44%)	30- to 44-year-olds (66%)
		Workers in privately held companies (45%)	6 to 10 years' tenure (66%)
		3 to 5 years' tenure (45%)	Employees who supervise others (64%)
		45- to 63-year-olds (47%)	Employees in U.S.-based multinationals (61%)
		18- to 29-year-olds (51%)	11 or more years' tenure (59%)
		Nonmanagement employees (51%)	1 to 2 years' tenure (59%)

(continued)

TABLE 4.2 *(Continued)*

Form of Retaliation	Percentage of Reports Who Experienced Retaliation	Groups LESS Likely to Experience This Form of Retaliation	Groups MORE Likely to Experience This Form of Retaliation
Almost lost job	48%	Employees who do not supervise others (38%) 11 or more years' tenure (39%) First-line supervisors (39%) 6 to 10 years' (40%) 45- to 63-year-olds (41%)	1 to 2 years' tenure (68%) 18- to 29-year-olds (64%) Employees who supervise others (56%)
Not given promotions or raises	43%	First-line supervisors (25%) Employees who do not supervise others (35%) Members of unions (36%) Workers in privately held companies (36%) Employees in domestic companies (38%) 30- to 44-year-olds (38%)	Employees in U.S.-based multinationals (63%) Workers in publicly traded companies (52%) 1 to 2 years' tenure (50%) Employees who supervise others (49%) Middle management (48%) Nonmanagement employees (47%)
Verbally abused by other employees	42%	Middle management (22%) 3 to 5 years' tenure (30%) 1 to 2 years' tenure (35%) 45- to 63-year-olds (37%) Members of unions (37%)	6 to 10 years' tenure (59%) First-line supervisors (52%) 18- to 29-year-olds (48%) 30- to 44-year-olds (46%) Employees in U.S.-based multinationals (46%)
Relocated or reassigned	27%	Workers in privately held companies (16%) 18- to 29-year-olds (18%) Nonmanagement employees (20%) Top management (20%) 6 to 10 years' tenure (22%) Middle management (23%) Members of unions (23%)	First-line supervisors (39%) Employees in U.S.-based multinationals (37%) Workers in publicly traded companies (36%) 11 or more years' tenure (36%) 45- to 63-year-olds (35%)

TABLE 4.2   *(Continued)*

Form of Retaliation	Percentage of Reports Who Experienced Retaliation	Groups LESS Likely to Experience This Form of Retaliation	Groups MORE Likely to Experience This Form of Retaliation
Demoted	18%	Men (9%)	1 to 2 years' tenure (38%)
		3 to 5 years' tenure (9%)	18- to 29-year-olds (27%)
		11 or more years' tenure (11%)	Women (26%)
			First-line supervisors (24%)
		30- to 44-year-olds (14%)	
			Employees in U.S.-based multinationals (22%)
Experienced physical harm to person or property	4%		Top management (11%)
			11 or more years' tenure (9%)

Source: © 2011, Ethics Resource Center. Used with permission of the Ethics Resource Center, 2345 Crystal Drive, Suite 201, Arlington, VA 22202, www.ethics.org.

dismissal has been characterized as a "poisoned benefit." It places the whistleblower in an environment that is, in all probability, quite hostile: "Reinstating the whistleblower in his previous job could lead to a continuation of his subtle daily torture. It has been suggested that this might even turn out to be a strong additional disincentive."[31]

Reinstatement of the whistleblower is an unrealistic remedy, considering both the psychological pressures and the dubious career advancement potential of that employee. Moreover, if the organization involved in a widespread fraud or crime is about to file bankruptcy proceedings, the job of the reinstated whistleblower will only be temporary.

 ## EMPIRICAL STUDY

An interesting empirical study of whistleblowers was made at Wright-Patterson Air Force Base in Ohio, which consisted of an air force unit with 9,900 employees, two-thirds of whom were civilians and one-third active-duty military.[32] Unit tasks ranged from the acquisition of high-tech aircraft and support systems to medical care to base support. Questionnaires were distributed to all employees, to be completed anonymously and be returned to the researchers. A total of 3,288 employees participated. The base commander provided a cover letter assuring employees of anonymity and suggesting that results might influence his future decision making.

Near the beginning of each questionnaire, respondents were asked whether, within the last 12 months, they had "personally observed or had direct evidence" of any of 17 types of wrongdoing involving their organizations.

The whistleblowers who reported wrongdoing (excluding those who reported wrongdoing anonymously) experienced the types of retaliation shown in Table 4.3.

Our next chapter deals with whether women are more likely than men to be whistleblowers and the factors motivating employees to go public with the information.

TABLE 4.3   Types of Retaliation Reported by Identified Whistleblowers

Retaliation	Experienced (%)
Poor performance appraisal	15
Tighter scrutiny of daily activities by management	14
Verbal harassment or intimidation	12
Coworkers not socializing with me	11
Withholding of information needed to successfully perform job	10
Denial of opportunity for training	9
Personnel/staff withdrawn	9
Assignment to less desirable or less important duties	8
Charged with committing an unrelated offense	7
Denial of award	7
Denial of promotion	7
Professional reputation was harmed	7
Reassignment to different job with less desirable duties	7

Source: Reprinted by permission from Michael T. Rehg, Marcia P. Miceli, Janet P. Near, and James R. Van Scotter, "Antecedents and Outcomes of Retaliation Against Whistleblowers: Gender Differences and Power Relationships," *Organization Science* 19, No. 2 (March–April 2008): 221–240, Copyright 2008, the Institute for Operations Research and the Management Sciences (INFORMS), 7240 Parkway Drive, Suite 300, Hanover, MD 21076 USA.

NOTES

1. Danny Westneat, "Nobody Likes a Snitch . . . Do They?" *Seattle Times*, July 20, 2008.
2. David M. Becker, Esq., General Counsel, Speech by SEC Staff, Remarks at the Practising Law Institute's Ninth Annual Institute on Securities Regulation in Europe, U.S. Securities and Exchange Commission, January 25, 2011.
3. Conversation with Patrick Burns, Director of Communications, Taxpayers Against Fraud, based on a review of whistleblower claims on the website: www.taf.org/abouttaf.htm.
4. Maarten De Schepper, "Setting the Right Incentives for Whistleblowers," August 10, 2009, paper submitted for European Master in Law and Economics, 2008–2009. www.emle.org/_data/Marten_De_Schepper_-_Setting_the_Right_Incentives_for_Whistleblowers.pdf.
5. Ibid., p. 22.
6. John Hechinger and James Bandler, "Former Xerox Officials in Mexico Assert Headquarters Ignored Fiscal Warnings," *Wall Street Journal*, February 9, 2001.
7. Alexander Dyck, Adair Morse, and Luigi Zingales, "Who Blows the Whistle on Corporate Fraud?" *Journal of Finance* 65, no. 6 (2010): 2213–2253. http://dx.doi.org/10.1111/j.1540-6261.2010.01614.x.
8. Ibid.
9. Kipling D. Williams, *Ostracism: The Power of Silence* (New York: Guilford Press, 2002), pp. 191–196.
10. De Schepper, "Setting the Right Incentives for Whistleblowers."
11. Geoffrey Christopher Rapp, "Beyond Protection: Invigorating Incentives for Sarbanes-Oxley Corporate and Securities Fraud Whistleblowers," *Boston University Law Review* 87, no. 91 (2007): 91–156.
12. Ibid.
13. William James, *Principles of Psychology* (New York: Dover Publications, 1950), p. 293. (Originally published 1890.)
14. Sonja L. Faulkner, "After the Whistle Is Blown: The Aversive Impact of Ostracism," PhD diss., August 1998, University of Toledo.
15. See Marcia P. Miceli and Janet P. Near, "Blowing the Whistle: The Organizational and Legal Implications for Companies and Employees" (New York: Lexington Books, 1992), p. 49.
16. Faulkner, "After the Whistle Is Blown."
17. C. Fred Alford, *Whistleblowers: Broken Lives and Organizational Power* (Ithaca, NY: Cornell University Press, 2002), p. 32.
18. Robert Howse and Ronald J. Daniels, "Rewarding Whistleblowers: The Costs and Benefits of an Incentive-Based Compliance Strategy," University of Pennsylvania Scholarly Commons, Department Papers (School of

Law), January 1, 1995, p. 533. http://works.bepress.com/cgi/viewcontent
.cgi?article=1017&context=ronald_daniels.

19. Dyck, Morse, and Zingales, "Who Blows the Whistle on Corporate Fraud?" p. 24.

20. Pamela H. Bucy, "Private Justice," *Southern California Law Review* 75, No. 1 (2002): 61–62; see also De Schepper, "Setting the Right Incentives for Whistle-blowers."

21. Alford, *Whistleblowers: Broken Lives and Organizational Power* (Ithaca, NY: Cornell University Press, 2002), pp. 31–32.

22. Becker, Speech by SEC Staff.

23. Vincent Keter and Louise Smith, "Whistleblowing: The Public Interest Disclosure Act of 1998." House of Commons Standard Note SN/BT/248, August 14, 1999.

24. See Terry Morehead Dworkin and Elletta Sangrey Callahan, "Buying Silence," *American Business Law Journal* 36 (1998): 151, 152.

25. See ibid. at p. 153.

26. See Leonard M. Baynes, "Just Pucker and Blow?: An Analysis of Corporate Whistleblowers, the Duty of Care, the Duty of Loyalty, and the Sarbanes-Oxley Act," *St. John's Law Review* 76 (2002): 884, 893.

27. Ethics Resource Center, Supplemental Research Brief, "2009 National Business Ethics Survey: Retaliation: The Cost to Your Company and Its Employees," 2010.

28. Michael T. Rehg, Marcia P. Miceli, Janet P. Near, and James R. Van Scotter, "Antecedents and Outcomes of Retaliation Against Whistleblowers: Gender Differences and Power Relationships," *Organization Science* 19, No. 2 (March-April 2008): 221–240. Copyright 2008, the Institute for Operations Research and the Management Sciences (INFORMS), 7240 Parkway Drive, Suite 300, Hanover, MD 21076 USA.

29. www.ethics.org/files/u5/Retaliation.pdf.

30. Ibid.

31. De Schepper, "Setting the Right Incentives for Whistleblowers."

32. Rehg et al., "Antecedents and Outcomes of Retaliation Against Whistleblowers."

CHAPTER FIVE

Women as Whistleblowers

Factors Motivating Public Whistleblowing

A NY SANE WHISTLEBLOWER POLICY encourages internal whistle-blowing so that the problems can be corrected before there is public disclosure of the illegal conduct. An effective whistleblower policy therefore considers what factors will induce a whistleblower to report misconduct externally rather than internally and attempts to eliminate or at least ameliorate those factors.

Because so many women have become famous as whistleblowers, we examine the role of gender in this chapter.[1] Female employee whistleblowers suffer more frequent retaliation than men, as discussed in this and the prior chapter. Because women are more likely to suffer retaliation for internal whistleblowing than men, women are more likely to become external whistleblowers.

In 2002, *TIME* magazine selected three individuals as "Person of the Year": Each was a whistleblower in a large organization, and all were women. These women were Sherron Watkins, Cynthia Cooper, and Coleen Rowley, and a brief profile of each follows.

 SHERRON WATKINS

Sherron Watkins was a whistleblower in Enron. On August 22, 2001, Kenneth Lay, Enron's chairman, received a letter from Enron accounting executive Sherron Watkins that contained the following allegations:

I am incredibly nervous that we will implode in a wave of accounting scandals. My eight years of Enron work history will be worth nothing on my resume, the business world will consider the past successes as nothing but an elaborate accounting hoax. [Enron president Jeff] Skilling is resigning now for "personal reasons" but I would think he wasn't having fun, looked down the road and knew this stuff was unfixable and would rather abandon ship now than resign in shame in two years. . . .

I realize that we have had a lot of smart people looking at this and a lot of accountants including AA & Co. [Arthur Andersen & Co.] have blessed the accounting treatment. None of that will protect Enron if these transactions are ever disclosed in the bright light of day. (Please review the late 90's problems of Waste Management—where AA paid $130 million plus in litigation re: questionable accounting practices.) . . .

Involve Jim Derrick and Rex Rogers [Enron's inside lawyers] to hire a law firm to investigate the Condor and Raptor transactions to give Enron attorney-client privilege on the work product. (Can't use V & E [the law firm of Vinson & Elkins] due to conflict—they provided some true sale opinions on some of the deals.)

Law firm to hire one of the big 6, but not Arthur Andersen or PricewaterhouseCoopers due to their conflicts of interest: AA & Co. (Enron); PWC (LJM).[2]

The actual timeline of what happened thereafter is presented next.

August–October 2001: The Watkins letter triggered an investigation by the firm of Vinson & Elkins (despite her request not to use V&E), which began in August and ended with a verbal report on September 21 and a written report on October 15. The report concluded that the facts so far revealed did not warrant a "further widespread investigation by independent counsel or auditors," although it did note that the "bad cosmetics" of the Raptor related-party transactions, coupled with the poor performance of the assets placed in the Raptor vehicles, created "a serious risk of adverse publicity and litigation."

October 16, 2001: Enron publicly announced a $44 million after-tax charge against earnings and a reduction of its shareholders equity by $1.2 billion.

December 2, 2001: Enron, then the seventh largest publicly traded corporation in the United States, declared bankruptcy.

According to one source, Watkins was "unsuccessful" at stopping Enron's fraud because the information she disclosed was "sanitized" by Ken Lay and the law firm of Vinson & Elkins before it made its way to the company's board.[3]

CYNTHIA COOPER

Cynthia Cooper was the vice president of internal audit for WorldCom, Inc. A series of obscure tips in the spring of 2002 led her and Gene Morse, a WorldCom internal audit manager, to suspect that their employer was cooking its books:

> Armed with accounting skills and determination, Ms. Cooper and her team set off on their own to figure out whether their hunch was correct. Often working late at night to avoid detection by their bosses, they combed through hundreds of thousands of accounting entries, crashing the company's computers in the process.
>
> By June 23, they had unearthed $3.8 billion in misallocated expenses and phony accounting entries. It all added up to an accounting fraud, acknowledged by the company, which turned out to be the largest in corporate history. Their discoveries sent WorldCom into bankruptcy, left thousands of their colleagues without jobs and shook the stock market.
>
> At a time when dishonesty at the top of U.S. companies was dominating public attention, Ms. Cooper and her team are a case of middle managers who took their commitment to financial reporting to extraordinary lengths. As she pursued the trail of fraud, Ms. Cooper time and again was obstructed by fellow employees, some of whom disapproved of WorldCom's accounting methods but were unwilling to contradict their bosses or thwart the company's goals.[4]

Ms. Cooper's job as an internal auditor was to disclose accounting wrongdoing to the WorldCom audit committee. In contrast to whistleblowers Cheryl Eckard or Sherron Watkins, Ms. Cooper was therefore less likely to suffer internal retaliation, as discussed later in this chapter.

COLEEN ROWLEY

Coleen Rowley was a whistleblower in the Federal Bureau of Investigation (FBI).

After the September 11, 2001 attacks, Rowley wrote a paper for FBI Director Robert Mueller documenting how FBI HQ [headquarters] personnel in Washington, D.C. had mishandled and failed to take action on information provided by the Minneapolis, Minnesota Field Office regarding its investigation of suspected terrorist Zacarias Moussaoui. This individual had been suspected of being involved in preparations for a suicide-hijacking similar to the December 1994 "Eiffel Tower" hijacking of Air France 8969. Failures identified by Rowley may have left the U.S. vulnerable to the September 11, 2001 attacks. Rowley was one of many agents frustrated by the events that led up to the attacks.[5]

The 9/11 Commission subsequently described Moussaoui as an "Al Qaeda mistake and missed opportunity," the investigation of whom may have led to the center of the Al Qaeda plot if it had been pursued in a timely and effective manner.[6]

EXTERNAL REPORTING BY INTERNAL WHISTLEBLOWERS

Research repeatedly has shown that the majority of internal whistleblowers who use external or public channels also have blown the whistle internally and suffered retaliation.[7] Cheryl Eckard, whose story is in Chapter 2 of this book, is a classic example.

Employees who report externally tend to suffer more retaliation than employees who report solely internally, and perceive a more retaliatory climate.[8] Although external whistleblowing by employees of both genders is related to perceived retaliation, the relationship is much stronger for women than for men.[9]

One empirical study of 9,900 employees at an air force base, referred to in Chapter 4, concluded:

Male whistleblowers were treated differently depending on their power in the organization, but female whistleblowers received the same treatment regardless of the amount of organizational power they held: Their status as women overrode their status as powerful or powerless organization members. This was consistent with earlier findings that female attorneys (a relatively powerful group) suffered greater levels of interpersonal mistreatment than male attorneys.[10] On the other hand, women who reported wrongdoing that was serious or which harmed them directly were more likely to suffer retaliation, whereas men were not. Again, we believe that women who blow the whistle are behaving in ways that are inconsistent with their status; when they blow the whistle about serious wrongdoing or about a higher-level wrongdoer, the whistle-blowing is even more at odds with the appropriate role for women, thereby causing them to be seen as deserving retaliation.[11]

The seriousness of wrongdoing also is related to the use of external channels by employee whistleblowers. This relationship is true for both men and women. Presumably, wrongdoing that is not serious is typically not pursued publicly, in light of the risk of retaliation. The empirical study supported these conclusions:

- There is a correlation between gender and retaliation, with women more likely to suffer retaliation than men when they are whistleblowers.
- Low whistleblower power (reflected in nonsupervisory status, low leverage, and no employee prescription for whistleblowing) was significantly related to retaliation for men but was unrelated to retaliation for women.
- The greater the seriousness of the wrongdoing, the greater the retaliation for women whistleblowers.
- Retaliation against the whistleblower was positively associated with the relationship of the whistleblower to his or her supervisor. The effect of the retaliation was stronger for women.

According to the study, the gender of the whistleblower was positively related to the chances of retaliation against a woman whistleblower, perhaps because whistleblowing represented a violation of the stereotypical role expectations for women.

The study also concluded that greater individual power within the organization did not help female whistleblowers avoid retaliation. For men, greater individual power and support from others was helpful but, contrary to the model, seriousness of wrongdoing was unrelated to retaliation.

This study has important implications for organizations that wish to use best practices. Retaliation may cause whistleblowers subsequently to use external channels for reporting, and female whistleblowers are more likely to suffer retaliation than male whistleblowers.

Also important to the employee's decision to report externally is his or her view of the organization's procedures for handling whistleblower complaints. A perception of procedural injustice results in retaliation against the organization by the whistleblower. The employee's direct supervisor hears the complaint first and is responsible for administering the whistleblower procedures.

Whistleblowers who perceive their supervisors as behaving unjustly are more likely to report externally. Likewise, if an employee whistleblower suffers retaliation or procedural injustice, he or she is more likely to retaliate against the organization through public disclosure.[12]

Another important driving force motivating external whistleblowing is revenge,[13] which apparently is very sweet to some disgruntled former employees who believe they have experienced internal retaliation. Therefore, it is important to prevent real or perceived retaliation against whistleblowers.

 WHISTLEBLOWER ANONYMITY

If internal retaliation (whether real or perceived) against internal whistleblowers actually causes them to report externally, it is obviously important to prevent such retaliation. Human nature being what it is, it is unlikely that there is any way to completely protect whistleblowers from retaliation by fellow employees or others unless the identity of the whistleblower is completely anonymous.

Numerous articles have been written about the necessity of not revealing the identity of whistleblowers.[14] There is almost universal agreement that this is the only method that has any chance of protecting whistleblowers from retaliation. Indeed, without a guarantee of anonymity, many potential whistleblowers will refuse to provide needed information to the organization for fear of retaliation.

In Part III of this book, we discuss why all organizations should establish a robust whistleblower policy and the content of that policy.

 NOTES

1. Brent R. MacNab and Reginald Worthley, "Self-Efficacy as an Intrapersonal Predictor for Internal Whistleblowing: A US and Canada Examination," *Journal of Business Ethics* 79 (2008): 407–421.
2. "Sherron Watkins eMail to Enron Chairman Kenneth Lay," January 20, 2002. www.itmweb.com/f012002.htm.
3. Richard E. Moberly, "Sarbanes-Oxley's Structural Model to Encourage Corporate Whistleblowers," *Brigham Young University Law Review* 1108, no. 5 (2006): 1123.

4. Susan Pulliam and Deborah Solomon, "Uncooking the Books: How Three Unlikely Sleuths Discovered Fraud at WorldCom," *Wall Street Journal*, October 30, 2002.

5. www.howtheworldchanged.org/speakers.html#.

6. www.coleenrowley.com/pages/about_coleen.php.

7. M. P. Miceli and J. P. Near, *Blowing the Whistle: The Organizational and Legal Implications for Companies and Employees.* (New York: Lexington Books, 1992).

8. J. P. Near and M. P. Miceli, "Retaliation against Whistleblowers: Predictors and Effects," *Journal of Applied Psychology* 71 (1986): 137–145.

9. Michael T. Rehg, Marcia P. Miceli, Janet P. Near, and James R. Van Scotter, "Antecedents and Outcomes of Retaliation Against Whistleblowers: Gender Differences and Power Relationships," *Organization Science* 19, no. 2 (March–April 2008): 221–240.

10. L. M. Cortina, K. A. Lonsway, V. J. Magley, L. V. Freeman, L. L. Collinsworth, M. Hunter, and L. F. Fitzgerald, "What's gender got to do with it? Incivility in the federal courts," *Law & Social Inquiry* 272 (2002): 235–270.

11. Rehg et al., "Antecedents and Outcomes of Retaliation Against Whistleblowers," p. 235.

12. D. P. Skarlicki and R. Folger, "Retaliation in the Workplace: The Roles of Distributive, Procedural and Interactional Justice," *Journal of Applied Psychology* 83 (1997): 434–443.

13. Phillip G. Clampitt, *Communicating for Managerial Effectiveness: Problems, Strategies, Solutions* (Thousand Oaks, CA: Sage Publications, 2004), p. 75.

14. A. Morse, A. Dyck, and L. Zingales, *Who Blows the Whistle on Corporate Fraud?* (Cambridge, MA: National Bureau of Economic Research, 2007); S. Ayers and S. Kaplan, "Wrongdoing by Consultants: An Examination of Employees' Reporting Intentions," *Journal of Business Ethics* 57 (2005): 121–37; J. Near and M. Miceli, "Whistle-Blowing: Myth and Reality," *Journal of Management* 22 (1996): 507–527; J. Near and M. Miceli, "Effective Whistle-Blowing," *Academy of Management Review* (1995): 679–708.

PART THREE

Organizational Best Practices

CHAPTER SIX

6

Why Should Organizations Adopt a Robust Whistleblower System?

THE FIVE PRIMARY REASONS that organizations should adopt a robust whistleblower system are:

1. To protect the organization from criminal indictment, conviction, and fines and from related civil liability
2. To protect the shareholders or other equity holders of the organization from loss of value of their equity interests
3. To protect the board of directors and officers from civil liability
4. To protect the chief executive officer (CEO) from both criminal and civil liability
5. To protect the business reputation of both the directors and the CEO

The purpose of a robust whistleblower system is to induce employees to use the internal compliance system to report illegal activity rather than report such activity externally to receive statutory rewards. Internal reporting permits the organization to prevent and correct the illegal behavior, thereby helping to safeguard the organization and its directors, officers, and equity holders from the consequences of such illegal behavior.

As discussed in this chapter, if a scandal occurs during the watch of a director or CEO, his or her business reputation will suffer, and it will be difficult to seek other comparable positions. This chapter also discusses the potential civil and criminal liability of both the organization and its directors and the CEO.

Many directors and CEOs believe that they and their organizations are protected by creating and disseminating a "paper" corporate compliance policy and designating a person as chief compliance officer. Nothing could be further from the truth. This chapter discusses the case of Charles Park, the CEO of Acme Markets, who did exactly that and still was found personally criminally liable.[1] Although Park-type cases are rare, prosecutors are becoming very frustrated with their inability to change corporate conduct solely through prosecution of the corporation and may elect to bring criminal prosecutions against CEOs and other responsible members of management.[2] This frustration has also led to attempts to oust longtime CEOs, particularly in the pharmaceutical industry.[3]

Both the board of directors and the CEO have fiduciary responsibilities to the corporation, and investors expect the board to have ultimate responsibility for risk oversight.[4] Any failure of corporate compliance may result in a shareholders' suit against both the CEO and the board of directors for the damage they have caused to the corporation. In addition, regulators, such as the U.S. Department of Justice (DOJ) and other federal and state agencies, also may bring direct actions against the CEO and the board of directors for their participation in unlawful activities.

 ## DIMINISHMENT OF SHAREHOLDER WEALTH

Criminal indictment or conviction of an organization has far-reaching negative consequences for the organization. The indictment or conviction results in adverse publicity for the organization and sullies its reputation. Indictment or conviction also may lead to a loss of important customers or suppliers. Governmental and other customers may suspend or bar the organization from doing business. The organization's ability to attract and retain competent executives may suffer. The organization may incur enormous legal fees and costs in contesting the indictment and any related shareholder lawsuits and suffer huge fines and penalties if convicted.

Melissa Baucus and David Baucus studied 68 Fortune 300 firms that were criminally convicted for five years, beginning with the year following the conviction.[5] The study used three performance measures: shareholder returns, return on assets, and return on sales. The 68 firms were then compared, using the same performance measurements, to unconvicted Fortune 300 firms during the same five-year period, controlling the comparison statistically for variables of size and industry membership. The study concluded:

> Convicted firms generate lower accounting returns (ROA [return on assets] and ROS [return on sales]) in the first year and over the five years after a conviction, possibly reflecting lower revenues or higher costs. These firms experience immediate and prolonged reductions in revenues as stakeholders (e.g., customers) exit the firms, and they may incur increased longer-term costs associated with acquiring capital, alleviating employee concerns, and attempting to stop the exodus of customers.
>
> Convicted firms experience reduced sales growth in the period three through five years after a conviction, indicating that customers may react more slowly to wrongdoing than other stakeholders. Managers employ defensive tactics . . . smoothing the immediate impact of convictions on sales by advertising, reducing prices, or shipping products within the fiscal year to overstate revenues. . . . Firms employing defensive initiatives experience immediate decreases in returns; however, defense initiatives and publicity have a temporary positive impact on sales, and the drop in sales shows up in years three through five.
>
> The seriousness of violations did not relate differentially to longer-term performance, suggesting stakeholders paint all convicted firms with the same brush. A conviction may stain a firm's image, sending a warning signal to stakeholders, or prompt stakeholders to reassess relationships with the firm, regardless of its seriousness.[6]

Other empirical studies have supported the thesis that indictment of a public corporation has at least a short-term negative impact on shareholder wealth.[7] Even Securities and Exchange Commission enforcement actions, to say nothing of criminal indictments, can have major negative impacts on share prices.[8]

BOARDS OF DIRECTORS

We now turn to why the board of directors should establish a robust whistleblower system. We begin with examples in which the boards of companies that had disasters were never given the proper information by senior management. We then discuss the legal standard applicable to directors.

The history of corporate scandals during the last 50 years shows that boards of directors, particularly the independent directors, were completely blindsided by impending scandals; they had no prior knowledge that problems were occurring. The independent directors were clueless because they relied on management to provide them with all necessary information, and management failed to do so, either purposely or negligently. Directors also relied on independent public accountants to detect illegal activity and to advise them of major risk exposures; unfortunately, the auditing procedures used by the independent accountants did not ensure that they could detect either illegal activity or major risk exposures.

WE WERE DUPED!

"We were duped!" is a common refrain by directors after every corporate scandal or financial disaster. For example:

- *Enron.* Sherron Watkins testified before Congress that the Enron board of directors was "duped."[9] "As for the Enron board, some directors pointed fingers of blame at company management, especially [Andrew] Fastow [Enron chief financial officer]."[10] One Enron director was quoted as saying "The board was duped."[11] Herbert S. "Pug" Winokur, Jr., former head of the Finance Committee, testified that Enron was "a cautionary reminder of the limits of a director's role," which is by nature a "part-time job." He stated, "We cannot, I submit, be criticized for failing to address or remedy problems that have been concealed from us."[12]
- *Tyco.* According to *USA Today*:

  Tyco directors' lack of awareness and events surrounding criminal charges against CEO Dennis Kozlowski underscore the lax oversight of management that plagues many company boards, corporate governance experts say. . . . The head of The Directorship Group, a director search firm, stated: "Just how do you hide this much money for so long from your board? . . . It's their job as a director to know what's going on."[13]

- *Merrill Lynch.* Stan O'Neal, the Merrill Lynch CEO prior to its forced merger with Bank of America, decided not to tell the board about an $8 billion write-down of its mortgage-backed securities. Other executives at the company were aware of its huge exposure to the subprime market and had warned O'Neal, but the board was in the dark allegedly because O'Neal did not initially believe the exposure was that large.[14] According to the book *All The Devils Are Here*:

> The board members were stunned. Their anger turned to fury. Some began grilling O'Neal on Merrill's exposure; others complained that his approaching Wachovia [Bank, another suitor,] was a terrible breach of corporate etiquette—a CEO is supposed to get a board's permission before approaching another company. "Their reaction was vitriolic," recalls one participant. "I've never seen that kind of interplay between a CEO and a board of directors."[15]

This huge exposure to the subprime mortgage market forced Merrill Lynch to disclose on October 24, 2007, a net loss of $7.9 billion on its collateralized debt obligations[16] and resulted in its merger in late 2008 with Bank of America, N.A.

■ *Lehman Brothers Holdings Inc.* According to the Bankruptcy Examiner's Report: "As their bad business decisions were pushing it toward collapse, top executives of the failed investment bank, Lehman Brothers Holding, Inc., repeatedly withheld information from their own board." The report states that in May 2008, a Lehman senior vice president, Matthew Lee, wrote a letter to management alleging accounting improprieties, asserting that Lehman used $50 billion of Repo 105 transactions (a questionable accounting technique) to temporarily move assets off balance sheet at quarter-end, but these allegations were never brought to the board's attention.[17] According to the report: "Senior executives did not disclose to the board of directors at the September 9, 2008 finance committee meeting the fact that a substantial portion of its liquidity pool was encumbered by clearing-bank pledge."[18] The report further states that "Lehman officers did not disclose to the board of directors that its liquidity position was substantially impaired by collateral held at clearing banks until the evening of September 14, 2008."[19] The bankruptcy filing occurred on September 15, 2008.

The board of directors is required to oversee and monitor the activities of an organization's executive officers. If board members rely solely on information provided to them by the senior executives, they are risking their business reputations. For example, Herbert Winokur, Jr., an Enron director, was forced to step down from his position at the Harvard Corporation, the governing body of Harvard University, as a result of the Enron bankruptcy.[20]

There have been numerous cases of CEOs and senior managers who lied on their resumes and subsequently were fired or disciplined. For example:

- On February 1, 2000, Jeffrey P. Papows quit as president of IBM's Lotus unit because of discrepancies in his education and military records.[21]
- In October 2002, Kenneth Lonchar, the chief financial officer (CFO) of Veritas Software, was forced to resign after making false claims that he was a Stanford MBA graduate.
- In November 2002, Bausch & Lomb, the eye care company, announced that chairman and chief executive Ronald Zarrella would forfeit $1.1 million because his resume falsely noted an MBA from New York University.
- In November 2002, MSG Capital chairman and CEO Brian Mitchell admitted falsifying a degree from Syracuse University. Although he continued on as CEO, the stock price fell 37 percent after the announcement, hitting a 52-week low.[22]
- In February 2006, the CEO of RadioShack Corp., David J. Edmondson, resigned following the revelation that he had lied on his resume about earning certain college degrees.

If some CEOs are willing to lie on their resumes, they also may be willing to lie to boards of directors. Accordingly, independent directors should not take as gospel anything that is said to them by the CEO or senior management.

EXECUTIVE WHISTLEBLOWERS

Lower-level executives typically are aware of potential scandals and major risk areas and bring these concerns to the attention of higher-level management. Higher-level management also may bring them to the attention of the CEO. The CEO, for one reason or another, may decide not to share these concerns with the board.

A major advantage of a robust whistleblower policy is to encourage greater communication of significant organizational risk exposures directly to the board of directors and particularly to the independent directors. Members of lower-level management often disagree with the CEO on risk exposures, but they have no opportunity to communicate their concerns directly to the board without fear of punishment by the CEO.

For example, prior to the collapse of AIG, certain executives recognized the major risks being undertaken through its derivatives business in credit default swaps[23] but had no incentive to reveal these risks to the directors. According to an article by Michael Lewis, an author, in mid-2005, an AIG executive named Eugene Park was fiddling around at work with his online trading account after reading about this wonderful new stock called New Century Financial with a terrific dividend yield. Park looked at New Century's financial statements and noticed something "frightening."[24] The average homeowner counted on to feed the interest on the A+ tranche of New Century mortgage-backed collateralized debt obligations (CDOs) had a credit score of only 598, with a 4.28 percent likelihood of being 60 days or more late on payment.[25] Park subsequently discovered that the AIG Financial Products Division was insuring a substantial portion of the New Century mortgages. He allegedly revealed this information to Joseph Cassano's (the AIG executive in charge of swaps) number-two person in the AIG financial products division and ultimately was blown off.[26] Had a robust whistleblower system existed at AIG at that time, Park might have used it to advise the AIG audit committee. Instead, the AIG financial products division did not reduce or hedge its existing supersenior tranches of subprime CDOs, although it stopped writing credit default swaps in late 2005–2006.[27]

Likewise, some senior officers at Merrill Lynch recognized its major exposure to subprime mortgages well before its forced merger into Bank of America; their warnings were ignored by the CEO.[28]

The Financial Crisis Inquiry Report notes that one of the two Bear Stearns executives stated in a diary in his personal e-mail account in 2006, long before the firm's collapse, that "a wave of fear set over [him]" when he realized that the Enhanced Fund "was going to subject investors to 'blow up risk'" and "we could not run the leverage as high as I had thought we could."[29]

A robust whistleblower system, as discussed in the next chapter, would create incentives for people to report such significant risk information anonymously to independent directors, thereby alleviating fear of retaliation from the CEO. A robust whistleblower system that guarantees anonymity and offers meaningful rewards might induce lower-level executives to provide independent directors with the same information. Without those guarantees, no one is going to risk their career by going over the head of the CEO.

Some directors believe that they can speak privately to lower-level company executives and obtain truthful and accurate information, even if that information contradicts information that the CEO or CFO has supplied to the board. What these directors do not realize is that lower-level executives are generally unwilling to jeopardize their careers with the company by contradicting the CEO or CFO even in private conversations with directors. The disincentives to whistleblowing, discussed earlier, make it unlikely that lower-level executives will be candid with directors unless their identity is completely protected. Only a naive or a very brave executive would take the risk that his or her name would not ultimately be revealed to higher-level executives after private conversations with directors.

The Enron case provides an example of private conversations between a director and a lower-level executive that failed to reveal important information. Director Winokur claims to have had several private conversations with an Enron risk management executive well before any problems with the company surfaced. Winokur claimed that the executive never advised him of problems at Enron, but that same executive testified publicly after the Enron bankruptcy that he did not like some of the derivative hedges that Enron was using.[30] Winokur should not have been surprised by the lack of candor of this risk management executive who would have risked his career by being candid with a director.

A robust whistleblower policy would have allowed the Enron executive to communicate with the independent directors in a manner that guaranteed anonymity. Although there is no assurance that this person would have used such a system, had it been available, the system would have provided the best chance for independent directors to obtain candid information from the executive ranks.

In summary, independent directors typically must rely on the CEO and CFO for almost all of their information about the company, subject to any additional information that they may receive from independent or internal auditors. It is difficult for independent directors to provide management oversight when most of their information comes from top management. This problem is exacerbated by the fact that a director's job is part time only and does not give him or her the necessary access to important corporate information.

 ## WHY INDEPENDENT DIRECTORS CANNOT RELY SOLELY ON INDEPENDENT OR INTERNAL AUDITORS

Absent the ability to receive communications from lower-level management executives, the board, and particularly the independent directors, must rely on independent or internal auditors to advise them of any law violation or major risk exposure. However, in each of the scandals discussed, that did not happen. Even in the WorldCom scandal, which ultimately was uncovered by the company's internal audit department, it took that department more than a year and a half to uncover the fraud.[31] Furthermore, under normal audit procedures, independent auditors do not necessarily have the ability to detect illegal activity or major risk exposures.

The Public Company Accounting Oversight Board (PCAOB) was established under the Sarbanes-Oxley Act of 2002 to provide oversight over the accounting profession as a result of the Enron, WorldCom, and other scandals from 2000 to 2002. The Investor Advisory Group, which was established by the PCAOB to provide views and advice to it, stated about the financial crisis from 2007 to 2009:

> The recent financial crisis presented auditors, and by extension the Sarbanes-Oxley Act audit reforms, with their first big test since these reforms were put into place. By any objective measure, they failed that test.
>
> ■ Dozens of the world's leading financial institutions failed, were sold in fire sales, or were prevented from failing only through a massive government intervention—all without a hint of advance warning on their financial statements that anything might be amiss.
> ■ Investors suffered devastating losses. Millions of Americans lost their homes or their jobs, and $11 trillion in household wealth has vanished, according to the Financial Crisis Inquiry Commission.
> ■ As a result, serious questions have been raised both about the quality of these financial institutions' financial reporting practices and about the quality of audits that permitted those reporting practices to go unchecked.[32]

The report of the Investment Advisory Group is contained in Table 6.1.

Although there were dissents from the report of the Investor Advisory Group, it is clear that there is substantial doubt about the ability of independent auditors, in a normal audit, to detect major risk areas within the business.

The PCAOB has clarified the limit of the auditor's duty to detect illegal acts in this passage:

> Entities may be affected by many other laws or regulations, including those related to securities trading, occupational safety and health, food and drug administration, environmental protection, equal employment, and price-fixing or other antitrust violations. Generally, these laws and regulations relate more to an entity's operating aspects than to its financial and accounting aspects, and their financial statement effect is indirect. An auditor ordinarily does not

TABLE 6.1 Sampling of Failed Financial Institutions (All of Which Received Unqualified Audit Opinions within Months of the Failure)

Company	Event	Event Date	Investor Losses ($m)*	Audit Firm
New Century	Bankruptcy	4/2/2007	2,576.40	KPMG LLP
Countrywide	Purchased	1/11/2008	22,776.00	KPMG LLP
Bear Stearns	Purchased	3/17/2008	20,896.80	Deloitte & Touche LLP
Freddie Mac	Government takeover	9/2/2008	41.50	PricewaterhouseCoopers
Fannie Mae	Government takeover	9/6/2008	64.10	Deloitte & Touche LLP
Lehman Bros.	Bankruptcy	9/15/2008	31,437.10	Ernst & Young
AIG	Troubled Asset Recovery Plan (TARP)	9/16/2008	155,499.60	PricewaterhouseCoopers
Washington Mutual	Bankruptcy	9/26/2008	30,558.50	Deloitte & Touche LLP
Citigroup	TARP	10/26/2008	212,065.20	KPMG LLP

* Calculated based on decline in market capitalization between one year prior to the event and the event date. Fannie Mae and Freddie Mac data are from October 9, 2007, and September 12, 2008.
Source: PCAOB Investor Advisory Group, "Report from the Working Group on: Lessons Learned from the Financial Crisis," March 16, 2011.

have sufficient basis for recognizing possible violations of such laws and regulations. . . . Even when violations of such laws and regulations can have consequences material to the financial statements, the auditor may not become aware of the existence of the illegal act unless he is informed by the client, or there is evidence of a governmental agency investigation or enforcement proceeding in the records, documents, or other information normally inspected in an audit of financial statements.[33]

Internal audit departments vary in size and competency and typically have dual reporting responsibilities: to both management and the audit committee of the board of directors. Indeed, some public companies have only a single employed internal auditor and use an outside service. Most internal audit services are performed for management as part of operational audits and do not necessarily reveal management accounting fraud or major risk exposures. For example, according to the Second Thornburgh Report, WorldCom management kept the internal audit department tied up in operational audits so that it did not have time to review or uncover the accounting manipulation occurring at the company.[34] There is no record that any of the internal audit departments in the companies listed in Table 6.1 ever warned the audit committee of problems the company faced.

 ## LEGAL STANDARD

As noted, boards of directors have a fiduciary duty to supervise and monitor management.

Many boards believe that they can delegate their supervisory responsibility for corporate compliance to management. From a legal point of view, this is generally true, unless a red flag is brought to the board's attention. Boards also tend to rely on legal exculpatory provisions contained in state corporate laws (such as Section 102(b)(7) of the Delaware General Corporation Law,[35] which permits the elimination of monetary liability for breach of the duty of care), indemnification provisions in the corporate charter and by-laws, favorable corporate law doctrines (such as the business judgment rule and Section 141(e) of the Delaware statute), and director and officer liability insurance policies.

Most corporate laws protect the directors legally to the extent that they rely in good faith on information supplied by officers of the company. Typical of these legal protections is the following quote from Section 141(e) of the Delaware General Corporation Law:

> A member of the board of directors, or a member of any committee designated by the board of directors, shall, in the performance of such member's duties, be fully protected in relying in good faith upon the records of the corporation and upon such information, opinions, reports or statements presented to the corporation by any of the corporation's officers or employees, or committees of the board of directors, or by any other person as to matters the member reasonably believes are within such other person's professional or expert competence and who has been selected with reasonable care by or on behalf of the corporation.

However, if the corporation gets into legal trouble, shareholders are going to blame the board. Even if the directors are completely exonerated from legal liability, their business reputations will suffer. The business reputation of a director is one of his or her most important assets. Once that reputation has been sullied, it is very difficult to repair. For example, I suspect that few of the pre-scandal Enron directors will use their position with Enron to obtain other directorships, even though they may not bear any blame in the scandal but rather were completely deceived by management.

 ## CAREMARK

In re Caremark International, Inc. Derivative Litigation (Caremark)[36] supports the idea that the board must establish systems to detect illegal behavior. A robust whistleblower system is exactly the type of system referred to in this case, as discussed below. However, an anemic whistleblower system that just barely complies with the requirements of Sarbanes-Oxley would not necessarily violate the *Caremark* standard (see italics below):

> Caremark was a large, for-profit health care corporation engaged in the business of providing patient care and managed care services. In 1994, Caremark and some of its officers and employees were criminally indicted in multiple jurisdictions for violations of federal health care laws, including the Anti-Kickback Act and criminal false claims statutes. Caremark pled guilty to various offenses and agreed to pay $250 million in civil penalties, criminal fines and restitution to private parties.
>
> Following the corporation's entry of the guilty plea and its payment of nearly $250 million in civil penalties and criminal fines, Caremark's shareholders filed suit against the company's directors, alleging that the directors breached their fiduciary duties to the corporation by allowing the criminal misconduct to occur. In evaluating this allegation, the court in Caremark analyzed the directors' duties to institute compliance programs to prevent and detect violations of the law. Notably, the court expressed its view that: *A director's obligation includes a duty to attempt in good faith to assure that a corporate information and reporting system, which the Board concludes is adequate, exists, and that failure to do so under some circumstances may, in theory at least, render a director liable for losses caused by non-compliance with applicable legal standards.*[37]

The court in *Caremark* carefully examined the corporation's compliance program and found the existence and effectiveness of that program crucial to its holding that the directors did not breach their duties. Absent the directors' development of Caremark's elaborate compliance program, the court suggested that the directors could have been held individually liable.[38]

 ## RECOMMENDED STRATEGY

Our recommended strategy for dealing with whistleblowers assumes that it is in the corporation's interest to correct any legal noncompliance problems *internally* before they are disclosed externally to the authorities. The strategy also assumes that members of the board of directors want to have major risk exposures brought to their attention promptly.

Our strategy rejects the "head-in-the-sand" approach, which says that since the detection risk by prosecutors and regulators is small, we should not encourage whistleblowing by employees internally, even though that risks the possibility of external whistleblowing (i.e., employee disclosure to prosecutors and regulators). The assumption behind the "head-in-the-sand" approach is that the company's profit from breaking the law will significantly exceed the penalties if discovered.

There are three problems with this approach (also called "audit roulette" in the tax field).

1. The potential loss of shareholder value and legal fees, fines, and penalties resulting from breaking the law may overwhelm whatever potential profits result from such unlawful activities.
2. The business reputation of the corporation may suffer severely from external prosecution, which may include being barred from certain kinds of business, such as from becoming U.S. government contractors and subcontractors.
3. Prosecutors who are not satisfied just with prosecuting corporations criminally, only to have them repeat the same conduct, may well criminally target the responsible members of management and the board of directors.[39]

An example of this frustration by the DOJ can be found in the criminal indictment on November 9, 2010, of Lauren Stevens, the former vice president and associate general counsel of Glaxo. Her indictment contained two counts of obstruction and four counts of making false statements to the U.S. Food and Drug Administration (FDA) relating to her denial in a series of letters to the FDA that Glaxo was promoting off-label uses for a prescription drug and her failure to provide the FDA with off-label slides used by company-paid speakers. Although the case was subsequently dismissed, this indictment reflects a much more aggressive attitude toward individual company officers.[40]

A proactive whistleblower policy encourages early detection and remediation of potentially illegal activity before it is reported to authorities. Early detection prevents the company from incurring huge legal fees, fines, potential imprisonment, and damage to its business and reputation from external prosecution of illegal activity.

The DOJ and other prosecutors encourage early detection of illegal activity and self-remediation of such illegal activity. A vigorous internal compliance program is the best protection for the company and its board and management against both civil and criminal prosecution.

In order to better understand CEO and board responsibilities for compliance, next we discuss the criminal liability of the organization and its executives.

 ## CRIMINAL LIABILITY OF AN ORGANIZATION

An organization may be held criminally liable for the illegal acts of its directors, officers, employees, and agents if the acts (1) are within the scope of their duties and (2) were intended, at least in part, to benefit the corporation. For example, in *United States v. Basic Construction Co.*,[41] the court held that "a corporation may be held criminally responsible for antitrust violations committed by its employees if they were acting within the scope of their authority, or apparent authority, and for the benefit of the corporation, even if . . . such acts were against corporate policy or express instructions." Employees may act for mixed reasons—both for self-aggrandizement (both direct and indirect) and for the benefit of the corporation—and a corporation may be held liable as long as one motivation of its agent is to benefit the corporation. *United States v. Potter*[42] states that the test to determine whether an agent is acting within the scope of employment is "whether the agent is performing acts of the kind which he is authorized to perform, and those acts are motivated, at least in part, by an intent to benefit the corporation." In *United States v. Automated Medical Laboratories, Inc.*,[43] for example, the Fourth Circuit affirmed a corporation's conviction for the actions of a subsidiary's employee despite the corporation's claim that the employee was acting for his own benefit, namely his "ambitious nature and his desire to ascend the corporate ladder."[44] The court stated, "[Hugo] Partucci was clearly acting in part to benefit AML [American Medical Laboratories, Inc.] since his advancement within the corporation depended on AML's well-being and its lack of difficulties with the FDA."[45] (See also *United States v. Cincotta*,[46] which upholds a corporation's conviction, notwithstanding the substantial personal benefit reaped by its miscreant agents, because the fraudulent scheme required money to pass through the corporation's treasury and the fraudulently obtained goods were resold to the corporation's customers in the corporation's name.) Moreover, the corporation need not even necessarily profit from its agent's actions for it to be held liable.[47]

The CEO can become, in rare cases, personally liable civilly and criminally for an ineffective corporate compliance program. In some regulated industries, directors and officers have been found personally liable for corporate wrongdoing in which they did not actively participate, pursuant to the Responsible Corporate Officer doctrine.[48] The doctrine originally arose in cases involving the Food, Drug and Cosmetic Act, which provided strict personal criminal liability for offenses, even though corporate officers may not have known about the alleged wrongful conduct. The doctrine also has been applied in connection with so-called public welfare offenses, when a statute is intended to improve the common good and the legislature eliminates the normal requirement for culpable intent, resulting in strict liability for all those who have a responsible share in the offense, such as in the case of certain environmental statutes.[49] Even in nonregulated industries, directors and officers can be held civilly liable for their mere failure to investigate criminal conduct. However, generally, directors and officers of a corporation are criminally liable only if they actively participate in, conspire to commit, or aid and abet in committing a crime.

 ## RESPONSIBLE CORPORATE OFFICER DOCTRINE

No CEO wants to be subject to a criminal conviction or fine. It is definitely not a resume builder. Likewise, jail time is a downer.

Aggressive prosecutors who believe that merely sanctioning the corporation is not sufficient to deter unlawful conduct are increasingly using the Responsible Corporate Officer Doctrine against CEOs and other corporate officers.

For example, in March 2003, the Minnesota Court of Appeals affirmed the criminal conviction of a construction company's CEO, John Arkell, for violations of the Minnesota Uniform Building Code. Arkell was sentenced to pay a fine, make restitution to condominium owners, and serve 90 days in jail (with 80 days stayed pending compliance with sentencing conditions).[50]

The trial court convicted Arkell, basing its decision on Minnesota Statute Section 16B.69. This statute provides for enforcement of the State Building Code and sets forth a misdemeanor penalty for code violations. The court found that Section 16B.69 is a public welfare statute, therefore warranting application of both strict liability and the Responsible Corporate Officer doctrine. Public welfare statutes are those that regulate conduct that is "potentially harmful or injurious" to human safety. The court held that Section 16B.69 falls within this definition, because the Building Code is "intended to protect the health, safety, and welfare of the citizens of this state."

THE *ACME MARKETS* CASE

The U.S. Supreme Court supported the Responsible Corporate Officer Doctrine in *United States v. Park* (the *Acme Markets, Inc.* case):

At the time of the case, Acme Markets, Inc. was a national retail food chain with approximately 36,000 employees, 874 retail outlets, 12 general warehouses, and four special warehouses. Its headquarters, including the office of the president and chief executive officer, John R. Park were located in Philadelphia, PA. The U.S. government criminally charged Acme and Park with violations of the Federal Food, Drug and Cosmetic Act. It was alleged that Acme and Park had received food that had been shipped in interstate commerce and that, while the food was being held for sale in Acme's Baltimore warehouse following shipment in interstate commerce, the defendants caused it to be held in a building accessible to rodents and to be exposed to contamination by rodents. These acts were alleged to have resulted in the food's being adulterated.

Acme pleaded guilty, but Park pleaded not guilty. The evidence presented at trial showed that, in April 1970, the FDA advised Park by letter of unsanitary conditions in Acme's Philadelphia warehouse. In 1971, the FDA discovered that similar conditions existed in the firm's Baltimore warehouse. An FDA consumer safety officer testified that there was evidence of rodent infestation and other unsanitary conditions discovered during a 12-day inspection of the Baltimore warehouse in November and December 1971.

That same officer stated that a second inspection of the warehouse had been conducted in March 1972 and the inspectors found that there had been improvement in the sanitary conditions, but that "there was still evidence of rodent activity in the building and in the warehouses and we found some rodent-contaminated lots of food items."

The prosecution also presented testimony by the Chief of Compliance of the FDA's Baltimore office, who advised Park by letter of the conditions at the Baltimore warehouse after the first inspection. An Acme Baltimore division vice-president responded to the letter on behalf of Acme and Park and described the steps taken to remedy the unsanitary conditions discovered by both inspections. The prosecution's final witness, Acme's vice-president for legal affairs and assistant secretary, identified Park as the president and chief executive officer of the company and read a bylaw prescribing the duties of the chief executive officer. He testified that Park functioned by delegating "normal operating duties," including sanitation, but that he retained "certain things, which are the big, broad, principles of the operation of the company," and had "the responsibility of seeing that they all worked together."

At the close of the prosecution's case, Park moved for a judgment of acquittal, which was denied.

Park was the only defense witness. He testified that although all of Acme's employees were in a sense under his general direction, Acme had an "organizational structure for responsibilities for certain functions," according to which different phases of its operations were "assigned to individuals who, in turn, have staff and departments under them." Park identified those individuals responsible for sanitation, and related that, upon receipt of a January 1972, FDA letter, he had conferred with the vice-president for legal affairs. The vice-president for legal affairs informed Park that the Baltimore division vice-president "was investigating the situation and would be taking corrective action and would be preparing a summary of the corrective action to reply to the letter."[51]

Park stated that he did not "believe there was anything [he] could have done more constructively than what [he] found was being done."[52] On cross-examination, Park conceded that providing sanitary conditions for food offered for sale to the public was something that he was "responsible for in the entire operation of the company." Park testified that it was one of many phases of the company that he assigned to "dependable subordinates."

Nevertheless, Park was convicted by the jury and fined $500. No jail time was imposed.

THE U.S. DEPARTMENT OF JUSTICE CRIMINAL GUIDELINES

The internal guidelines of the DOJ[53] state that there are nine factors in determining whether to criminally indict a corporation, including "the existence and adequacy of the corporation's compliance program." Although the DOJ recognizes that no compliance program can ever prevent all criminal activity by a corporation's employees, the critical factors in evaluating any program are whether it is adequately designed for maximum effectiveness in preventing and detecting wrongdoing by employees and whether corporate management is enforcing the program or is tacitly encouraging or pressuring employees to engage in misconduct to achieve business objectives. The DOJ has no formal guidelines for corporate compliance programs. The fundamental questions any prosecutor should ask, according to the guidelines, are: "Is the corporation's compliance program well designed?" and "Does the corporation's compliance program work?" For example, do the corporation's directors exercise independent review over proposed corporate actions rather than unquestioningly ratifying officers' recommendations? Are the directors provided with information sufficient to enable the exercise of independent judgment? Are internal audit functions conducted at a level sufficient to ensure their independence and accuracy? Have the directors established an information and reporting system in the organization reasonably designed to provide management and the board of directors regarding the organization's compliance with the law?[54]

According to the guidelines, prosecutors should attempt to determine whether a corporation's compliance program is merely a "paper program" or whether it was designed and implemented in an effective manner. In addition, prosecutors will determine *"whether the corporation has provided for a staff sufficient to audit, document, analyze, and utilize the results of the corporation's compliance efforts"*[55] (emphasis added). Moreover, prosecutors will determine *"whether the corporation's employees are adequately informed about the compliance program and are convinced of the corporation's commitment to it"*[56] (emphasis added). Doing this will enable prosecutors to make informed decisions as to whether the corporation has adopted and implemented a truly effective compliance program that, when consistent with other federal law enforcement policies, may result in a decision to indict only the corporation's employees and agents, not the corporation itself.

The U.S. Sentencing Guidelines were amended in November 2010 to permit organizations to obtain reduced criminal sentences (including fines), despite high-level personnel involvement in the illegal activity, if the organization has an effective compliance and ethics program that meets certain requirements.[57] These requirements are discussed in Chapter 7.

THE DISADVANTAGES OF A ROBUST WHISTLEBLOWER SYSTEM

Most labor and employment attorneys will tell you that many whistleblower complaints are spurious. The employee may misunderstand either the facts or the law and see violations where there are none. Some employees may use the whistleblower system to protect their positions under the anti-retaliation provisions of the whistleblower laws. Thus, if employees think they are about to be fired for poor performance, they may decide to abuse the whistleblower system by creating fictitious or frivolous whistleblower complaints in order to slow up the firing process or as a defense against being terminated.

Therefore, the question arises as to whether an organization should encourage whistleblower complaints, including anonymous ones.

There are two issues to consider. First, the overwhelming majority of hotline complaints *do* warrant investigation. According to the 2010 Corporate Governance and Compliance Hotline Benchmarking Report, in 2009, out of 117,303 hotline reports to The Network (a national hotline center) from 1,101 organizations, 73 percent were viewed as warranting an investigation, for those reports where the case outcome was provided.[58] A total of 40 percent of these hotline reports resulted in corrective action taken (see Table 6.2).

TABLE 6.2   Frequency of Case Outcome

Case Outcome	2009
No investigation warranted	17%
Investigated, corrective action taken	40%
Investigated, no corrective action taken	33%
Referred/Advised	7%
Other	3%

Source: 2010 Corporate Governance and Compliance Hotline Benchmark Report, "A Comprehensive Examination of Organizational Hotline Activity from The Network."

Therefore, the argument that whistleblower systems encourage spurious reports is unsubstantiated. Spurious hotline reports will occur whether there is a robust whistleblower system or not. Moreover, there is nothing wrong with an organization providing for disciplinary action for employees who intentionally make false accusations over the hotline.

Second, the benefits to the organization and its shareholders from the legitimate complaints far outweigh the cost of investigating the fictitious or frivolous complaints. A public company with a $1 billion market capitalization can easily lose 5 percent of its shareholder value if it is indicted for a serious crime. That means that shareholders collectively lose $50 million in shareholder value. If properly managed, the additional cost of investigating more complaints under a robust whistleblower system should be only a tiny fraction of the amount. Even a small public company that has a market capitalization of $50 million can easily lose 10 percent of its shareholder value if it is criminally indicted for a serious crime, and the additional cost of a properly managed whistleblower system should be only a small fraction of that amount.

Accordingly, the additional cost of investigating spurious hotline complaints is far outweighed by the detrimental effects to shareholder value from uncorrected illegal or high-risk behavior within the organization.[59]

The problem of spurious complaints is a cost of any effective whistleblower system. Indeed, public companies that currently have ineffective whistleblower systems still will receive meritless whistleblower complaints. Therefore, it is not clear that there will be a significant increase in spurious complaints solely as a result of a more robust whistleblower system.

Chapter 7 discusses how to establish a robust whistleblower system.

 NOTES

1. *United States v. Park*, 421 U.S. 658 (1975).
2. For example, see "Hogan Lovells' Peter Spivack on the Rise of the Park Doctrine," *Corporate Crime Reporter*, November 2, 2010. www.corporatecrime reporter.com/spivack110210.htm.
3. Alicia Mundy, "U.S. Effort to Remove Drug CEO Jolts Firms," *Wall Street Journal*, April 26, 2011, p. 1.
4. Section 2.7 of "Corporate Governance Policies" of Council of Institutional Investors. www.cii.org/UserFiles/file/council%20policies/CII%20Corp%20 Gov%20Policies%20Full%20and%20Current%204-13-10.pdf.

5. Melissa S. Baucus and David A. Baucus, "Paying the Piper: An Empirical Examination of Longer-Term Financial Consequences of Illegal Corporate Behavior," *Academy of Management Journal* 40, no. 1 (February 1997): 129–151.
6. Ibid.
7. D. Murphy, R. Shrieves, and S. Tibbs, "Determinants of the Stock Price Reaction to Allegations of Corporate Misconduct: Earnings, Risk, and Firm Size Effects," http://bus.utk.edu/corp_gov/Research/DetShrMurTib.pdf; Alan K. Reichert, Michael Lockett, and Ramesh P. Rao, "The Impact of Illegal Business Practice on Shareholder Returns," *Financial Review* 1 (1996): 67–85.
8. Barry Ritholz, "Indictment to Settlement: $15 Billion Market Cap Loss," the Big Picture, July 17, 2010. www.ritholtz.com/blog/2010/07/indictment-to-settlement-15-billion-market-cap-loss.
9. Benson Smith and Tony Rutigliano, "Enron and You—A Lesson for Sales Execs: You Don't Have the Luxury of Invoking the Fifth," *Gallup Management Journal*, February 25, 2002. http://gmj.gallup.com/content/313/enron.aspx.
10. Bethany McLean and Peter Elkind, *The Smartest Guys in the Room: The Amazing Rise and Scandalous Fall of Enron* (New York: Penguin, 2004). See also Andrea Redmond and Patricia Crisafulli, *Comebacks: Powerful Lessons from Leaders Who Endured Setbacks and Recaptured Success on Their Terms* (San Francisco: Jossey-Bass, 2010), p. 104.
11. Ibid.
12. Permanent Subcommittee of Investigations of the Committee on Governmental Affairs United States Senate, "The Role of The Board of Directors in Enron's Collapse," July 8, 2002, p. 6. http://fl1.findlaw.com/news.findlaw.com/cnn/docs/enron/senpsi70802rpt.pdf.
13. Gary Strauss, "Tyco Events Put Spotlight on Directors' Role," *USA Today*, September 15, 2002.
14. Bethany McLean and Joe Nocera, *All the Devils Are Here: The Hidden History of the Financial Crisis* (New York: Portfolio/Penguin, 2010), pp. 166, 308.
15. Ibid., p. 320.
16. Peter Evans, "Merrill's $3.4 Billion Balance Sheet Bomb," CNNMoney.com, October 24, 2007. http://money.cnn.com/2007/10/24/news/companies/merrill_eavis.fortune/index.htm.
17. "Report of Anton R. Valukas, Examiner," March 11, 2010, p. 21. http://lehmanreport.jenner.com.
18. Ibid., p. 1460.
19. Ibid., p. 1464.
20. Redmond and Crisafulli, *Comebacks*, p. 102.
21. Copeland, "Lotus CEO Resigns," *Computerworld*, January 10, 2000. www.computerworld.com/s/article/40601/Lotus_CEO_Resigns.
22. Olean, "Resume Fraud in the Corner Office," Smeal College of Business, Penn State College of Business (November 2002). http://news.smeal.psu.edu/

news-release-archives/2002/nov02/resume.html; see also Gross, "Schools Lie: Why Do So Many Executives Lie about Their Education?" *Slate*, October 22, 2002. www.slate.com/id/2072961.

23. McLean and Nocera, *All the Devils Are Here*, p. 190.
24. Michael Lewis, *The Great Hangover: 21 Tales of the New Recession from the Pages of Vanity Fair* (New York: Harper Perennial, 2010; see also the Financial Crisis Report Commission, "The Financial Crisis Inquiry Report" (January 2011): 200–201. www.gpoaccess.gov/fcic/fcic.pdf.
25. Moe Tkacik, "That AIG Story, for Readers Who Are Sick of AIG Already," July 6, 2009. http://trueslant.com/moetkacik/2009/07/06/.
26. Lewis, *The Great Hangover*.
27. Financial Crisis Report Commission, "The Financial Crisis Inquiry Report," pp. 200–201; Andrew Simpson, "Greenberg: AIG's Risky Subprime Activity 'Exploded' after He Left," *Insurance Journal*, Oct. 10, 2008. www.insurancejournal.com/news/national/2008/10/10/94544.
28. McLean and Elkind, *The Smartest Guys in the Room*, pp. 166, 308.
29. Financial Crisis Report Commission, "The Financial Crisis Inquiry Report," p. 238.
30. Redmond and Crisafulli, *Comebacks*, p. 104.
31. "Second Interim Report of Dick Thornburgh, Bankruptcy Court Examiner" (Bankr. SDNY June 9, 2003), *In re WorldCom, Inc., et al*, Chapter 11 Case No. 02-15533 (AJG), Jointly Administered.
32. PCAOB Investor Advisory Group, "Report from the Working Group on: Lessons Learned from the Financial Crisis," March 16, 2011. http://pcaobus.org/News/Events/Documents/03162011_IAGMeeting/The_Watchdog_That_Didnt_Bark.pdf.
33. AU Section 317.06 http://pcaobus.org/Standards/Auditing/Pages/AU317.aspx.
34. "Second Interim Report of Dick Thornburgh."
35. "Title 8: Corporations." State of Delaware. http://delcode.delaware.gov/title8/c001/sc01/index.shtml.
36. *Caremark International, Inc. Derivative Litigation*, 1996 WL 549894 [Del. Ch.].
37. www.kutakrock.com/publications/litigation/CORPORATEDIRECTORS.doc.
38. *Caremark International, Inc. Derivative Litigation*, 1996 WL 549894 [Del. Ch.].
39. Lisa Krigsten, "Criminalizing Management Decisions: Prosecuting the Responsible Corporate Officer," American Bar Association, Section of Litigation: Criminal Litigation, December 22, 2010. http://apps.americanbar.org/litigation/committees/criminal/articles/122210_responsible-corporate-officer.html.
40. *United States v. Lauren Stevens*, Case No. 10CR694-RWT(D. Md.), November 9, 2010. The indictment was dismissed on May 10, 2011.
41. *United States v. Basic Construction Co.*, 711 F.2d 570 (4th Cir. 1983).
42. 463 F.3d 9, 25 (1st Cir. 2006).
43. 770 F.2d 399 (4th Cir. 1985).

44. Ibid. at 407.

45. Ibid.

46. See *United States v. Cincotta*, 689 F.2d 238, 241–42 (1st Cir. 1982).

47. See *United States v. Automated Medical Laboratories*, 770 F.2d 399 (4th Cir. 1985); 770 F.2d at 407 (emphasis added; quoting *Old Monastery Co. v. United States*, 147 F. 2d 905, 908 (4th Cir.) *cert. denied*, 326 U.S. 734 (1945)).

48. *United States v. Dotterweich*, 320 U.S. 277 (1943).

49. See *Commissioner, Indiana Department of Environmental Management v. RLG, Inc.*, 755 N.E.2d 556, 560 (Ind. 2001), citing *Matter of Dougherty*, 482 N.W.2d 485, 489 (Minn. Ct. App. 1992).

50. *State v. Arkell*, 657 N. W.2e 883 (Minn. Ct. App. 2003).

51. *U.S. v. Park*, 421 U.S. 658 (1975).

52. Ibid.

53. "Principles of Federal Prosecution of Business Organizations," Memorandum from Mark R. Filip, Deputy Attorney General, to Heads of Department Components and United States Attorneys, August 28, 2008. www.justice.gov/opa/documents/corp-charging-guidelines.pdf.

54. *In re: Caremark*, 698 A.2d 959 (Del. Ct. Chan. 1996).

55. "Principles of Federal Prosecution of Business Organizations."

56. Ibid.

57. U.S. Sentencing Guidelines Manual Section 8C2.5(f)(3)(C) (2010); U.S. Sentencing Guidelines Manual Section 8C2.5, cmt. n.11 (2010).

58. 2010 Corporate Governance and Compliance Hotline Benchmark Report, "A Comprehensive Examination of Organizational Hotline Activity from the Network." http://tnwinc.com/files/2011TNWbenchmarkingreport .pdf?webSyncID=24de8b7c-92b9-3074-a566-921c84284727&session GUID=bcd27041-3405-c274-b7bd-071a4be99052.

59. Deloitte Forensic Center, "Whistleblowing and the New Race to Report: The Impact of the Dodd-Frank Act and 2010's Changes to U.S. Federal Sentencing Guidelines," 2010. www.deloitte.com/view/en_US/us/Services/Financial-Advisory-Services/Forensic-Center/fb02b4b17deaa210VgnVC-M2000001b56f00aRCRD.htm.

Establishing a Robust Whistleblower System

THIS CHAPTER DESCRIBES a robust whistleblower system. Such a system should be adopted not only by public companies but by all organizations of any significant size, including not-for-profit organizations and government entities. Indeed, Internal Revenue Service (IRS) Form 990 (Part VI, Line 13) for tax-exempt organizations specifically asks whether the organization has a "written whistleblower policy." Even smaller organizations should adopt a robust whistleblower system, but they may tailor the system recommended in this chapter to their size.

The object of a robust whistleblower system is to encourage legitimate whistleblowers to provide valuable information to the board of directors (or other controlling group) of the organization, which is not being supplied to the directors by the chief executive officer (CEO) or chief financial officer (CFO) or through the internal auditor or the independent auditor. This information can help the organization prevent or cease illegal activities and identify major risks that it may incur. Whistleblower information permits the board of directors (or other controlling group) of an organization to more effectively fulfill their fiduciary obligations to the organization.

Many organizations, particularly public companies, have installed employee hotlines that are used only occasionally. Independent directors may incorrectly assume that the lack of employee hotline usage is an indication of a lack of illegal activity. That is not necessarily the case. As explained later in this chapter, the lack of hotline usage may merely indicate the lack of an effective whistleblower system, including the failure to provide incentives to employees sufficient to overcome the substantial disincentives of using the hotline and becoming known as a whistleblower.

A robust whistleblower system can encourage internal reporting of illegal activities or major risk exposures so that the problems can be corrected internally. Empirical studies have indicated that nearly all whistleblowers first report perceived wrongdoing to parties within their organizations.[1] Unfortunately, too often these initial reports are ignored within the organization.

Equally important, a robust whistleblower system helps to prevent financial disasters where the board must claim that "we were duped" by the CEO or CFO. Director claims of being duped are not effective to prevent damage to their business reputations. More important, as noted in Chapter 6, such a system prevents criminal and civil liability of both the organization and its directors and officers.

As discussed, many boards of directors that relied solely on the CEO, CFO, and the internal and independent auditors for information have been misled. The history of scandals starting with Enron and ending with Lehman reveals that the board is often the last to know of the company's problems. The essential information that could have prevented these scandals was possessed by lower-level executives who had no incentive to go over the head of the CEO or CFO and "squeal" to the independent directors. A robust whistleblower system with independent directors in charge provides the best opportunity for the board to avoid unpleasant surprises.

An effective whistleblower system is really an internal control mechanism for accounting and auditing purposes. A whistleblower system should be considered an entity-level internal control, similar to the audit committee.[2]

 ## PROBLEMS WITH THE CURRENT WHISTLEBLOWER SYSTEM

Although Congress, when passing the Sarbanes-Oxley Act of 2002 (SOX), may have contemplated an active and effective whistleblower program, this goal has not been uniformly realized.

There are seven major problems with the current whistleblower systems:

1. The tone at the top tolerates but does not encourage whistleblowers.
2. There is no meaningful reward or recognition for legitimate whistleblowers.
3. The inability to communicate with anonymous whistleblowers results in failure to fully investigate anonymous information.
4. The system does not guarantee anonymity.
5. The system is not well advertised.
6. The audit committee uses employee administrators and investigators who are not viewed as independent by whistleblowers and who cannot use legal privileges to preserve confidentiality.
7. Whistleblowers' motivations and personalities affect the investigation.

Many public companies have a "paper" whistleblower system. In such a system, the company has complied with the letter of the SOX requirements and exchange listing rules but has done nothing more. Management tolerates the whistleblower system but does not encourage whistleblowers. Whistleblowers are almost never recognized as employees of the month. As a result, potential whistleblowers, facing daunting disincentives, refuse to participate in the system.

Concerning the SOX whistleblower statute, the former general counsel of the Securities and Exchange Commission (SEC) has stated:

> Not all corporate compliance programs work well. Some—no matter how elaborately conceived and extensively documented—exist only on paper. Some small number are shams. I once knew of an ostensibly anonymous employee hotline that actually rang on the desk of the CEO's secretary. I'm not at all sure that Congress intended that a whistleblower at this company would have to avail himself of this hotline before coming to the Commission and getting an award.[3]

Very few, if any, whistleblower systems provide meaningful rewards or recognition for whistleblowers. Given the real possibility that the employment of persons disclosing wrongful activity may be terminated and even if not terminated such person could be socially ostracized, employees have no reason to assume those risks without a meaningful incentive. Internal whistleblower systems do not have to compete economically with the size of awards available under the whistleblower statutes since there are many disincentives to employee whistleblowing, as detailed in Chapter 4. However, the lack of any meaningful reward or other recognition for whistleblowers reflects an organizational attitude that is not conducive to whistleblowing.

Although the SOX whistleblower system allows for anonymous whistleblowers, that system does not work well because the audit committee or its counsel may need to further question the person whose identity has been hidden. As discussed later in this chapter, the result is that audit committees tend to provide fewer resources to investigating anonymous complaints.[4] Unfortunately, approximately half of whistleblower calls in 2009 were anonymous, a fact that suggests that many employees fear retaliation.[5]

Moreover, some current whistleblower systems do not guarantee anonymity. Voice recognition techniques can be used to trace hotline calls. Private detectives can use handwriting analysis to trace anonymous letters. Anonymous e-mails can be traced back to the whistleblower's computer. The best practices described in this chapter provide greater guarantees of anonymity by permitting communication only through the whistleblower's personal counsel and permitting the whistleblower to form an entity to further hide his or her identity.

A study of fraud cases in large U.S. companies found that the percentage of employee whistleblowers dropped significantly after SOX compared to before SOX. It has been speculated that the job protection provisions of SOX were inadequate in light of the social ostracism and negative career impact on whistleblowers. This study emphasized the importance of both whistleblower anonymity and monetary rewards for whistleblowers.[6]

Many companies do not adequately communicate the whistleblower system except in a policy contained in an SEC filing or on their websites. As a result, average employees may not realize that the company even has an anonymous whistleblower system. A survey by the Institute of Internal Auditors indicates that employee familiarity with the organization's hotline is a key factor in encouraging its use.[7] The best practices described in this chapter provide for much better methods to communicate the whistleblower system to employees.

Investigations of whistleblower complaints are typically performed initially by the internal auditor, director of compliance, human resources (HR) head, or general counsel. All of these individuals are company employees whose compensation is determined by management (with the possible exception of the internal auditor). Potential whistleblowers do not have confidence in the independence or impartiality of these investigators. Moreover, many of these individuals are not skilled forensic investigators.

The best practices described in this chapter advise companies to use employees only to investigate lower-level complaints that do not involve executives (e.g., discrimination and sexual harassment complaints and reports of minor financial discrepancies) but use independent counsel (or other ombudsmen) to investigate all other complaints. Internal auditors remain the eyes and ears of the audit committee under a robust whistleblower system but will not investigate any whistleblower complaints, except for minor ones.

A key factor in employee willingness to use hotlines is the communication of the results of investigations of hotline tips and the actions taken.[8] Many companies do not adequately communicate this information to the whistleblower.

Moreover, whistleblowers with difficult personalities or who have obviously ulterior motives may receive short shrift in any investigation, even though their complaints may be valid. SEC officials made this mistake in ignoring Harry Markopolos's revelations about Bernie Madoff approximately 10 years before his Ponzi scheme was revealed.

In summary, most current SOX whistleblower systems are not sufficiently robust to attract potential internal whistleblowers. Internal compliance systems do not have to compete monetarily with available statutory awards since most potential internal whistleblowers prefer not to suffer the disincentives of going public with their information, including waiting many years for any bounties from litigation. However, it is necessary for the SOX whistleblower systems to provide sufficient incentives to potential internal whistleblowers to induce them to provide to the organization the information necessary to correct law violations and to reveal significant risk exposures.

 ## INITIAL STEPS

Two initial steps that should be taken in order to establish a robust whistleblower system are described next.

> **Best Practice**
>
> The company's employee booklet and any agreements signed by employees should include references to the company's zero-tolerance policy for violations of applicable law. ■

It is a no-brainer that the company's employee booklet should contain a reference to its zero-tolerance policy for law violations. However, a similar provision should be inserted in confidentiality agreements, invention disclosure agreements, and other agreements typically signed by employees in order to emphasize the importance of this policy to employees.

> **Best Practice**
>
> Employees at all levels should be required to report major risk exposures of the organization in addition to any potential law violations. ■

A robust whistleblower system should require employees at all levels to report law violations and major risk exposures of the organization. These reports may, at the employee's option, be provided anonymously. As discussed later, the reports should go directly to the independent directors or independent counsel (or an ombudsman).

It is important for the independent directors to obtain information about any major risk exposures of the organization. Senior executives may be aware of these risk exposures and may have reported them to the CEO or CFO only to have these officers ignore the warning. Normally senior executives are not willing to go over the head of the CEO or CFO directly to the board of directors or the independent directors. Such actions would likely lead to very short careers and may even result in blacklisting in the industry. However, conscientious senior executives who are absolutely assured of anonymity may be willing to take that risk.

ELEMENTS OF A ROBUST WHISTLEBLOWER POLICY

An effective compliance program requires the following elements, each of which is discussed in this chapter:

- Independent directors must be in charge and must be given the resources to fulfill their responsibilities.
- The whistleblower system must be independently administered.
- Whistleblower complaints should be investigated by independent counsel (or other ombudsman) reporting directly to the independent directors.
- There should be no presumption that anonymous complaints are less deserving of investigation.
- The motivations and personality of the whistleblower are not relevant to the truth of the allegations.

- Absolute protection of whistleblowers' identity is essential
- Periodically assess the effectiveness of any employee hotline and provide employee compliance training.
- Independent counsel should report to the whistleblower the status and results of the investigation and the organization should provide annual reports to all employees as to actions taken.
- Legitimate employee whistleblowers should receive meaningful monetary rewards.
- The whistleblower policy must be communicated effectively.
- There should be milder sanctions for whistleblowers involved in illegal group activity.
- Retaliation claims should be independently investigated.
- The director of corporate compliance (if any) should report to the independent directors and become their eyes and ears within the organization.
- The tone at the top of the organization must support an ethical, law-abiding culture. (See "Do's and Don'ts for CEOs" section below).

 ## INDEPENDENT DIRECTORS MUST BE IN CHARGE

SOX requires the audit committees of companies whose securities are listed on a national securities exchange to establish procedures for the "receipt, retention, and treatment of complaints received by the issuer regarding accounting, internal accounting controls, or auditing matters and the confidential, anonymous submission by employees of the issuer of concerns regarding questionable accounting or auditing matters."[9] Congress thereby established a public policy that the independent directors who constitute the audit committee would be in charge of accounting and similar complaints.

Prior to SOX, independent directors had no such responsibility, although many companies voluntarily used the audit committee to receive whistleblower complaints. SOX rejected the idea that management should be in charge of receiving and investigating such complaints.

Legitimate whistleblower complaints are typically bad news for companies. Such complaints may reduce company profits significantly. Incentive compensation plans, which may be based on earnings growth, are adversely affected by legitimate whistleblower complaints. Indeed, significant legitimate allegations can affect the tenure of the CEO. Civil and criminal lawsuits can be the result of a whistleblower complaint. Accordingly, Congress elected in SOX to remove this issue from management control.

On April 12, 2011, the chief operating officer (COO) of Renault SA resigned as a result of an embarrassing episode in which the company falsely accused and wrongfully fired three senior managers for alleged corporate espionage. The COO told the media that the company had evidence, resulting from an internal investigation by security personnel, that the three fired managers had taken money in return for divulging aspects of the company's business model for electric cars. Subsequently, a prosecutor determined that the allegations were without substance, and an apology and reinstatement was offered to the three fired senior managers. The audit committee of Renault SA's board of directors was not informed of the investigation by internal security personnel until after the executives were fired, and roundly criticized management for a series of missteps in connection with the internal investigation, ultimately leading to the resignation of the COO. The moral of this story is that the independent directors must be in charge of any serious internal investigations.[10]

Best Practice

Independent directors must be in charge of the whistleblower system and must be given adequate resources to fulfill their responsibilities. ■

Having independent directors actively in charge of the whistleblower system enables potential whistleblowers to feel confident that some objective person will pay attention to their information. The organization must give independent directors adequate resources to fulfill their responsibilities, including the ability to hire independent counsel (or an ombudsman), forensic accountants, and other consultants to assist them.

Using independent directors to monitor the whistleblower system is not without its weaknesses. As academic studies have noted, serious whistleblower allegations can reflect badly on the business reputation of the independent director who may have failed in his or her oversight responsibility and result in the loss of board seats and future directorship opportunities.[11] Notwithstanding that weakness, independent directors still have the highest potential for objective and meaningful investigations of whistleblower information.

Independent directors typically make up the only constituency in a public or private company who do not participate in an incentive compensation plan that can be adversely affected by a whistleblower complaint. It is unusual for independent directors' fees to be based on company revenues or profits. Moreover, independent directors are concerned about their business reputations and usually would be horrified to learn that lawbreaking occurred on their watch. Conscientious independent directors should, therefore, be at the heart of any effective whistleblower program.

THE WHISTLEBLOWER PROGRAM MUST BE INDEPENDENTLY ADMINISTERED

Independent directors typically rely on the internal auditor, the director of compliance, or internal general counsel to administer the whistleblower program. This is a mistake. Internal auditors, the director of compliance, and internal general counsel are employees of the company and participate in incentive compensation plans that may be adversely affected by a whistleblower complaint. Although these employees may be very conscientious in performing their duties, both the perception and the reality that they are part of management taints their objectivity. Potential whistleblowers may well be unwilling to assume the substantial risks of whistleblowing when employees are administering the system.

Some public companies have internal audit teams that are highly respected within the organization and viewed as independent by the employees. Unfortunately, this is not always the case. In this regard, there is an interesting quote, allegedly from the chief internal auditor of Fannie Mae, who was told by the CEO that the company could double its earnings per share over the next five years from $3.23 to $6.46. The chief internal auditor, who is supposed to be independent of management, is quoted as saying to his staff:

> By now, every one of you must have 6.46 branded in your brains. You must be able to say it in your sleep, you must be able to recite it forwards and backwards, you must have a raging fire in your belly that burns away all doubts, you must live, breathe, and dream 6.46. . . . After all, thanks to Frank [Raines, the Fannie Mae CEO], we all have a lot of money riding on it.[12]

This anecdote does not mean that every internal auditor lacks independence. However, it does reflect the fact that whistleblower fears about the impartiality of internal auditors may not be unjustified.

The current practice of having inside counsel, the internal auditor, the compliance director, or HR person determine which complaints are worthy of

Best Practice

The whistleblower program should be independently administered. Hotline calls and other whistleblower communications should be directed to the chair of the independent directors' committee, to independent counsel, or to another independent party acting as an ombudsman. ■

independent investigation undermines the integrity of the whistleblower system. It permits employees of the organization, whose compensation is determined by upper management, to make these sensitive judgments, despite the fact that such judgments may adversely affect their salaries, bonuses, profit sharing, and stock options.

To assure potential whistleblowers of the integrity of the whistleblower system, the system should be independently administered. Some companies have whistleblower complaints go directly to the chair of the audit committee; however, this person has many other duties and responsibilities to perform. Therefore, the audit committee chair should assign the administration of the system to an independent party, preferably independent counsel or another disinterested party, such as an internal audit outsourcer that provides no services to management. This disinterested party can act as a trusted intermediary between the organization and the potential whistleblower.

If administration of the whistleblower program is assigned to independent counsel or some other disinterested party, such independent counsel or other party should report directly to the independent directors. The independent counsel or other disinterested party should be able to determine which complaints are worthy of independent investigation and which complaints are of such a routine nature that they should be investigated by internal personnel.

For example, if an employee claims sexual harassment by a fellow employee or discrimination by a supervisor, independent counsel or another ombudsman normally should assign that claim to the HR department to handle. Doing this helps to reduce the costs of using independent counsel or other ombudsmen. However, if the employee claims sexual harassment or discrimination by the CEO or some other executive officer, independent counsel should investigate that claim. For example, on August 7, 2010, Mark Hurd, CEO of Hewlett-Packard, resigned after an investigation found that he had falsified expense reports to conceal a "close personal relationship" with a female contractor.[13] Obviously, that type of investigation must be performed by independent counsel. The point is that the decision as to how a claim is handled should be made by an independent person or another ombudsman.

According to a 2009 survey of 117,303 hotline reports from 1,101 organizations with more than 13 million employees, approximately 48 percent of all reports were related to personnel management.[14] Thus, even though the administration of the whistleblower system is handled independently, approximately 48 percent of the investigations will be performed by internal personnel, with the exception of personnel complaints involving senior executives.

The administration of the whistleblower system by internal personnel undermines the confidence of potential employee whistleblowers in the independence and objectivity of the program, thereby discouraging them from taking action. For example, if an employee claims to be sexually harassed by an executive officer, it is absurd to have someone who reports or is subordinate to that executive officer decide how the claim will be investigated.

Hotline calls should go directly to the chair of the independent directors' committee or to independent counsel or another third party selected by the independent directors. Currently, many hotline calls go to the internal auditor, who, as mentioned, may not have the confidence of potential whistleblowers.

Some may argue that it is too expensive to have independent counsel or other ombudsmen administer the whistleblower system. It is true that there is less expense if internal employees administer the system. However, the purpose of a whistleblower system is to encourage employees with important information to report it directly to the independent directors if they have not received an adequate response internally. The additional cost of independent administration of the system must be weighed against the potential loss of shareholder value in the event of illegal or fraudulent activity or excessive risk taking by the corporation, the damage to the organization's business reputation, the criminal and civil liabilities of directors and officers, and the loss of contributors in the case of nonprofit organizations. In this context, unless the organization is extremely small, the potential risk to shareholder value far outweighs the additional cost of an independent administration of the whistleblower system.

 ## WHISTLEBLOWER COMPLAINTS SHOULD BE INVESTIGATED BY INDEPENDENT COUNSEL REPORTING DIRECTLY TO THE INDEPENDENT DIRECTORS

A current practice of many public company whistleblower systems is to assign an internal auditor, director of compliance, HR head, or internal general counsel to initially investigate any whistleblower complaints. These investigators are all employees of the company and are considered part of the management structure. They are salaried employees and may have stock options and incentive bonuses based on the financial results of operations.

Is it any wonder that whistleblowers do not view these investigators as impartial? The whistleblower may be risking his or her career with the company, and possibly in the entire industry, by providing damaging information through the whistleblower system. He or she may be viewed as a disloyal snitch and have a difficult time ever getting another job, even outside of the industry. Therefore, the least that the company can do is to provide whistleblowers with an impartial investigation of their complaints, even though the company may have to pay the fees of independent counsel.

Many internal auditors are not equipped to perform an independent investigation. They do not have the necessary background to interview witnesses and do not have the experience of a trained investigator. The same argument may be made about internal general counsel. Thus, neither the internal auditor nor the internal general counsel is the best choice to investigate serious whistleblower complaints.

The company's regular outside law firm is also not the best choice for serious whistleblower complaints, particularly those that might involve top management. The regular outside law firm typically is chosen by management and normally will not do anything to jeopardize that relationship.

Unfortunately, even supposedly good whistleblower systems today use company employees at least initially to investigate whistleblower complaints. The use of these employee investigators tends to deter potential whistleblowers from participating in the whistleblower system.

Best Practice

Independent counsel, reporting directly to the independent directors, should investigate all whistleblower complaints, except for obviously minor or routine complaints. ■

A key element in establishing a robust whistleblower system is the appointment of independent counsel by the independent directors. Independent counsel should, as a best practice, be an attorney or law firm that does not provide any legal work for the company, either currently or in the future, except for legal services for the independent directors. Potential whistleblowers will not have confidence in the impartiality of outside counsel that provides significant legal services requested by management, even though such outside counsel may be extremely ethical and have a great deal of integrity.

The independent counsel must have skilled forensic investigators, preferably attorneys who have previously served in a government law enforcement position.

Any investigation of whistleblower complaints must be done by independent counsel or under the auspices of independent counsel. The only exception should be obviously minor or routine complaints, such as complaints against fellow employees (other than executives) and reports of minor financial discrepancies. Moreover, independent counsel may be able to protect the information that is gathered from subsequent discovery in a lawsuit, since such counsel may have the benefit of the attorney/client privilege or the work product doctrine. The independent auditor, the director of compliance, or the head of HR normally will not have these legal privileges available to protect the information that is gathered.

The independent counsel may not have the skills necessary to investigate the complaint fully. For example, a complaint about a complex accounting issue will require the use of an accounting expert. Likewise, some complaints will require the use of a forensic accountant or an investigator. The independent counsel, with the permission of the independent directors, must have the authority and funding to hire these experts.

If the independent counsel (possibly with the help of experts) determines the complaint to be without foundation or otherwise spurious, independent counsel should so notify the whistleblower after the completion of the investigation. The independent counsel's decision as to the merits of the whistleblower complaint will be more meaningful to the employee than any decision by management personnel or by regular outside counsel.

An example of the worst practices in investigating whistleblower complaints is presented next.

On August 22, 2001, Kenneth Lay, Enron's chairman, received a letter from an Enron accounting executive, Sherron Watkins,[15] which requested an internal investigation of her allegations of accounting fraud. She specifically requested that the investigation not be conducted by the regular outside counsel for Enron.

The subsequent investigation of Enron by Vinson & Elkins is a classic example of a bad investigation. The board delegated the investigation to the company's general counsel, even though Watkins's complaints implicated top management at Enron. Vinson & Elkins, the primary outside counsel for

Enron, and the Enron general counsel agreed on a very limited investigation that did not involve obtaining an independent accountants' opinion on the work of Arthur Andersen & Co., even though accounting issues were the heart of Watkins's complaint and even though she had specifically requested that Arthur Andersen not be involved in the investigation. Indeed, Watkins also requested that Vinson & Elkins *not* be involved in the investigation; this request also was ignored by Enron's general counsel. At the end of the very limited investigation, Vinson & Elkins gave Enron a report that in general found no substance to Watkins's complaint. A separate investigation completed shortly after Enron's bankruptcy by an independent board committee, using completely independent counsel, found significant substance to her complaint.[16]

Thus, to investigate serious whistleblower complaints, the independent directors should select an independent counsel that has no relationship to the management of the company and does not intend to have such a relationship.

It is important that the independent counsel be chosen solely by the independent directors. Although there is nothing wrong with the independent directors obtaining the views of the internal general counsel, the independent counsel must owe entire allegiance to the independent directors who selected him or her. Potential whistleblowers need confidence that their complaints will be investigated objectively.

Best Practice

Before acting on a whistleblower complaint, take the time to perform a thorough investigation. ■

Some organizations are so eager to appear to act responsibly that they act prematurely on a whistleblower complaint before they have thoroughly investigated the situation. Acting on a complaint before completing an investigation can be just as harmful to the organization as never acting at all or unreasonably delaying action.

For example, as noted previously, in August 2010, several top managers of Renault SA received an anonymous tip accusing a senior Renault executive of negotiating a bribe. In return for the bribe, the executive allegedly sold secrets of Renault's electric car technology to the Chinese. After a four-month investigation overseen by Renault's internal security personnel, Renault dismissed the executive and two other managers, despite their professions of innocence, and instituted criminal action against them. In March 2011, Renault's COO stated that he may have been tricked by members of Renault's security department and that Renault was prepared to exonerate the three managers for lack of evidence. Renault apologized to the three managers, pledging to repair the injustice against them.[17] On April 12, 2011, the COO of Renault SA resigned.[18] One blogger characterized Renault's investigation as "Ready, Fire, Aim."[19]

THERE SHOULD BE NO PRESUMPTION THAT ANONYMOUS COMPLAINTS ARE LESS DESERVING OF INVESTIGATION

An academic study of audit committee members of large publicly traded U.S. firms indicated that they would allocate fewer resources to anonymous reports relative to attributed reports, because they would place little faith in the credibility of the anonymous source.[20] These audit committee members also express concerns about anonymous whistleblower reports because they had dealt with many false accusations arising from anonymous sources. This study consisted of 83 participants, 22 female and 61 male, with an overall average of approximately 23 years of business experience. All participants actively served on at least one board and at least one audit committee, and 75 percent of the participants were considered financial experts.[21]

> **Best Practice**
>
> Anonymous complaints should have the same resources devoted to them as other complaints. ■

Some of the most meaningful information to board members is likely to come from junior executives. These executives will provide this type of information only if they have complete assurance of anonymity. If their identity is known to the CEO or CFO, it is likely that their career at both that organization and within the same industry will be very short.

Audit committee members who believe that junior executives will provide meaningful information without such assurance of anonymity need to rethink their position. Without a guarantee of anonymity, there is generally no incentive for junior executives to jeopardize their careers by becoming whistleblowers.

It is true that many spurious complaints are made by whistleblowers anonymously, and audit committee members hate to waste company resources in investigating allegations that lack factual or legal substance. Nevertheless, audit committees should refer all complaints, whether anonymous or not, to independent counsel (or other ombudsmen) to determine who should investigate the claim. If the claim is obviously routine, such as discrimination or sexual harassment claims or a minor financial discrepancy not involving an executive officer, independent counsel (or other ombudsmen) should refer the investigation to the internal auditor, HR, or internal counsel to investigate. If there is doubt as to whether the complaint is "obviously minor," that doubt should be resolved in favor of an independent investigation.

No presumption should be created against devoting resources to anonymous complaints.

MOTIVATIONS AND PERSONALITY OF THE WHISTLEBLOWER ARE NOT RELEVANT TO THE TRUTH OF THE ALLEGATIONS

Best Practice

The motivations and personality of whistleblowers should not be considered when determining the truth of their allegations. ■

It is not unusual for some members of management to assign nefarious motivations to whistleblowers and to try to denigrate their legitimacy. Indeed, the SEC made exactly that same mistake in refusing to take seriously the complaint of Harry Markopolos, who claimed that he had discovered the Madoff Ponzi scheme.[22] The SEC likely viewed Markopolos as motivated by a desire to obtain a bounty and to hurt a competitor, namely Madoff, who was allegedly producing better returns for his investors than Markopolos was producing for his company.[23]

A passage from Markopolos's book reads:

Certainly one reason that office [the SEC's New York office] paid so little attention to my submission is that they believed my motive for pursuing Madoff was to collect a big reward. Bachenheimer [Doria Bachenheimer, assistant director of the SEC's New York branch office] described me to SEC Inspector General David Kotz as "a competitor of Madoff's who had been criticized for not being able to meet Madoff's returns, and . . . was looking for a bounty"—information she probably got from my previous public testimony. She added, "If the first thing I hear from someone is what's in it for me, then it raises my antenna a little bit."[24]

Academic researchers[25] have long studied the various motivations of whistleblowers. These motivations vary from very honorable and honest motivation, such as altruistic behavior[26] to do the right thing or to resolve an injustice,[27] to devious motivations, such as taking advantage of statutory protections of whistleblowers or revenge.

In the end, however, whistleblower motivations are not relevant in determining whether the allegations are true or false.

Likewise, the personality of the whistleblower is irrelevant to the truth of the allegations. The fact that the whistleblower is an arrogant "know-it-all" or has other displeasing personality characteristics should not be considered in determining the validity of the allegations. Indeed, the report by SEC Inspector General David Kotz on the Madoff scandal indicates that one of the SEC investigators personally disliked Harry Markopolos and that may have played a role in her skepticism about his Madoff allegations.[28]

 ## ABSOLUTE PROTECTION OF WHISTLEBLOWERS' IDENTITY IS ESSENTIAL

Fellow employees and supervisors typically view whistleblowing as an act of disloyalty. This is particularly true in the executive suite, where many times loyalty is prized over other qualities. Chapter 4 discussed a variety of disincentives to whistleblowers, including potential harassment by fellow employees and supervisors, poor performance reviews, and isolation.

Given the disincentives to whistleblowing, it is important that the identity of the whistleblower remain confidential as long as possible. Absent such a guarantee, many potential whistleblowers will refuse to subject themselves to the possible negative repercussions of disclosing illegal activity. In 2009,

50 percent of the whistleblowers using The Network national hotline center elected to remain anonymous, which represented a 4 to 6 percent increase over the past five years.[29]

Best Practice

The anonymity of the employee whistleblower must be protected unless the whistleblower agrees to the disclosure of his or her identity. ■

The question then remains as to the nature of the confidentiality guarantee. One possibility is to have whistleblowers directly disclose the information solely to independent counsel for the independent directors' committee. However, many potential whistleblowers still would not trust that their identity would remain confidential, especially once the investigation by independent counsel began.

Another option is to permit whistleblowers to remain completely anonymous, an option that has been suggested as the best practice by one academic paper.[30] The difficulty with maintaining complete anonymity lies in the fact that investigating counsel often must ask further questions of whistleblowers in order to obtain more details and to respond to questions arising during the course of the investigation.

In the investigation of the complaints, independent counsel must represent the company and its independent directors, not the whistleblower. Therefore, the whistleblower will not be entitled to the protection of the attorney/client privilege in his or her communications with independent counsel.

One way around this problem is to have whistleblowers submit communications through a personal attorney of their own choosing and to have the company fund the legal fees of that attorney, up to a reasonable limit. This solution enables whistleblowers' identity to be protected by the attorney/client privilege while at the same time providing, through the personal counsel, answers to queries by the independent counsel. To avoid abuse of this provision, the independent directors should give the independent counsel authority to establish such an arrangement with whistleblowers' personal attorneys, subject to the understanding that no personal attorney fees will be paid if the complaint is completely without substance.

Some hotline services permit further questions to be asked of anonymous whistleblowers. However, it is likely that some employee whistleblowers will not be comfortable with this direct communication, even through a hotline service, and will prefer speaking only through their personal counsel to avoid disclosure of their identity.

> **Best Practice**
>
> Permit legitimate whistleblowers to form entities to protect their identity. ■

Another method of protecting the identity of legitimate whistleblowers is to permit them to form an entity. Typically, the entity is a Delaware limited liability company (LLC) or limited partnership (LP) since these entities are more tax efficient than corporations. The entities can be formed by law firms or outside services so that the name of the whistleblower does not appear in any public document. Qui tam plaintiffs typically form general partnerships.

Entities are particularly useful in cases where external whistleblowers partner with internal whistleblowers who do not wish their identity to be revealed. It was reported that Harry Markopolos formed entities to share the rewards with other whistleblowers in connection with an accusation against banks concerning the conversion of foreign currencies.[31] The external whistleblower who is willing to have his or her identity revealed can become the president of the LLC or the general partner of the LP, with the internal whistleblowers serving as equity owners of the LLC or LP.

The company should permit potential legitimate employee whistleblowers to form entities and, if the accusations have merit, pay the reasonable costs of forming the entity. The reimbursement for the reasonable costs of forming an entity would not apply unless independent counsel determined that the complaint had some merit.

Laws in certain European countries, such as France and Germany, limit the use of and discourage the emphasis on anonymity for whistleblower reports.[32] The confidentiality issue has posed significant problems for multinational United States–based corporations attempting to create whistleblower hotlines in compliance with SOX. For example, when McDonald's Corporation and Wal-Mart attempted to establish hotlines in France and Germany, a German labor court ruled that the proposed hotline violated German law, and the French Data Protection Authority (Commission Nationale de l'Informatique et des Libertés) refused to approve the proposed whistleblowing programs. For France, in particular, the concept of anonymous reporting carries historical implications related to Nazi informants during World War II, and there remains fear that an anonymous whistleblowing system could give way to an organized system of professional denunciation.[33] Therefore, whistleblower policies must be tailored for these countries.

Best Practice

Organizations should permit the whistleblower to communicate information by a multitude of methods, including e-mail, the Internet, hotlines, and letters (which may be anonymous). Organizational hotlines should operate 24 hours a day, 365 days a year; accommodate languages other than English; and permit use by customers and suppliers. ■

It is important to permit e-mail and Internet communication by whistleblowers. Some companies limit communications to hotlines where it is necessary to speak to a live operator. In some parts of the world, particularly Asia and Latin America, there are cultural biases against speaking directly to a hotline operator.[34] Therefore, it is important to permit communication by e-mail or through an Internet website, since potential whistleblowers throughout the world typically are comfortable with this mode of communication.

According to one major hotline operator, almost 50 percent of calls from employees are received outside of normal business hours. Presumably whistleblowers are fearful of using the hotline during normal business hours since they may be overheard by fellow employees, have their name show up on a caller ID, or be tracked on telephone call logs. Accordingly, the best practice is to permit the anonymous hotline to be used outside of business hours, preferably 24 hours a day.[35]

Many organizations have employees who do not speak English as their first language. In addition, large public companies may have international subsidiaries and operations that have employees who do not speak English at all. Therefore, in such cases, hotlines with live operators should have operators who speak foreign languages. Moreover, in the case of foreign operations, input should be obtained from foreign employees in designing the whistleblower system in order to accommodate different cultures.

Finally, consideration should be given to permitting customers and suppliers to use the hotline anonymously. For example, customers may become aware of illegal activity by employees of the sales department of the organization. The ability to communicate this illegal activity anonymously to the highest level of the organization may encourage the customer to use the hotline. Likewise, suppliers who have been gouged for a kickback or solicited to engage in other illegal activity by a member of the organization's purchasing department will be permitted to communicate these facts anonymously to the independent directors.

As discussed later in this chapter, customers and vendors account collectively for close to 30 percent of all tips, second only to employees as the source of tips.

ASSESS THE EFFECTIVENESS OF HOTLINES AND PROVIDE EMPLOYEE COMPLIANCE TRAINING

Many organizations have hotlines that receive very few calls. The organization then may incorrectly assume that there is no illegal activity occurring and that all is well.

This is not necessarily the case. The receipt of very few hotline calls may be the result of an ineffective whistleblowing program, which may include ineffective communication of the availability of the hotline service and a lack of incentives to employees to use it. This situation is particularly true in organizations that provide no recognition or rewards to legitimate whistleblowers. The lack of hotline activity may indicate only the failure of the organization to provide incentives to employee whistleblowing that are sufficient to outweigh the substantial disincentives.

> **Best Practice**
>
> Periodically assess the effectiveness of any employee hotline and provide employee compliance training. ■

The Deloitte Forensic Center (a think tank sponsored by Deloitte Advisory Services LLP) suggests that organizations should periodically assess hotline effectiveness through any one of these methods:

- Anonymous employee surveys
- Benchmarking
- Focus groups

- Feedback from hotline users
- Employee interviews
- Incident logs
- Exit interviews

The advantage of employee surveys is that they remind employees that a hotline exists. Employee surveys, which should be anonymous, should ask questions such as whether the employee has witnessed illegal activity and not reported it on the hotline. The surveys should also ask whether the organization is assuming major risks that have not been reported on the hotline. Exit interviews are particularly helpful since employees tend to be more candid with the interviewer when they are leaving the organization.

Each of these methods is useful in assessing hotline effectiveness. The actual methods used should be tailored to the nature of the workforce.

Periodic employee compliance training is essential to maintaining an ethical, law-abiding culture. A compliance evaluation component should be included in annual job performance assessments.

INDEPENDENT COUNSEL SHOULD REPORT THE STATUS AND RESULTS OF THE INVESTIGATION

One reason why whistleblowers report externally (i.e., to government authorities) is their belief, which may be mistaken, that no one investigated their complaint adequately. Whistleblowers who believe that they are not being taken seriously are much more likely to report externally.

Best Practice

Whistleblowers (if their identity is known) should receive periodic reports on the status of the investigation and at least a summary of the results of the investigation. All employees should receive an annual report of the actions taken in response to whistleblower complaints. ▪

Accordingly, the best practice is for independent counsel to keep whistleblowers continually advised as to the status of the investigation, which may take several months, if not longer. In addition, whistleblowers should be given at least an abbreviated report of the results of the investigation and, if feasible, the full report. Obviously, if whistleblowers are anonymous and do not have an attorney or other representative, it is not possible to keep them advised of developments.

To encourage the use of hotlines, annual reports should be given by the organization to all employees summarizing the actions taken as a result of whistleblower reports.[36]

INTERNAL WHISTLEBLOWERS SHOULD RECEIVE MEANINGFUL MONETARY REWARDS

It is to the company's advantage to encourage internal whistleblowing.[37] The substantial rewards available to external whistleblowers can entice people to report externally rather than internally. Indeed, the Internet is full of plaintiff law firms advertising for whistleblowers. Internal whistleblowing gives the company the opportunity to remedy the problem well before any inquiry by public authorities.

Once the government opens an inquiry, the costs to the company rise steeply. If the law violation is remedied because of the internal whistleblower, there is a substantial benefit to the company. Indeed, it is possible that there will never be an external investigation.

Best Practice

The company should provide meaningful rewards for legitimate internal whistleblowers and advertise the availability of these internal rewards. ■

A meaningful bounty not only enriches the whistleblower but also provides needed recognition for him or her within the organization. The psychological pressures on whistleblowers within organizations can be very serious. Rewards help to offset the social disincentives to whistleblowers, such as ostracism, by providing the organization's blessing on them.

The use of rewards has long been advocated to motivate whistleblowers.[38] Congress has created significant rewards for whistleblowers who go public with their allegations. It is in the organization's interest to provide meaningful bounties for whistleblowers who report internally instead of externally reporting their allegations.

What Is a Meaningful Reward?

Some whistleblowers do not need a meaningful reward to induce them to blow the whistle. Enron's Sherron Watkins is one such person. Glaxo's Cheryl Eckard is another. The Federal Bureau of Investigation's Coleen Rowley is a third. Eckard initially was an internal whistleblower who would have received no reward but went external only after she was ignored and her employment was terminated. However, given the huge disincentives to being a whistleblower, many employees will not risk their careers and their livelihoods without both a guarantee of anonymity and a meaningful reward.

A meaningful reward to the whistleblower whose allegations prove true helps create an atmosphere that encourages internal whistleblowing, which clearly benefits the company.

If the board of directors intends to encourage direct communication to the board by lower-level executives, a $1,000 reward is not going to be meaningful. Such an amount may be meaningful to someone making less than $50,000 per year but not to an executive making $200,000 a year.

A meaningful reward should be at least 10 to 30 percent of any savings to the company from the use of the information. Rewards equal to 100 percent of the whistleblower's salary should be considered. The company's compliance policy should indicate the reward percentages, with the understanding that the amounts are not legally binding. In cases where the information does not provide savings to the company but helps it avoid damage to its reputation, discretion would have to be exercised in determining the amount of the reward.

Independent counsel should recommend the amount of the award to the independent directors for their final decision. The full board of directors should give the independent directors complete discretion in making decisions about awards.

Some would argue that the amount of internal rewards could never compete economically with rewards available to whistleblowers from public or external whistleblowing. This argument assumes that there is an applicable statutory incentive for the whistleblowers, that they are willing to wait for years of litigation to be concluded, and that they are willing to risk the social ostracism and other disincentives, including possible unemployment, resulting from external whistleblowing.

Although there are many statutory incentives to whistleblowing, these incentives do not apply to every type of whistleblower. For example, if an executive at Merrill Lynch in 2007 complained to public authorities that the company was taking excessive risk with its large subprime mortgage portfolio, there would have been no applicable statutory reward. Even after the enactment of the Dodd-Frank Act, there would be no applicable statutory award for disclosure of excessive risk taking unless there had been a violation of the federal securities laws and the monetary sanctions exceeded $1 million.

Many potential internal whistleblowers do not want to be stigmatized as "squealers" by making public disclosures but would be willing to respond to a robust internal whistleblower system that rewarded them and treated them as heroes. Even though the economic rewards to an internal whistleblower may not match the statutory awards, the internal whistleblower avoids years of litigation and the social ostracism and other disincentives of external whistleblowing.

THE WHISTLEBLOWER POLICY MUST BE COMMUNICATED EFFECTIVELY

One of the major problems of the SOX whistleblower provisions is that they are not widely and frequently communicated to employees. As previously noted, an empirical study by the Institute of Internal Auditors indicates that greater employee familiarity with the hotline encourages its use.[39]

> **Best Practice**
>
> Communicate the provisions of the whistleblower policy widely and frequently, and recognize legitimate whistleblowers who are willing to be identified. ■

At a minimum, the CEO should send a memorandum to all employees describing the whistleblower system at least once a year. The memorandum should include a description of the bounty provisions of the internal whistleblower policy and the methods by which whistleblowers can make anonymous submissions to protect their identity. The independent counsel for the independent directors should be named in the memorandum. The memorandum should also discuss the arrangements that can be made to further safeguard the identity of anonymous whistleblowers through communication with their personal counsel and the fact that the company will pay personal counsel fees directly if the allegations are legitimate.

This form of communication from the CEO helps to establish the tone at the top and helps create an ethical, law-abiding culture within the organization.

The memorandum should also recognize the achievements of legitimate whistleblowers and the benefits of their actions to the organization. In order to protect their identities, the names of specific whistleblowers should be disclosed only with their written consent.

The best method of further communicating a whistleblower policy to employees depends on the company's business and the nature of its workforce. For example, posters are very effective in the construction industry to communicate whistleblower policies whereas intranet messages are much more effective in technology businesses.

According to a 2010 report, the following are the overall means of communicating awareness of the organization's hotline in all industries:[40]

Means of Caller Awareness	2009
Brochure	2%
Employee	14%
HR	5%
Handbook	9%
Intranet	11%
Manager	5%
Poster	32%
Sign	2%
Unknown	2%
Video	0%
Wallet card	4%
Other	14%

The 2010 report then breaks down the chart by industry. The charts for the industries with regard to "means of awareness" of the organization's hotline that are over 10 percent frequency are presented next.

Construction

Means of Awareness	2009
Employee	12%
Poster	45%
Other	13%

Finance, Insurance, and Real Estate

Means of Awareness	2009
Employee	11%
Intranet	26%
Unknown	15%
Other	14%

Manufacturing

Means of Awareness	2009
Employee	13%
Poster	33%
Other	12%

Mining

Means of Awareness	2009
Employee	16%
Intranet	11%
Poster	32%
Other	15%

Public Administration

Means of Awareness	2009
Employee	13%
Intranet	14%
Unknown	15%
Other	39%

Retail Trade

Means of Awareness	2009
Poster	35%
Unknown	19%
Other	10%

Service Industries

Means of Awareness	2009
Employee	10%
Poster	21%
Unknown	36%

Transportation, Communication, and Utilities

Means of Awareness	2009
Employee	15%
Intranet	17%
Poster	18%
Unknown	17%
Other	16%

Wholesale Trade

Means of Awareness	2009
Employee	13%
Poster	52%
Other	10%

THERE SHOULD BE MILDER SANCTIONS FOR WHISTLEBLOWERS INVOLVED IN ILLEGAL GROUP ACTIVITY

There are occasions when a division of an organization or a group of employees becomes involved in a minor fraud or crime. What starts out as a minor fraud or crime might soon turn out to be a large-scale fraud or crime.

It has been suggested that "the leaders of the fraud or crime within the organization have a strong incentive to induce other employees to engage in wrongdoing so as to immunize them against becoming whistleblowers."[41] This conspiracy, which involves pressuring others to engage in the fraud or crime, can be revealed only if the employees involved in the fraud or crime are given special inducements or immunity to blow the whistle.

Best Practice

Whistleblowers who are themselves involved in illegal group activity should receive milder sanctions from the organization in order to encourage internal whistleblowing. ■

To induce employees who are themselves involved in a fraud or crime to inform the organization of what is transpiring, milder sanctions or possible immunity should be given to such whistleblowers. This is the same procedure used in criminal law enforcement, which metes out milder sanctions to informants who may themselves be involved in the crime.

The organization that does not treat informants better than other participants in a fraud or crime is not likely to receive the necessary information to prevent further harm to the organization.

RETALIATION CLAIMS SHOULD BE INDEPENDENTLY INVESTIGATED

Once a whistleblower's complaint is determined to have some merit, the whistleblower must be protected from any perceived retaliation, direct or indirect. Similar protection should be given to the whistleblower during the period that his or her accusations are being investigated. This protection is important not only to avoid violating anti-retaliation laws but also to maintain the integrity of the whistleblower system. If legitimate whistleblowers are not protected from either direct or subtle retaliation, other potential whistleblowers will be discouraged from using the internal whistleblower system.

Any claim of retaliation against a whistleblower should be investigated by the independent counsel reporting directly to the independent directors.

Best Practice

Any retaliation claim by a whistleblower should be investigated by independent counsel reporting to the independent directors. Any decision to terminate the employment of a legitimate whistleblower should be approved by the independent directors. ■

An organization may have good reasons for laying off or otherwise terminating employment of a legitimate whistleblower. The whistleblower may be part of a group of employees who have become redundant because of plant closure or other good reasons. The whistleblower's job performance may have suffered sufficiently so that the termination is more than justified.

To protect legitimate whistleblowers from either direct or subtle retaliation through employment termination, any such termination decision should be submitted to the independent directors for approval. These directors can, with the help of independent counsel, make reasonable inquiries as to whether the termination is justified.

It should be remembered that Cheryl Eckard, whose story is discussed in Chapter 2, had her employment terminated for "redundancy" after she reported problems at the Cidra, Puerto Rico, plant to Glaxo. Had the decision to terminate her employment been subject to approval by the Glaxo independent directors, the company may not have had to pay $750 million in penalties, to the detriment of its shareholders and Glaxo's reputation.

THE DIRECTOR OF CORPORATE COMPLIANCE SHOULD BECOME THE EYES AND EARS OF THE INDEPENDENT DIRECTORS

Best Practice

The director of corporate compliance should report directly to the independent directors not less frequently than annually and should become their eyes and ears within the organization.

In many organizations today, the director of corporate compliance reports to a higher-level executive within the organization. The compensation of the director of corporate compliance is determined by the top officers of the organization. Is it any wonder that potential whistleblowers may have very little confidence in making disclosures to the director of corporate compliance, since he or she is viewed as part of management?

A robust whistleblower system requires the director of corporate compliance to report to the independent directors and become their eyes and ears within the organization. This is a similar role to the internal auditor with respect to the audit committee of the board of directors. The primary task of the corporate compliance director should be to report to the independent directors on the corporate culture tone within the organization. Is there an ethical, law-abiding culture within the organization?

The director of corporate compliance should also have the following tasks:

- Advertising whistleblower policies within the organization on a continual basis
- Helping to identify risk areas or problems within the organization and reporting them to the CEO and the independent directors
- Searching for legal compliance disasters within the organization's industry and determining whether the organization is engaged in similar conduct
- Updating the compliance policies for changes in law and for new product or service launches

The independent directors and the CEO should set the compensation of the corporate compliance director.

An incentive has been created under the U.S. Sentencing Guidelines for the corporate compliance director to have "direct reporting obligations" to the independent directors. Under amendments to the U.S. Sentencing Guidelines, effective November 2010, organizations can obtain reduced criminal sentences (including fines) despite high-level personnel involvement if the organization has an effective compliance and ethics program, which contains these four elements:

1. the individual or individuals with operational responsibility for the compliance and ethics program . . . have direct reporting obligations to the governing authority or an appropriate subgroup thereof (e.g., an audit committee of the board of directors);
2. the compliance and ethics program detected the offense before discovery outside the organization or before such discovery was reasonably likely;
3. the organization promptly reported the offense to appropriate governmental authorities; and
4. no individual with operational responsibility for the compliance and ethics program participated in, condoned, or was willfully ignorant of the offense.[42]

The corporate compliance director is considered to have "direct reporting obligations" to the governing authority or an appropriate subgroup thereof if the individual has express authority to communicate personally to the

governing authority or appropriate subgroup thereof (1) promptly on any matter involving criminal conduct or potential criminal conduct, and (2) no less
than annually on the implementation and effectiveness of the compliance and
ethics program.[43]

MAJOR DOs AND DON'Ts FOR CEOs

A few major dos for the CEO are listed next.

- *Do* establish a robust whistleblower system as described in this chapter.
- *Do* maintain a good tone at the top by periodically reporting to your staff
  the fact that the corporation has investigated whistleblower complaints
  (without necessarily naming names or the content of the allegations) so
  that employees understand that such complaints are treated seriously
  by top management. Together with the independent directors, authorize
  meaningful rewards and recognition to whistleblowers whose information
  provides a substantial benefit to the corporation.
- *Do* remember that the U.S. Department of Justice guidelines require a determination of "whether the corporation's employees are adequately informed
  about the compliance program and are convinced of the corporation's commitment to it."
- *Do* pay attention to legal compliance disasters in the corporation's industry. It is likely that prosecutors of other firms in your industry will seek to
  determine whether your corporation is engaged in similar conduct.
- *Do* have the corporate compliance director report to you any increase in
  the activities of the federal, state, and foreign prosecutors. According to the
  New York Times of October 27, 2010, the U.S. Department of Justice opened
  more investigations in the last two years than in any other two-year period
  and had under consideration hundreds of lawsuits.
- *Do* make certain that corporate compliance policies and procedures are
  reviewed and updated periodically for new laws or regulations affecting
  existing products and services. New laws and regulations that can affect
  the corporation's business are constantly being created. Thus, compliance
  policies and procedures must be updated regularly.
- *Do* advise the corporate compliance director and the legal department of all
  new proposed products and services so that there is adequate time before
  the launch date to perform the necessary research on applicable laws and
  regulations and to create compliance procedures.

A few major don'ts for the CEO are listed next.

■ *Don't* fail to provide adequate resources to conduct investigations of whistleblower complaints, as described in Chapter 6.[44] Such a failure can be viewed as causing an ineffective compliance policy. Remember that the U.S. Department of Justice criminal guidelines require a determination of "whether the corporation has provided for a staff sufficient to audit, document, analyze and utilize the results of the corporation's compliance efforts."[45] The corporate compliance director should be encouraged to speak directly to you and the independent directors concerning staff or budget inadequacies.
■ *Don't* fail to periodically test the effectiveness of your organization's employee hotline and provide employee compliance training.
■ *Don't* undermine the tone at the top by having your personal actions be inconsistent with the ethical culture that you are advocating to employees. Nothing is more damaging to an ethical corporate culture than a CEO who violates his or her own rules or permits or tolerates others in top management to violate the company compliance program.
■ *Don't* fail to schedule periodic presentations by the corporate compliance director to the board of directors or an appropriate committee of the board in charge of compliance.[46] A November 2010 amendment to the U.S. Federal Sentencing Guidelines requires reports to the board of directors or the audit committee "no less than annually . . . on the implementation and effectiveness of the compliance and ethics program."[47]

In Part IV of the book, we review the qui tam private actions under the False Claims Act, IRS whistleblower bounties, other statutory incentives and protections of whistleblowers, and a step-by-step guide to SEC whistleblowing under the Dodd-Frank Act.

NOTES

1. Marcia P. Miceli and Janet P. Near, "What Makes Whistleblowers Effective? Three Field Studies," *Human Relations* 55, No. 4 (2002): 455–479.
2. Public Company Accounting Oversight Board Standard No. 5. http://pcaobus .org/Standards/Auditing/Pages/Auditing_Standard_5.aspx.
3. David M. Becker, Esq., General Counsel, "Speech by SEC Staff: Remarks at the Practicing Law Institute's Ninth Annual Institute on Securities Regulation in Europe," U.S. Securities and Exchange Commission, January 25, 2011.

4. James E. Hunton and Jacob M. Rose, "Effects of Anonymous Whistle-Blowing and Perceived Reputation Threats on Investigations of Whistle-Blowing Allegations by Audit Committee Members," *Journal of Management Studies* 1, no. 48 (2011): 75–98.

5. Deloitte Forensic Center, "Whistleblowing and the New Race to Report: The Impact of the Dodd-Frank Act and 2010's Changes to U.S. Federal Sentencing Guidelines," 2010. www.deloitte.com/view/en_US/us/Services/Financial-Advisory-Services/Forensic-Center/fb02b4b17deaa210VgnVCM2000001b56f00aRCRD.htm.

6. Alexander Dyck, Adair Morse, and Luigi Zingales, "Who Blows the Whistle on Corporate Fraud?" Compliance Building.com, April 29, 2010. www.compliancebuilding.com/2010/04/29/who-blows-the-whistle-on-corporate-fraud.

7. Mary B. Curtis, "Whistleblower Mechanisms: A Study of the Perceptions of 'Users' and 'Responders,'" Dallas chapter of the Institute of Internal Auditors, April 2006.

8. Ibid.

9. Section 10A of the Securities Exchange Act of 1934.

10. Sebastian Moffett, "Renault's No. 2 Executive Quits," *Wall Street Journal*, April 12, 2011.

11. James E. Hunton and Jacob M. Rose, "Do Audit Committee Members' Self-Interests Influence Accounting Choice?" *Accounting, Organizations and Society* 33 (2008): 783–800; E. Fama and M. Jenson, "Separation of Ownership and Control," *Journal of Law and Economics* 26 (1983): 301–325.

12. Bethany McLean and Joe Nocera, *All The Devils Are Here: The Hidden History of the Financial Crisis* (New York: Portfolio/Penguin 2010).

13. "Hewlett-Packard CEO Mark Hurd Resigns after Sex Harassment Investigation," *Telegraph*, August 7, 2010. www.telegraph.co.uk/news/worldnews/northamerica/usa/7932100/Hewlett-Packard-CEO-Mark-Hurd-resigns-after-sex-harassment-investigation.html.

14. J. Greenberg, "Reactions to Procedural Justice in Payment Distributions: Do the Ends Justify the Means?" *Journal of Applied Psychology* 72 (1987): 55–71.

15. "Sherron Watkins eMail to Enron Chairman Kenneth Lay," January 20, 2002. www.itmweb.com/f012002.htm.

16. Dan Ackman, "Sherron Watkins Had Whistle, But Blew It," *Forbes*, February 14, 2002. www.forbes.com/2002/02/14/0214watkins.html.

17. Ashby Jones and Joann S. Lublin, "Firms Revisit Whistleblowing," *Wall Street Journal*, March 14, 2011; see also Gerard Bon, "Renault Security Manager under Fraud Investigation," Reuters, March 13, 2011.

18. Sebastian Moffett, "Renault's No. 2 Executive Quits," *Wall Street Journal*, April 12, 2011.

19. Thomas R. Fox, "Ready, Fire, Aim: L'Affaire Renault," FCPA Compliance and Ethics Blog, March 15, 2011. http://tfoxlaw.wordpress.com/2011/03/15/ready-fire-aim.

20. Hunton and Rose, "Effects of Anonymous Whistle-Blowing."
21. Ibid.
22. Harry Markopolos with Frank Casey, Neil Chelo, Gaytri Kachroo, and Michael Ocrant, *No One Would Listen: A True Financial Thriller* (Hoboken, NJ: John Wiley & Sons, 2010), p. 171.
23. Ibid.
24. Ibid., p. 156.
25. Michael J. Gundlach et al., "The Decision to Blow the Whistle: A Social Information-tion Process Framework," *Academy of Management Review* 28, No. 1 (January 2003): 107–123; Marcia P. Miceli and Janet P. Near, "The Incident of Wrong-doing, Whistle-Blowing, and Retaliation: Results of a Naturally Occurring Field Experiment," *Employee Responsibilities and Rights Journal* 2, No. 2 (1989); Janet P. Near and Tamila C. Jensen, "The Whistleblowing Process: Retaliation and Perceived Effectiveness," *Work and Occupations* 10, No. 1 (February 1983): 3–28.
26. A. P. Brief and S. Motowidlo, "Prosocial Organizational Behaviors," *Academy of Management Review* 11 (1986): 710–725.
27. Greenberg, "Reactions to Procedural Justice in Payment Distributions."
28. U.S. Securities and Exchange Commission, Office of Investigations, "Investigation of Failure of the SEC to Uncover Bernard Madoff's Ponzi Scheme—Public Version," Report No. OIG-509, August 2009, p. 250. www.sec.gov/news/studies/2009/oig-509.pdf.
29. 2011 Corporate Governance and Compliance Hotline Benchmark Report, "A Comprehensive Examination of Organizational Hotline Activity from The Network." http://tnwinc.com/files/2011TNWbenchmarkingreport .pdf?webSyncID=24de8b7c-92b9-3074-a566-921c84284727&session GUID=bcd27041-3405-c274-b7bd-071a4be99052.
30. Maarten De Schepper, "Setting the Right Incentives for Whistleblowers," paper submitted for (European Master in Law and Economics, 2008–2009). www .emle.org/_data/Marten_De_Schepper_-_Setting_the_Right_Incentives_for_ Whistleblowers.pdf.
31. Carrick Mollenkamp, Lingling Wei, and Gregory Zuckerman, "States Widen Currency-Trade Probes," *Wall Street Journal*, February 3, 2011.
32. Deloitte Forensic Center, "Whistleblowing and the New Race to Report."
33. Patrick Collins, Lee Stein, and Caryn Trombino, "Consider the Source: How Weak Whistleblower Protection Outside the United States Threatens to Reduce the Impact of the Dodd-Frank Reward Among Foreign Nationals," Third Annual National Institute on the Foreign Corrupt Practices Act, Washington, D.C., 2010.
34. Ibid.
35. Ibid.
36. Curtis, "Whistleblower Mechanisms."

37. Robert Howse and Ronald J. Daniels, "Rewarding Whistleblowers: The Costs and Benefits of an Incentive-Based Compliance," University of Pennsylvania Scholarly Commons, Department Papers (School of Law), January 1, 1995. http://works.bepress.com/cgi/viewcontent.cgi?article=1017&context=ronald_daniels.

38. Richard E. Moberly, "Sarbanes-Oxley's Structural Model to Encourage Corporate Whistleblowers," *Brigham Young University Law Review* (2006): 1108, n. 5.

39. Curtis, "Whistleblower Mechanisms."

40. 2011 Corporate Governance and Compliance Hotline Benchmarking Report by The Network, Inc. and BDO Consulting. Reprinted with permission.

41. Howse and Daniels, "Rewarding Whistleblowers," p. 538.

42. U.S. Sentencing Guidelines Manual, § 8C2.5(f)(3)(C) (2010). www.ussc.gov/Guidelines /2010_guidelines/index.cfm.

43. U.S. Sentencing Guidelines Manual, § 8C2.5, cmt. n. 11 (2010).

44. "Principles of Federal Prosecution of Business Organizations," Memorandum from Mark R. Filip, Deputy Attorney General, to Heads of Department Components and United States Attorneys, August 28, 2008. www.usdoj.gov/opa/documents/corp-charging-guidelines.pdf.

45. Ibid.

46. www.corporatecomplianceinsights.com/2011/dos-and-donts-for-ceos-on-compliance-issues/.

47. 2010 Federal Sentencing Guidelines Manual, § 8B2.1, Commentary.

PART FOUR

Statutory Incentives and SEC Award Regulations

CHAPTER EIGHT

The False Claims Act: Qui Tam Cases

T HE FALSE CLAIMS ACT[1] (Act) is a U.S. federal law that permits people who are not affiliated with the government to file actions against federal contractors, claiming fraud against the government. The Act provides a reward or bounty (usually 15 to 25 percent, but it can reach as high as 30 percent) of any recovered damages. The Act protects against fraudulent billings turned in to the federal government. Claims under the Act are filed by persons with insider knowledge of false claims, which typically have involved healthcare, military, or other government spending programs.[2]

During the American Civil War (1861–1865), fraud was rampant in both the Union North and the Confederate South. Some argue that the False Claims Act came about because of bad mules. During the war, unscrupulous contractors sold the Union Army decrepit horses and mules in ill health, faulty rifles and ammunition, and rancid rations and provisions, among other fraudulent actions.[3] The Act was passed by Congress on March 2, 1863, in an effort by the United States to respond to these fraudulent practices in obtaining payments from the U.S. government. A bounty was offered in what is called the qui tam provision, which permits individuals to sue on behalf of the government and be paid a percentage of the recovery.

It should be noted that private qui tam actions are not permitted under the Dodd-Frank Act for violations of federal securities laws or under the whistleblower provisions of the Internal Revenue Code. Only the Securities and Exchange Commission, the Internal Revenue Service (IRS), or the U.S. Department of Justice can bring an action for violation of such laws.

 ## WHAT IS A FALSE CLAIM?

The term "false claim" refers to any of these acts relating to a claim involving the U.S. government:

§ 3729. False claims
  (a) Liability for certain acts.
      (1) In general. Subject to paragraph (2), any person who—
          (A) knowingly presents, or causes to be presented, a false or fraudulent claim for payment or approval;
          (B) knowingly makes, uses, or causes to be made or used, a false record or statement material to a false or fraudulent claim;
          (C) conspires to commit a violation of subparagraph (A), (B), (D), (E), (F), or (G);
          (D) has possession, custody, or control of property or money used, or to be used, by the Government and knowingly delivers, or causes to be delivered, less than all of that money or property;
          (E) is authorized to make or deliver a document certifying receipt of property used, or to be used, by the Government and, intending to defraud the Government, makes or delivers the receipt without completely knowing that the information on the receipt is true;
          (F) knowingly buys, or receives as a pledge of an obligation or debt, public property from an officer or employee of the Government, or a member of the Armed Forces, who lawfully may not sell or pledge property; or
          (G) knowingly makes, uses, or causes to be made or used, a false record or statement material to an obligation to pay or transmit money or property to the Government, or knowingly conceals or knowingly and improperly avoids or decreases an obligation to pay or transmit money or property to the Government,
      is liable to the United States Government. . . .

The statute provides for a civil penalty of not less than \$5,000 and not more than \$10,000, as adjusted by the Federal Civil Penalties Inflation Adjustment Act of 1990 (28 U.S.C. § 2461 note; Public Law 104-410), plus 3 times the amount of damages which the Government sustains because of the act of that person.[4]

The statutory definition of a "false claim" that creates liability is extremely broad. A partial list of examples follows.[5]

- Billing for goods and services that were never delivered or rendered.
- Billing for marketing, lobbying or other non-contract related corporate activities.
- Submitting false service records or samples in order to show better-than-actual performance.
- Presenting broken or untested equipment as operational and tested.
- Performing inappropriate or unnecessary medical procedures in order to increase Medicare reimbursement.
- Billing for work or tests not performed.
- Billing for premium equipment but actually providing inferior equipment.
- Automatically running a lab test whenever the results of some other test fall within a certain range, even though the second test was not specifically requested.
- Defective testing—Certifying that something has passed a test, when in fact it has not.
- "Lick and stick" prescription rebate fraud and "marketing the spread" prescription fraud, both of which involve lying to the government about the true wholesale price of prescription drugs.
- Unbundling—Using multiple billing codes instead of one billing code for a drug panel test in order to increase remuneration.
- Bundling—Billing more for a panel of tests when a single test was asked for.
- Double billing—Charging more than once for the same goods or service.
- Upcoding—Inflating bills by using diagnosis billing codes that suggest a more expensive illness or treatment.
- Billing for brand—Billing for brand-named drugs when generic drugs are actually provided.

- Phantom employees and doctored time slips: Charging for employees that were not actually on the job, or billing for made-up hours in order to maximize reimbursements.
- Upcoding employee work: Billing at doctor rates for work that was actually conducted by a nurse or resident intern.
- Yield burning—Skimming off the profits from the sale of municipal bonds.
- Falsifying natural resource production records—Pumping, mining, or harvesting more natural resources from public lands than is actually reported to the government.
- Being overpaid by the government for sale of a good or service, and then not reporting that overpayment.
- Misrepresenting the value of imported goods or their country of origin for tariff purposes.
- False certification that a contract falls within certain guidelines (i.e., the contractor is a minority or veteran).
- Billing in order to increase revenue instead of billing to reflect actual work performed.
- Failing to report known product defects in order to be able to continue to sell or bill the government for the product.
- Billing for research that was never conducted; falsifying research data that was paid for by the U.S. government.
- Winning a contract through kickbacks or bribes.
- Prescribing a medicine or recommending a type of treatment or diagnosis regimen in order to win kickbacks from hospitals, labs, or pharmaceutical companies.
- Billing for unlicensed or unapproved drugs.
- Forging physician signatures when such signatures are required for reimbursement from Medicare or Medicaid.

 FALSE CLAIMS ACT BOUNTIES

The False Claims Act provides incentive to so-called relators (private persons who bring qui tam claims under the Act) by granting them between 15 and 30 percent of any award or settlement amount. In addition, the statute provides an award of the relator's attorneys' fees, making qui tam actions a popular topic for the plaintiffs' bar. An individual bringing suit pro se—that is, without the representation of a lawyer—may not bring a qui tam action under the False Claims Act.[6] There is no requirement in the statute that a relator be a U.S. citizen.

The bounty provisions of the False Claims Act are presented next.

(d) Award to qui tam plaintiff.

    (1) If the Government proceeds with an action brought by a person under subsection (b), such person shall, subject to the second sentence of this paragraph, receive at least 15 percent but not more than 25 percent of the proceeds of the action or settlement of the claim, depending upon the extent to which the person substantially contributed to the prosecution of the action. Where the action is one which the court finds to be based primarily on disclosures of specific information (other than information provided by the person bringing the action) relating to allegations or transactions in a criminal, civil, or administrative hearing, in a congressional, administrative, or Government [General] Accounting Office report, hearing, audit, or investigation, or from the news media, the court may award such sums as it considers appropriate, but in no case more than 10 percent of the proceeds, taking into account the significance of the information and the role of the person bringing the action in advancing the case to litigation. Any payment to a person under the first or second sentence of this paragraph shall be made from the proceeds. Any such person shall also receive an amount for reasonable expenses which the court finds to have been necessarily incurred, plus reasonable attorneys' fees and costs. All such expenses, fees, and costs shall be awarded against the defendant.

    (2) If the Government does not proceed with an action under this section, the person bringing the action or settling the claim shall receive an amount which the court decides is reasonable for collecting the civil penalty and damages. The amount shall be not less than 25 percent and not more than 30 percent of the proceeds of the action or settlement and shall be paid out of such proceeds. Such person shall also receive an amount for reasonable expenses which the court finds to have been necessarily incurred, plus reasonable attorneys' fees and costs. All such expenses, fees, and costs shall be awarded against the defendant.

    (3) Whether or not the Government proceeds with the action, if the court finds that the action was brought by a person who planned and initiated the violation of section 3729 upon which the action was brought, then the court may, to the extent the court considers appropriate, reduce the share of the proceeds of the action which the person would otherwise receive under paragraph (1) or (2) of this subsection, taking

into account the role of that person in advancing the case to litigation and any relevant circumstances pertaining to the violation. If the person bringing the action is convicted of criminal conduct arising from his or her role in the violation of section 3729, that person shall be dismissed from the civil action and shall not receive any share of the proceeds of the action. Such dismissal shall not prejudice the right of the United States to continue the action, represented by the Department of Justice.

(4) If the Government does not proceed with the action and the person bringing the action conducts the action, the court may award to the defendant its reasonable attorneys' fees and expenses if the defendant prevails in the action and the court finds that the claim of the person bringing the action was clearly frivolous, clearly vexatious, or brought primarily for purposes of harassment.[7]

According to statistics provided by the Taxpayers Against Fraud Education Fund, in 2010, there were 573 new qui tam cases and settlements and judgments totaling close to $2.4 billion. In 2010, the relators' share of these settlements or judgments totaled over $385 million.

 ## U.S. DEPARTMENT OF JUSTICE MEMORANDUM

The next memorandum, provided by the U.S. Department of Justice, contains a general overview of the government's decision to intervene in private qui tam litigation under the False Claims Act.[8] The U.S. government's decision to intervene is usually very helpful in forcing a settlement:

The False Claims Act, 31 U.S.C. § 3729 et seq., provides for liability for triple damages and a penalty from $5,500 to $11,000 per claim for anyone who knowingly submits or causes the submission of a false or fraudulent claim to the United States.

The statute, first passed in 1863, includes an ancient legal device called a "qui tam" provision (from a Latin phrase meaning "he who brings a case on behalf of our lord the King, as well as for himself"). This provision allows a private person, known as a "relator," to bring a lawsuit on behalf of the United States, where the private person has information that the named defendant has knowingly submitted or caused the submission of false or fraudulent claims to the United States. The relator need not have been personally harmed by the defendant's conduct.

The False Claims Act has a very detailed process for the filing and pursuit of these claims. The qui tam relator must be represented by an attorney. The qui tam complaint must, by law, be filed under seal, which means that all records relating to the case must be kept on a secret docket by the Clerk of the Court. Copies of the complaint are given only to the United States Department of Justice, including the local United States Attorney, and to the assigned judge of the District Court. The Court may, usually upon motion by the United States Attorney, make the complaint available to other persons.

The complaint, and all other filings in the case, remain under seal for a period of at least sixty days. At the conclusion of the sixty days, the Department of Justice must, if it wants the case to remain under seal, file a motion with the District judge showing "good cause" why the case should remain under seal. In the usual course, these motions request an extension of the seal for six months at a time.

In addition to the complaint filed with the District Court, the relator through his or her council [sic] must serve upon the Department of Justice a "disclosure statement" containing substantially all the evidence in the possession of the relator about the allegations set forth in the complaint. This disclosure statement is not filed in any court, and is not available to the named defendant.

Under the False Claims Act, the Attorney General (or a Department of Justice attorney) must investigate the allegations of violations of the False Claims Act. The investigation usually involves one or more law enforcement agencies (such as the Office of Inspector General of the victim agency, the Postal Inspection Service, or the FBI.) In some investigations where state agencies are victims, state attorneys general with expertise and interest will participate in the investigation and work closely with the federal agencies.

The investigation will often involve specific investigative techniques, including subpoenas for documents or electronic records, witness interviews, compelled oral testimony from one or more individuals or organizations, and consultations with experts. If there is a parallel criminal investigation, search warrants and other criminal investigation tools may be used to obtain evidence as well.

At the conclusion of the investigation, or earlier if so directed by the Court, the Department of Justice must choose one of three options named in the False Claims Act:

- intervene in one or more counts of the pending qui tam action. This intervention expresses the Government's intention to participate as a plaintiff in prosecuting that count of the complaint. Fewer than 25% of filed qui tam actions result in an intervention on any count by the Department of Justice.
- decline to intervene in one or all counts of the pending qui tam action. If the United States declines to intervene, the relator and his or her attorney may prosecute the action on behalf of the United States, but the United States is not a party to the proceedings apart from its right to any recovery. This option is frequently used by relators and their attorneys.
- move to dismiss the relator's complaint, either because there is no case, or the case conflicts with significant statutory or policy interests of the United States.

In practice, there are two other options for the Department of Justice:

- settle the pending qui tam action with the defendant prior to the intervention decision. This usually, but not always, results in a simultaneous intervention and settlement with the Department of Justice (and is included in the 25% intervention rate).
- advise the relator that the Department of Justice intends to decline intervention. This usually, but not always, results in dismissal of the qui tam action.

There are no statistics reported on the length of time the average qui tam case remains under seal. In this District, most intervened or settled cases are under seal for at least two years (with, of course, periodic reports to the supervising judge concerning the progress of the case, and the justification of the need for additional time).

Intervention by the Department of Justice in a qui tam case is not undertaken lightly. Intervention usually requires approval by the Department in Washington. As part of the decision process, the views of the investigative agency are solicited and considered, and a detailed memorandum discussing the relevant facts and law is prepared. This memorandum usually includes a discussion of efforts to advise the named defendant of the nature of the potential claims against it, any response provided by the defendant, and settlement efforts undertaken prior to intervention. This memorandum is considered to be attorney work product exempt from disclosure.

Upon intervention approval, the Department of Justice files:

- a notice of intervention, setting forth the specific claims as to which the United States is intervening;
- a motion to unseal the qui tam complaint filed by the relator and the notice of intervention. All other documents filed by the Department of Justice up to that point remain under seal.

The decision by the Department of Justice to intervene in a case does not necessarily mean that it will endorse, adopt or agree with every factual allegation or legal conclusion in the relator's complaint. It has been the usual practice of the Department to file its own complaint about 60 days after the intervention, setting forth its own statement of the facts that show the knowing submission of false claims, and the specific relief it seeks. In addition, the Department of Justice has the ability to, and often will, assert claims arising under other statutes (such as the Truth in Negotiation Act or the Public Contracts Anti-Kickback Act) or the common law, which the relators do not have the legal right to assert in their complaint, since only the False Claims Act has a qui tam provision.

After the relator's complaint is unsealed, the relator through his or her attorney has the obligation under the Federal Rules of Civil Procedure to serve its complaint upon each named defendant within 120 days.

Each named defendant has the duty to file an answer to the complaint or a motion within 20 days after service of the government's complaints. Discovery under the Federal Rules of Civil Procedure begins shortly thereafter.[9]

The U.S. Department of Justice, based on one source, has elected to intervene in approximately 18 percent of private qui tam actions.[10]

 ## STATUTE OF LIMITATIONS

Whistleblowers must bring qui tam claims within the statute of limitations provided in the False Claims Act. The Act contains this statute of limitations:

(b) A civil action under section 3730 [which provides for actions by private persons and by the Attorney General under the False Claims Act] may not be brought—

    (1) more than 6 years after the date on which the violation of section 3729 [the definition of false claims previous quoted] is committed, or

    (2) more than 3 years after the date when facts material to the right of action are known or reasonably should have been known by the official of the United States charged with responsibility to act in the circumstances, but in no event more than 10 years after the date on which the violation is committed, whichever occurs last.

(c) If the Government elects to intervene and proceed with an action brought under 3730(b), the Government may file its own complaint or amend the complaint of a person who has brought an action under section 3730(b) to clarify or add detail to the claims in which the Government is intervening and to add any additional claims with respect to which the Government contends it is entitled to relief. For statute of limitations purposes, any such Government pleading shall relate back to the filing date of the complaint of the person who originally brought the action, to the extent that the claim of the Government arises out of the conduct, transactions, or occurrences set forth, or attempted to be set forth, in the prior complaint of that person.[11]

The next chapter reviews IRS bounties for whistleblowers.

 NOTES

1. 31 U.S.C. §§ 3729–3733, also called "Lincoln Law." www.law.cornell.edu/uscode/31/3729.html, www.law.cornell.edu/uscode/31/3733.html.

2. www.ethicspoint.com/article/federal-false-claims-act.

3. Larry D. Lahman, "Bad Mules: A Primer on the Federal False Claims Act," 76 *Oklahoma Bar Journal* 901, (April 9, 2005). www.okbar.org/obj/articles_05/040905lahman.htm.

4. www.law.cornell.edu/uscode/31/3729.html.

5. www.taf.org/whyfca.htm.

6. See, for example, *United States ex Rel. Lu v. Ou*, 368 F.3d 773 (7th Cir. 2004).

7. www.law.cornell.edu/uscode/31/3730.html.
8. www.justice.gov/usao/pae/Documents/fcaprocess2.pdf.
9. Ibid.
10. John T. Boese, *Civil False Claims and Qui Tam Actions*, 3rd ed. (New York: Aspen Publishers, 2007), pp. 1–7.
11. www.law.cornell.edu/uscode/31/3730.html.

CHAPTER NINE

IRS Whistleblowers

T HE FALSE CLAIMS ACT explicitly excludes tax fraud and other tax claims. Section 3729(e) states that the Act "does not apply to claims, records, or statements made under the Internal Revenue Code." However, on December 20, 2006, the Tax Relief and Healthcare Act was signed into law, which inserted a provision in the Internal Revenue Code (Code) mandating that the Internal Revenue Service (IRS) pay rewards to whistleblowers who exposed major tax underpayments. The IRS was also required to establish a Whistleblower Office and permitted an appeal by the whistleblower to the U.S. Tax Court ("tax court") if the whistleblower was arguably entitled to a mandatory award. The congressional effort to expand rewards to whistleblowers was led by a conservative Republican, Iowa senator Charles Grassley.

Prior to December 20, 2006, the IRS had a discretionary whistleblower award system, which is now embodied in Section 7623(a) of the Code. The mandatory system adopted on December 20, 2006, is embodied in Section 7623(b) of the Code.

On April 8, 2011, the first whistleblower award was made under the mandatory system in the amount of $4.5 million (less withholding) to an in-house accountant who tipped off the IRS that his employer was skimping on taxes.[1] The accountant's tip netted the IRS $20 million in taxes and interest from the employer, a financial services firm and a Fortune 500 company. The accountant had filed the complaint with the IRS in 2007 but had heard nothing for two years. Frustrated, he hired an attorney to push the issue. According to his lawyer, the accountant was given the third highest category of IRS whistleblower reward under the new law, namely 22 percent of the proceeds that the IRS collected. The IRS mailed the accountant's lawyer a check for $3.24 million, the sum that represents the award less a 28 percent tax withholding. The accountant's identity was not disclosed, and his lawyer made the announcement in a television interview. According to the accountant's lawyer, the accountant continues to work as an in-house certified public accountant and never wants to be known as a whistleblower.[2]

Unlike the False Claims Act, private qui tam actions by whistleblowers are not permitted under the Code. Only the IRS may proceed against a taxpayer. In this respect, the Code whistleblower provisions are similar to those under the Dodd-Frank Act, which only permits the Securities and Exchange Commission or the U.S. Department of Justice to proceed against a violator of the federal securities laws.

The IRS reportedly receives approximately 40 to 50 tips per month alleging liability in excess of $2 million, which is one of the requirements for a mandatory award to the whistleblower.[3] In fiscal years 2007 through 2009, the IRS Whistleblower Office reported receiving more than 12,000 new cases.[4] The discrepancy in the number of cases versus the number of tips likely results from the fact that there are multiple taxpayers who are alleged to be underpaying taxes with each tip.[5]

The recent turnover of Swiss bank account data highlights the role of whistleblowers in U.S. enforcement. Bradley Birkenfeld, a banker at UBS (a Swiss investment bank), brought the extent of offshore tax evasion to the attention of the Department of Justice and the IRS. Unfortunately for Birkenfeld, he was given a 40-month sentence for conspiring to commit tax fraud because of his counseling of UBS clients.

Awards by the IRS may be paid to people who provide specific and credible information that results in the collection of taxes, penalties, interest, or other amounts from the noncompliant taxpayer. In certain cases to be described, the award is mandatory. The IRS claims that it is looking for solid information, not an "educated guess" or unsupported speculation. The IRS also states that it is looking for a significant federal tax issue: "[T]his is not a program for resolving personal problems or disputes about a business relationship."[6]

The law provides for two types of awards, mandatory and discretionary.

SECTION 7623(b): MANDATORY WHISTLEBLOWER AWARDS

If the IRS proceeds with any administrative or judicial action relating to violation of the internal revenue laws or "conniving" at the same *based on* information brought to the IRS's attention by an individual, that individual will, subject to the monetary thresholds and other provisions to be described, receive as an award at least 15 percent but not more than 30 percent of the collected proceeds (including penalties, interest, additions to tax, and additional amounts) resulting from the action (including any related actions) or from any settlement in response to such action. The determination of the amount of such award by the Whistleblower Office depends on the extent to which the individual substantially contributed to such action.

Under Code Section 7623(b), a mandatory whistleblower award is required only if the tax, penalties, interest, additions to tax, and additional amounts in dispute exceed $2 million. If the case deals with a taxpayer who is an individual, his or her annual gross income must be more than $200,000 for any tax year subject to the IRS action. If the annual gross income of the individual taxpayer is $200,000 or less for the relevant tax year, the mandatory whistleblower awards do not apply, but the whistleblower may proceed under the discretionary Code Section 7623(a), to be discussed. If the case deals with a taxpayer that is not an individual (such as a corporation or other entity), the more-than-$200,000 annual gross income requirement is inapplicable.

The IRS Manual[7] defines the words "based on," which are emphasized above, in this way:

> An action is *based on* the information provided by the whistleblower if the IRS would not have acted but for the receipt of the information from the whistleblower. Action by the IRS may include the initiation of an examination or investigation that would not otherwise have been undertaken, or the modification of a pending or planned examination or investigation as a result of information provided by the whistleblower. (Emphasis added.)

The determination of the amount of the award between 15 percent and 30 percent is made by the IRS Whistleblower Office and depends on the extent to which the whistleblower substantially contributed to such administrative or judicial action against the taxpayer. The IRS Manual states that "all relevant factors, including the value of the information furnished in relation to the facts developed by the investigation of the violation, will be taken into account in determining whether an award will be paid, and, if so, the amount of the award."[8]

REDUCTION OF AWARD PERCENTAGE

If the administrative or judicial action is one that the Whistleblower Office determines to be based principally on disclosures of specific allegations (other than information specifically provided by the whistleblower) resulting from a judicial or administrative hearing; from a governmental report, hearing, audit, or investigation; or from the news media, the Whistleblower Office may award such sums as it considers appropriate, but in no case more than 10 percent of the collected proceeds (including penalties, interest, additions to tax, and additional amounts) resulting from the action (including any related actions) or from any settlement in response to such action, taking into account the significance of the individual's information and the role of such individual and any legal representative of such individual in contributing to such action. The reduction to a 10% bounty does not apply if the information resulting in the initiation of the administrative or judicial action was "originally provided" by the whistleblower, even though "based principally" on a government report or the like.

If the Whistleblower Office determines that the claim for an award is brought by an individual who planned and initiated the actions that led to the underpayment of tax or violating the Code or "conniving" at the same, then the Whistleblower Office may appropriately reduce such award. If such individual is convicted of criminal conduct arising from the role describe in the preceding sentence, the Whistleblower Office must deny any award.

If the whistleblower disagrees with the outcome of the claim, he or she can appeal to the tax court.

The IRS states on its website that the following examples of whistleblower claims will *not* be processed under Code Section 7623(b), which mandates whistleblower awards:

- The informant is an employee of the Department of Treasury, or is acting within the scope of his or her duties as an employee of any Federal, State, or local Government.
- The individual is required by federal law or regulation to disclose the information, or the individual is precluded by federal law or regulation from making the disclosure.
- The individual obtained or was furnished the information while acting in his or her official capacity as a member of a State body or

commission having access to such materials as Federal returns, copies, or abstracts.

- The individual had access to taxpayer information arising out of [a] contract with the federal government that forms the basis of the claim.
- The claim is found to have no merit or the claim lacked sufficient specific and credible information.
- The claim was submitted anonymously or under an alias.
- The claim was filed by a person other than an individual (e.g., corporation or partnership).
- The alleged noncompliant taxpayer is an individual whose gross income is below $200,000.[9]

SECTION 7623(a): DISCRETIONARY AWARDS

The IRS also has a discretionary award program for other whistleblowers—generally those who do not meet the dollar thresholds of $2 million in dispute or cases involving individual taxpayers with gross income of $200,000 or less. The awards through this program are less, with a maximum award of 15 percent up to $10 million. In addition, the informant cannot dispute the outcome of the claim in tax court. The rules for these cases are found at Code Section 7623(a)—Informant Claims Program, and some of the rules are different from those that apply to cases involving more than $2 million.

The IRS has stated that the following examples of whistleblower claims will *not* be processed in Section 7623(a) for a discretionary whistleblower award:

- The individual is an employee of the Department of Treasury, or is acting within the scope of his or her duties as an employee of any Federal, State, or local Government.
- The individual is required by federal law or regulation to disclose the information, or the individual is precluded by federal law or regulation from making the disclosure.
- The individual obtained or was furnished the information while acting in his or her official capacity as a member of a State body or commission having access to such materials as Federal returns, copies, or abstracts.
- The individual had access to taxpayer information arising out of [a] contract with the federal government that forms the basis of the claim.

- The claim is found to have no merit or the claim lacked sufficient specific and credible information.
- The claim was submitted anonymously or under an alias.
- The claim was filed by a person other than an individual (e.g., corporation or partnership).[10]

 FORM 211

If you decide to submit information and seek either a mandatory or a discretionary award for doing so, use IRS Form 211, The Application for Award for Original Information. This form, together with its instructions, is attached as Appendix 1 of this book and is executed under penalties of perjury. Form 211 is required to be mailed to:

Internal Revenue Service
Whistleblower Office
SE:WO
1111 Constitution Ave., NW
Washington, DC 20224

Form 211 may also include the submission of the information on which the whistleblower relies. If the claim meets the criteria under the statute after an initial review, the IRS Whistleblower Office will acknowledge receipt of the claim and identify the analyst assigned to process the claim. Further, a whistleblower must sign a confidentiality agreement before receiving access to the preliminary award report package.

The IRS Manual states that the following must be included in Form 211:

A. The date the claimant submits the claim;
B. Claimant's name;
C. Name of claimant's spouse (if applicable);
D. Claimant's contact information, including address with zip code and telephone number;
E. Claimant's date of birth;
F. Claimant's Taxpayer Identification Number (e.g., Social Security Number or Individual Taxpayer Identification Number) and Taxpayer Identification Number of claimant's spouse, if applicable; and
G. Explanation of how the information that forms the basis of the claim came to the attention of the claimant, including the date(s)

on which this information was acquired, and a complete description of the claimant's present or former relationship (if any) to the person that is the subject of the claim (e.g., family member, acquaintance, client, employee, accountant, lawyer, bookkeeper, customer). If the claimant identifies multiple person(s) as the subject of a claim, the claimant must describe his or her relationship to each person.[11]

The IRS Manual further states that Form 211 and any attachments must include specific and credible information concerning the person(s) that the claimant believes will lead to the collection of unpaid taxes. To the extent known by the whistleblower, the information should include:

- The legal name of the person(s) (e.g., individual or entity), and any related person(s), that failed to pay taxes;
- The person's aliases, if any;
- The person's address;
- The person's Taxpayer Identification Number(s);
- A description of the amount(s) and tax year(s) of Federal tax claimed to be owed, and facts supporting the basis for the amount(s) claimed to be owed;
- Documentation to substantiate the claim (e.g., financial data; the location of bank accounts, assets, books, and records; transaction documents or analyses relevant to the claim); and
- Any and all other facts and information pertaining to the claim.[12]

 ## IRS WHISTLEBLOWERS AWARDS

The IRS has made these statements concerning Form 211:[13]

- If the whistleblower withholds available material information, the whistleblower bears the risk that withheld information may not be considered by the Whistleblower Office in making any bounty determination.
- If there are documents or supporting evidence known to the whistleblower but not in her/her possession, the whistleblower should describe these documents and identify their location to the best of his or her ability.
- Except in the most unusual cases involving voluminous data, the whistleblower should include the evidence with the initial submission.

- The whistleblower is advised to contact the Whistleblower Office for guidance if there is a question on what to submit. The IRS states that it does not expect or condone illegal actions taken to secure documents or supporting evidence.
- Although no specific format is required, an index to documents exhibits, particularly when they are voluminous, is suggested helpful.[14]

 ## IRS AWARD DETERMINATIONS

The IRS Manual states that the starting point for the Whistleblower Office's analysis of the amount of the award will be the statutory minimum of 15 percent of collected proceeds. The office then will apply the factors noted below to the facts of a case to determine whether the case merits a larger award percentage. The factors are described as positive or negative factors, but the analysis will not be reduced to a simple mathematical equation. The factors are not exclusive and are not weighted. In the particular circumstances of a case, one factor may outweigh several others and result in a unique or exceptional award determination. Negative factors can offset positive factors but cannot result in an award that is less than the statutory minimum. The absence of negative factors does not mean that the award percentage will be larger than 15 percent.

The Whistleblower Office will determine awards of 15 percent, 18 percent, 22 percent, 26 percent, or 30 percent, based on the positive and negative factors.

These positive factors can increase the amount of the bounty:

Positive Factors (applicable to mandatory award determinations under Section 7623(b)):

A. Did the whistleblower take prompt action to advise the Government or the taxpayer of the tax noncompliance ? If so, this may, depending on the acts, be a positive factor. For example, providing the IRS with an opportunity to address the tax noncompliance early can help mitigate the impact of the taxpayer's noncompliance.

B. Did the whistleblower submit information that identifies an issue of a type previously unknown to the Government or a taxpayer behavior that the

Government was unlikely to identify or was especially difficult to detect through the exercise of reasonable diligence?

C. Did the whistleblower thoroughly present the details of the noncompliance in a clear and organized manner? For example, a detailed submission may save the IRS work and resources, thereby increasing the incentive for a larger reward.

D. Did the whistleblower (and/or his/her representative) provide exceptional cooperation and assistance during the audit, investigation, or trial, including useful technical or legal analysis of the taxpayer's records?

E. Has the whistleblower identified assets that could be used to pay the taxpayer's liability or assets not otherwise known to the IRS?

F. Has the whistleblower identified connections between transactions, or parties to transactions, which enabled the IRS to understand tax implications that might not otherwise have been disclosed?

G. Is there a positive impact of the report on the behavior of the taxpayer? For example, the whistleblower's report may, directly or indirectly, cause the taxpayer to correct an improper position.[15]

Negative factors that reduce the amount of the bounty are listed next.

Negative Factors (providing an offset against positive factors) (applicable to Section 7623(b) mandatory award determinations):

A. Has the whistleblower delayed reporting after learning the relevant facts, and the delay had an adverse impact on the ability of the IRS to pursue the issues raised? Delayed reporting can permit the noncompliant activity to be repeated, increasing the magnitude of the taxpayer's noncompliance and, in some cases, compromising the ability of the Government to assess and collect.

B. What was the whistleblower's role in the underpayment of tax reported, such as when a whistleblower actively and knowingly participated in carrying out the tax noncompliance? If the whistleblower directly or indirectly profits from the noncompliance, this may also be considered a negative factor in computing the award.

C. Did the whistleblower place the tax case at risk? For example, a whistleblower's premature disclosure to the taxpayer of the existence or scope of IRS planned enforcement activity may be a negative factor if the whistleblower revealed information regarding the IRS interest in a matter in such a way that permitted the affected taxpayer(s) to impede IRS access to relevant information and thus impeded the exam or audit.

D. Since whistleblowers will normally be given specific instructions regarding permissible and impermissible activities, violations of these instructions may be a negative factor in determining the bounty and percentage if it causes the IRS to expend additional resources it would not otherwise have spent.[16]

 ## AWARD ADMINISTRATIVE PROCEEDINGS

The IRS Manual contains a detailed whistleblower award process, which is described generally below. The administrative proceeding for the award review and determination process begins on the date the claim for award is received by the Whistleblower Office. The purpose of a preliminary recommendation package is to obtain input from the whistleblower regarding the a preliminary award recommendation before a final determination is made by the director.

After the statutory period for filing a claim for refund expires or there is an agreement between the taxpayer and the IRS that there has been a final determination of tax for the specific period and the right to file a claim for a refund has been waived, the director of the Whistleblower Office prepares a preliminary recommendation regarding an award to the whistleblower. Prior to communicating the preliminary recommendation to the whistleblower, the director shares the preliminary recommendation with the Whistleblower Executive Board for concurrence. Upon concurrence, the preliminary recommendation is communicated to the whistleblower in a package containing these documents:

- A notice of opportunity to comment letter
- A proposed summary award report
- An award consent form
- A confidentiality agreement

Whistleblowers are then given 10 days to respond to the preliminary recommendation package in one of four ways:

1. If no action is taken by the whistleblower, the director makes a final award determination.

2. If the whistleblower signs, dates, and returns a form consenting to the proposed award recommendation, the director makes a final award determination.
3. If the whistleblower submits comments on the proposed award recommendation but does not sign, date, and return the confidentiality agreement, the comments will be reviewed for purposes of making a final award determination.
4. If the whistleblower signs, dates, and returns the confidentiality agreement, the director affords the whistleblower the additional administrative review opportunity described earlier.

If the whistleblower signs, dates, and returns the confidentiality agreement, the director provides the whistleblower with a preliminary award report package. The preliminary award report package contains a preliminary award report that discloses the amount of the recommended award and provides an explanation of the recommended award. The report includes the recommended amount of proceeds to be attributed to the whistleblower information, the recommended specific award percentage, the recommended specific award amount, and a summary of the factors considered in making the specific bounty percentage recommendation. The recommendation package also contains instructions on scheduling an appointment for the whistleblower (and the whistleblower's representative, if there is one) to review the documents supporting the recommendation. If scheduled, this review will take place at the IRS Whistleblower Office in Washington, DC, and whistleblowers will not be permitted to make copies of the documents.

Whistleblowers are then given 30 days to respond to the preliminary award report package in one of three ways:

1. If no action is taken by the whistleblower, the director makes a final award determination.
2. If the whistleblower schedules an appointment to review the documents supporting the recommendation, the Whistleblower Office supervises the document review meeting. The whistleblower then is given 30 days from the date of the meeting to provide a written response to the Whistleblower Office. The written response is reviewed by the director for purposes of making a final award determination.
3. If the whistleblower fails to schedule an appointment but does submit written comments on the award report, the Whistleblower Office adds the

comments to the file and includes them for review by the director for purposes of making a final award bounty determination.[17]

APPEAL TO TAX COURT

Any appeal from a determination regarding an IRS whistleblower award that is pursuant to Section 7623(b) mandatory awards must be made within 30 days after a determination by the IRS Whistleblower Office. There is no appeal from a determination under Section 7623(a), which deals with discretionary awards.

DURATION OF PROCESS AND AWARD PAYMENT

The IRS's comments concerning the duration of process and award payment make note of the following:

- It may take several years to complete the process from submission of complete information to the IRS until the proceeds are collected.
- Payments of awards will not be made until after the taxes, penalties, interest, additions to tax, and additional amounts that are finally determined to be owed to the IRS have been collected.
- Examples of when a final determination of tax liability can be made include but are not limited to:
  - If the taxpayer does not petition the tax court, the process is complete when the IRS and the taxpayer enter into a closing agreement wherein the taxpayer conclusively waives the right to appeal or otherwise challenge a deficiency or additional tax liability determined by the IRS.
  - If a taxpayer petitions the tax court, the process is complete when a decision becomes final within the meaning of Code Section 7481.
- The process is completed after the expiration of the statutory period for a taxpayer to file a claim for refund and to file a refund suit based on the claim against the United States, or if a refund suit is filed when the judgment in that suit becomes final.
- The IRS advises that a finding of fraud in a tax case carries some significant additional implications for penalties, fines, and jail time. In the context of whistleblower claims, it also has statute of limitations implications that can make a significant difference for the whistleblower.[18]

CONFIDENTIALITY OF WHISTLEBLOWER

The IRS Manual states the next points concerning confidentiality of the identity of the whistleblower:

1. The IRS will safeguard the identity of the whistleblower to the fullest extent permitted by the law.
2. To the extent that the IRS Whistleblower Office determines that an individual is a "whistleblower" under IRC section 7623, such individual is considered to be a confidential informant whose identity shall be protected in accordance with IRC section 6103(h)(4). . . .
3. Under some circumstances, such as when the whistleblower is an essential witness in a judicial proceeding, it may not be possible to pursue the investigation or examination without revealing the whistleblower's identity. These circumstances are rare, and the Service [IRS] will consult with the whistleblower before deciding whether to proceed in such a case.[19]

 ## RIGHT TO COUNSEL

An individual whistleblower has a right to counsel, whether the information is submitted under the mandatory award program or discretionary award program. *The author recommends that whistleblowers obtain sophisticated tax counsel to represent them in this process.*

 ## IRS CONTRACTS

The IRS may determine that it requires the assistance of the whistleblower or the legal representatives of the whistleblower and, in this connection, may, in rare cases, disclose tax return information to the whistleblower. The Congressional Joint Committee on Taxation (JCT) has noted that "[t]o the extent the disclosure of returns or return information is required [for the whistleblower or his or her legal representative] to render such assistance, the disclosure must be pursuant to an IRS tax administration contract."[20] The JCT has further noted that "[i]t is expected that such disclosures will be infrequent and will be made only when the assigned task cannot be properly or timely completed without the return information to be disclosed."[21] The whistleblower who receives such information is subject to civil and criminal penalties for the unauthorized inspection or disclosure of any such tax return information.

 ## DISQUALIFICATION OF U.S. TREASURY DEPARTMENT FEDERAL EMPLOYEES

According to Treasury Regulation Section 301.7623-1(b)(2):

> No person who was an officer or employee of the U.S. Department of the Treasury at the time the individual came into possession of information relating to violations of the internal revenue laws, or at the time the individual divulged such information, is eligible for a reward under Section 7623. Any other current or former federal employee is eligible to file a claim for reward if the information provided came to the individual's knowledge other than in the course of the individual's official duties.[22]

Table 9.1 provides information on informant claims paid from fiscal year 2005 to fiscal year 2009. Except for the anonymous accountant who received

TABLE 9.1 Amounts Collected and Awards Paid under Section 7623(a), Fiscal Years 2005 to 2009

	2005	2006	2007	2008	2009
Cases received	2,740	4,295	2,751	3,704	5,678
Awards paid	169	220	227	198	110
Collections over $2 million	NA	NA	12	8	5
Amounts of awards paid	$7,602,685	$24,184,458	$13,600,205	$22,370,756	$5,851,608
Amounts collected	$93,677,606	$258,590,435	$181,784,287	$155,985,834	$206,032,872

Source: FY 2009 Annual Report to Congress on the Use of Section 7623. See also www.irs.gov/pub/irs-utl/whistleblowerfy09rtc.pdf.

the $4.5 million on April 8, 2011, to August 1, 2011, all awards the IRS has paid have been based on information received before December 20, 2006, the date of the enactment of Code Section 7623(b). Therefore, all of the awards, including those paid in fiscal year 2009, were governed by the prior law, what is now Code Section 7623(a), the so-called discretionary award section. Thus, the applicable award percentages were those established in prior IRS policy, not the higher percentages set by the law that was adopted on December 20, 2006 which is contained in Code Section 7623(b).

The number and amount of awards paid each year can vary significantly, especially when a small number of high-dollar claims are resolved in one year (as was the case in fiscal years 2006 and 2008). The IRS states that one factor contributing to the lower award payments in fiscal year 2009 was a change in the IRS definition of the point at which proceeds in a tax case are available to make an award payment.

The IRS states that the "Whistleblower Office determined that in cases where the taxpayer had not filed an appeal, the IRS should not pay the claim until the period for filing an appeal has lapsed."[23] A taxpayer may generally file a claim for refund within two years of the last payment, unless he or she has waived that right. The effect of this rule is that until two years have passed after the last payment, the case is still subject to the possibility of appeal through the process of filing a claim for a refund. Thus, beginning in July 2009, the IRS monitors cases both for collection and then for the expiration of the period for filing a claim for refund.[24]

In January 2011, the IRS proposed a rule to correct an anomaly in its award procedure as a result of a letter sent by Senator Charles Grassley to the Treasury secretary. Under the new proposed rule, rewards may now be paid on "amounts" collected prior to receipt of the information if the information provided by the whistleblower "results in the denial of a claim for refund that otherwise would have been paid; and a reduction of an overpayment credit balance used to satisfy a tax liability incurred because of the information provided."[25]

The next chapter deals with state false claim statutes that provide whistleblower bounties and various whistleblower protection statutes.

 ## NOTES

1. Michael Cohn, "CPA Receives $4.5M IRS Whistleblower Award," *Accounting Today*, April 8, 2011. www.accountingtoday.com/news/CPA-Receives-IRS-Whistleblower-Award-57972-1.html.
2. Ibid.

3. Ryan Donmoyer, "IRS Reward Lures More Americans to Turn in Tax Cheats," May 4, 2010. www.bloomberg.com/news/2010-05-04/americans-sic-irs-on-suspected-tax-cheaters-eight-times-a-day-agency-says.html.
4. Cohn, "CPA Receives $4.5M IRS Whistleblower Award."
5. FY 2009 Annual Report to Congress on the Use of Section 7623.
6. www.irs.gov/compliance/article/0,,id=180171,00.html.
7. www.irs.gov/IRM/part25.
8. Ibid. at 25.2.2.2.
9. www.irs.gov/compliance/article/0,,id=181292,00.html.
10. Ibid.
11. 25.2.2.3.8 at www.irs.gov/irm/part25/irm_25-002-002.html#d0e753.
12. Ibid. at 25.2.2.3.9.
13. www.irs.gov/compliance/article/0,,id=181290,00.html.
14. Ibid. at 25.2.2.8.1, 3, 4, and 5.
15. Ibid. at 25.2.2.9.2.5.
16. Ibid.
17. Ibid.
18. www.irs.gov/compliance/article/0,,id=181290,00.html.
19. www.irs.gov/irm/part25/irm_25-002-002.html#d0e1046.
20. Joint Committee on Taxation, *Technical Explanation of H.R. 6408, The "Tax Relief and Health Care Act of 2006,"* as introduced in the House on December 7, 2006, at 89 (JCX-50-06), December 7, 2006.
21. Ibid.
22. Treasury Regulation § 301.7623-1(b)(2); see also http://law.justia.com/cfr/title26/26-18.0.1.1.2.19.68.17.html.
23. FY 2009 Annual Report to Congress on the Use of Section 7623.
24. www.irs.gov/pub/irs-utl/whistleblowerfy09rtc.pdf.
25. www.irs.gov/irb/2011-08_IRB/ar14.html.

Other Statutory Incentives and Protections for Whistleblowers

A VARIETY OF FEDERAL and state statutes provide bounties to whistleblowers or protect whistleblowers from retaliation. Many of these statutes are not well known.

ACT TO PREVENT POLLUTION FROM SHIPS

For example, in September 2010, four crew members of the M/V *Iorana*, a Greek-flagged cargo ship, were awarded $500,000 ($125,000 each) under the Act to Prevent Pollution from Ships, which provides that whistleblowers may receive an award of up to one-half of the fine collected under that statute.[1] A crew member passed a note to the Customs and Borders Protection inspector upon the ship's arrival in Baltimore alleging that the ship's chief engineer had directed the dumping of waste oil overboard through a bypass hose that circumvented pollution prevention equipment required by law. The whistleblower's note stated: "We are asking help to any authorities concerned about this, because we must protect our environment and our marine lives." A fine of $1 million was levied against Irika Shipping S.A. for violation of the statute, and the four crew members were entitled to one-half of that amount.

In May 2011, an even larger reward was made under the Act to Prevent Pollution from Ships. Three crew members of the Greek tanker vessel M/T *Kriton* received more than $1 million for cooperating with federal authorities in an investigation that led to the company's conviction for repeatedly dumping waste oil in the ocean and lying about it. A federal judge awarded $550,000 to Alexander Gueverra, and two other crew members received $350,000 each. Gueverra, an electrician, called the U.S. Coast Guard to report the discharges, leading to the investigation. He acknowledged that one of his motives in calling the Coast Guard was that he had read a magazine article describing how crew members on other ships received rewards for reporting such activity. Prosecutors supported the awards, saying the three provided crucial evidence and that ship pollution is difficult to prosecute because it may take place in the middle of the ocean at night. Prosecutors further stated that cooperating employees may lose job prospects in the industry by being "blackballed" as a result of their cooperation with the government.[2]

Although this statutory provision is not new, the recent increase in the frequency and amount of such awards shows that the provision is likely to encourage crew members to report environmental violations.[3]

FALSE PATENT MARKING STATUTE

Recently, an obscure federal statute dealing with false patent marking has become a cottage industry for bounty hunters. The statute reads:

35 U.S.C. 292 False Marking.
(a) Whoever, without the consent of the patentee, marks upon, or affixes to, or uses in advertising in connection with anything made, used, offered for sale, or sold by such person within the United States, or imported by the person into the United States, the name or any imitation of the name of the patentee, the patent number, or the words "patent," "patentee," or the like, with the intent of counterfeiting or imitating the mark of the patentee, or of deceiving the public and inducing them to believe that the thing was made, offered for sale, sold, or imported into the United States by or with the consent of the patentee; or Whoever marks upon, or affixes to, or uses in advertising in connection with any unpatented article the word "patent" or any word or number importing the same is patented, for the purpose of deceiving the public; or Whoever marks upon, or affixes to, or uses in advertising in

connection with any article the words "patent applied for," "patent pending," or any word importing that an application for patent has been made, when no application for patent has been made, or if made, is not pending, for the purpose of deceiving the public—Shall be fined not more than $500 for every such offense.

(b) Any person may sue for the penalty, in which even one-half shall go to the person suing and the other to the use of the United States.

Falsely marking as patented a product that is not, in fact, patented by the seller deters innovation and stifles competition, and the statute contains a civil fine for such behavior, if intentional. The civil fine is "not more than $500" for each "offense" (i.e., each improperly marked article). The statute permits "any person to sue for the penalty, in which event one-half shall go to the person suing and the other to the use of the United States."[4]

Prior to a 2009 case called *The Forest Group, Inc. v. Bon Tool Co.,*[5] the courts had severely limited the false marking damage awards by holding that the sale of thousands of falsely marked items constituted a single offense under the statute. This precedent was rejected in the *Forest Group* case.

Bon Tool bought and sold construction stilts that were manufactured by Forest. However, Bon Tool eventually dropped Forest as a supplier and began importing a duplicate knock-off version from China, even though Forest's stilts were marked with its patent number, 5,645,515. Forest sued for infringement and lost. Bon Tool counterclaimed for false marking on the ground that the construction stilts sold by Forest were not covered by the patent number marked on them, since the patent required a "resiliently lined yoke," which the stilts did not contain. During litigation on the Bon Tool counterclaim, another U.S. District Court on November 15, 2007, in another patent infringement case filed by Forest involving the same stilts but a different defendant, held that the same patent was not violated because of the absence of the resiliently lined yoke. In 2009, the U.S. District Court in the Bon Tool case held that Forest was liable to Bon Tool for false marking because it knowingly continued to mark its products as patented even after the November 15, 2007, decision that held that the patent did not apply to the stilts. However, the U.S. District Court awarded only $500 in damages. On appeal, the Federal Circuit Court reversed the U.S. District Court and held that *each* falsely marked article can serve as a basis for up to a maximum of $500 per article.

The per-article approach to the computation of the maximum fine of $500 was a game-changer. It permits a huge potential bounty to the plaintiff. Under the false patent marking statute: "Any person may sue for the penalty, in which event one-half shall go to the person suing and the other to the use of the United States." There is no requirement in the statute that the plaintiff be harmed by the false marking of the article. This case has resulted in an avalanche of false marking lawsuits.

Solo Cup (Solo) found itself the target of a potential $10.8 trillion judgment for continuing to mark approximately 21 billion coffee lids for years after knowing the lids were no longer covered by any existing patents.[6] In 2010, the Federal Circuit Court, however, issued Solo a reprieve by finding that its actions did not constitute "false marking" as Solo did not have the requisite intent to deceive.[7]

A listing of the numerous false marking cases that have been filed since the *Forest Group* decision can be found at www.grayonclaims.com/false-marking-case-information. As of September 9, 2011, a bill was passed by Congress that will eliminate qui tam actions for violations of this statute, effective upon enactment.

U.S. TARIFF ACT OF 1930

The U.S. Tariff Act of 1930 provides for bounties up to a maximum $250,000 for any case. The statute provides:

    (a) In general,
        If—
        (1) any person who is not an employee or officer of the United States—
            (A) detects and seizes any vessel, vehicle, aircraft, merchandise, or baggage subject to seizure and forfeiture under the customs laws or the navigation laws and reports such detection and seizure to a custom officer, or
            (B) furnishes to a United States attorney, the Secretary of the Treasury, or any customs officer original information concerning—
                (i) any fraud upon the customs revenue, or
                (ii) any violation of the customs laws or the navigation laws which is being, or has been, perpetrated or contemplated by any other person; and
        (2) such detection and seizure or such information leads to a recovery of—
            (A) any duties withheld, or
            (B) any fine, penalty, or forfeiture of property incurred;

the Secretary [of the Treasury] may award and pay such person an amount that does not exceed 25 percent of the net amount so recovered.

(b) Forfeited property not sold

If—

(1) any vessel, vehicle, aircraft, merchandise, or baggage is forfeited to the United States and is thereafter, in lieu of sale—

(A) destroyed under the customs or navigation laws, or

(B) delivered to any governmental agency for official use, and

(2) any person would be eligible to receive an award under subsection (a) of this section but for the lack of sale of such forfeited property,

the Secretary [of the Treasury] may award and pay such person an amount that does not exceed 25 percent of the appraised value of such forfeited property [but limited to $250,000 for any case].[8]

STATE FALSE CLAIMS STATUTES

In about 30 states,[9] whistleblower laws permit whistleblowers to collect as much as 15 to 30 percent of any government recovery in certain cases in which they assist.

Of the approximately 30 states, 11 have false claims laws that are limited to fraud involving Medicaid or other state healthcare funds. The remaining states have laws that apply to fraud involving a broad range of state-funded programs and are not limited to Medicaid. As with awards under the U.S. False Claims Act, the awards are limited to information about false claims that are made against state or local governments or their entities.

On February 3, 2011, the *Wall Street Journal* reported that state prosecutors were getting help from an organized group of whistleblowers regarding whether banks overcharged state public pension funds by tens of millions of dollars for foreign-exchange transactions. The whistleblowers used Delaware shell companies to remain anonymous.[10]

According to the article:

U.S. investors trading in global stock markets must convert dollars into the currencies of the foreign countries in which they invest. If a pension fund, for instance, buys stock in a South Korean auto maker, it converts U.S. dollars to [South Korean] won, and reverses that exchange when selling the stock. The suits claim the banks didn't charge the pension funds the currency rates that the banks paid, but consistently charged them the highest currency-conversion prices of the day, and pocketed the difference. The suits say the banks similarly overcharged when the pension funds exited the trades.[11]

Helping orchestrate the whistleblower effort is none other than Harry Markopolos, the whistleblower in the Madoff scandal who failed to convince the Securities and Exchange Commission of his allegations.

The website of the law firm of Phillips & Cohen (www.phillipsandcohen .com/CM/StateFalseClaimsLaws/StateFalseClaimsLaws152.asp) contains a short description of the state false claims laws.

Next we discuss the state false claims statutes in certain major states.

New York

The New York State False Claims Act creates liability for persons who knowingly present false or fraudulent claims for payment to the state or local governments, misappropriate state or local government property, or deceptively avoid binding obligations to pay the state or a local government. The Act also covers violations of the tax law, including submission of a fraudulent return if the violator has an income over $1 million and the harm to the state exceeds $350,000. A defendant may be required to pay up to three times both the actual harm to the state and consequential damages as well as a fine of between $6,000 and $12,000 for each violation of the Act.

A whistleblower who files a successful claim may receive between 15 and 25 percent of any recovery to the state if the New York attorney general intervenes in the matter. If the state does not intervene and the whistleblower proceeds with the case on his or her own, the whistleblower may receive between 25 and 30 percent of the recovery. The award may be reduced if the whistleblower planned or initiated the fraud, or if the action is largely based on information disclosed in the media or public hearings.

The Act also "protects whistleblowers from retaliation by their employers or prospective employers for filing a claim or assisting the state with its own claim. Plaintiffs may not file their complaint more than ten years after the date on which the violation was committed."[12]

In January 2011, the New York attorney general announced an $18 million Medicaid fraud settlement with the state's largest residential service provider.[13] Each year, the Young Adult Institute, Inc. (YAI) submits requests to the New York State Office for People with Developmental Disabilities, seeking funding for losses incurred to operate its programs. The amount of such rate appeals, or whether YAI is eligible to receive any adjustment at all, is based on an annually submitted consolidated fiscal report—a lengthy report detailing all of the organization's expenses. As a result, over the past 10 years, YAI received more than $8 million in additional funding from Medicaid.

However, beginning in at least 1999, YAI allegedly artificially inflated the expenses on its annual consolidated fiscal reports to the state in order to receive additional funding that it was not entitled to receive. Specifically, according to the attorney general's press release, YAI allocated the expenses related to certain employees to programs and sites at which those employees never worked. The company also listed high-level administrative staff as clinic social workers and improperly categorized fundraising expenses—all to inflate YAI's expenses and extract more money from the Medicaid program.

The investigation began after a whistleblower filed a complaint that YAI had improperly inflated its expense reports. Of the $18 million YAI will pay in damages, $10.8 million will be returned to the New York State Medicaid program. The investigation was conducted in cooperation with the U.S. Attorney for the Southern District of New York.

The New York statute has a very broad definition of what is a false claim:

> "Claim" means any request or demand, whether under a contract or otherwise, for money or property which is made to any employee, officer, or agent of the state or a local government, or to any contractor, grantee or other recipient, if the state or a local government provides any portion of the money or property which is requested or demanded or will reimburse such contractor, grantee, or other recipient for any portion of the money or property which is requested or demanded.[14]

California

On December 18, 2009, California state attorney general Edmund G. Brown Jr. announced a $21.3 million settlement with Schering-Plough Corporation, resolving allegations the company "deliberately inflated" the price of Albuterol and other drugs, causing California's Medicaid (Medi-Cal) program to overpay millions of dollars in pharmacy reimbursement. The settlement stemmed from a lawsuit filed by a whistleblower against predecessor companies of Schering-Plough Corporation.

The California False Claims Act:

> makes it a civil offense for persons to, among other violations, knowingly submit false or fraudulent claims for payment; misappropriate

public property, or deceptively avoid obligations to pay or return funds to the State of California. A defendant may be ordered to pay up to three times the actual harm to the state, plus a fine of between $5,000 and $10,000 for each violation of the Act.[15]

The term "claim" is defined as follows:

"Claim" means any request or demand, whether under a contract or otherwise, for money, property, or services, and whether or not the state or a political subdivision has title to the money, property, or services that meets either of the following conditions:
(A) Is presented to an officer, employer, or agent of the state or of a political subdivision.
(B) Is made to a contractor, grantee, or other recipient, if the money, property, or service is to be spent or used on a state or any political subdivision program or interest, and if the state or political subdivision meets either of the following conditions:
    (i) Provides or has provided any portion of the money, property, or service requested or demanded.
    (ii) Reimburses the contractor, grantee, or other recipient for any portion of the money, property, or service that is requested or demanded.[16]

An individual who provides information that establishes a violation of the Act may receive an award between 15% and 33% of any recovery obtained by the California Attorney General or political subdivision. If the state does not intervene and the whistleblower successfully prosecutes the case on his own, he will receive between 25% and 50% of the proceeds of the settlement. The Act also may provide a cause of action for whistleblowers who suffer employment retaliation because of their whistleblowing.

The California False Claims Act has been utilized in a wide variety of cases, both Medicaid and non-Medicaid. In most cases, plaintiffs must file a complaint within ten years of the violations they are reporting.[17]

Texas

On February 1, 2011, a Travis County jury returned a record-setting verdict for damages, finding that drug manufacturer Actavis Mid-Atlantic, LLC (Actavis) misrepresented its drug process to the taxpayer-funded Medicaid program. The jurors determined that Actavis and codefendant Actavis Elizabeth, LLC should pay Texas and the federal government $170.3 million for defrauding Medicaid. The state's legal action against Actavis stems from a whistleblower lawsuit that was filed under seal by a small Florida-based pharmacy called Ven-a-Care. The pharmacy owners pursued their claim after discovering Actavis reported artificially inflated prices to Medicaid for its drugs. Although the state attorney general's office has investigated multiple fraudulent drug pricing cases and successfully recovered hundreds of millions of dollars through the prelitigation settlements, the case against Actavis was the first to go to trial.

Under Texas's Medicaid Fraud Prevention Act, persons may be liable for knowingly submitting false or fraudulent claims to the state's Medicaid program. Defendants may also be liable for paying or receiving bribes in exchange for referrals or ordering of supplies. The statute provides that a defendant may be ordered to pay damages equal to up to three times the actual harm to the state, plus a fine between $5,000 and $10,000 for each violation of the Act, escalated to $15,000 if the violation results in harm to an elderly person.

A whistleblower in a Texas Medicaid Fraud action may recover between 15 and 25 percent of proceeds recovered in the matter if the government intervenes in the case. If the whistleblower proceeds with the case on his or her own, the plaintiff may receive between 25 and 30 percent of the amounts recovered. The court may reduce the value of the award "if the whistleblower planned or initiated the fraud, or if the action is largely based on information disclosed in the media or public hearings."

Texas also has a provision that permits an award to a whistleblower who reports activity that constitutes fraud or abuse of funds in the state Medicaid program or reports overcharges in the program if the disclosure results in the recovery of an administrative penalty. "The award may not exceed five percent of the amount of the administrative penalty that resulted from the individual's disclosure."

Additionally, the Texas Act provides whistleblowers with protection from retaliation by their employers for filing a claim or assisting the government with its own investigation.[18]

The term "claim" is defined in this way:

"Claim" means a written or electronically submitted request or demand that:
(A) is signed by a provider or a fiscal agent and that identifies a product or service provided or purported to have been provided to a Medicaid recipient as reimbursable under the Medicaid program,

without regard to whether the money that is requested or demanded is paid; or

(B) states the income earned or expense incurred by a provider in providing a product or a service and that is used to determine a rate of payment under the Medicaid program.[19]

Florida

On February 26, 2010, Florida state attorney general Bill McCollum announced that several public port authorities in Florida would receive a total of $707,000 from a settlement with marine product manufacturer Virginia Harbor Services, Inc. and its predecessor, Trelleborg Engineered Products, Inc. The settlement resolved allegations that the companies conspired to allocate business, rig bids, and fix prices of marine equipment. According to the lawsuit, Trelleborg sold foam-filled marine fenders and buoys to public port authorities in Florida for prices that were unlawfully inflated by collusion, bidding, and price-fixing. The settlement and preceding investigation by the attorney general's office evolved from a whistle-blower complaint that alleged the conduct violated the Florida False Claims Act.

The Florida False Claims Act creates liability for people and corporations that, among other violations, "knowingly present fraudulent or false claims for payment to the state; misappropriate state property; or deceptively conceal or avoid an obligation to pay the state."

A defendant may be ordered to pay "up to three times the actual harm to the state, plus a fine of between $5,500 and $11,000 for each violation of the Act." A whistleblower filing a False Claims Act case may receive between 15 and 25 percent of any recovery in matters joined by the Florida attorney general and between 25 and 30 percent of the recovery if the whistleblower proceeds on his or her own. The court may "reduce the amount of the award if the whistleblower's allegations are based on publicly disclosed information," or if the whistleblower "planned or initiated the fraud."

The Act also protects whistleblowers from retaliation by their employers. The whistleblower should be an "original source" of information on the fraud in order to have a valid claim.

Whistleblowers may not file their complaint more than 10 years after the date on which the violation occurred.[20]

The term "claim" is defined in this way:

"Claim" includes any written or electronically submitted request or demand, under a contract or otherwise, for money, property, or services, which is made to any employee, officer, or agent of any agency, or to any contractor, grantee, or other recipient if the agency provides any portion of the money or property requested or demanded, or if the agency will reimburse the contractor, grantee, or other recipient for any portion of the money or property requested or demanded.[21]

 ## WHISTLEBLOWER PROTECTIONS

Both U.S. federal and state laws provide substantial protections to whistleblowers against retaliation. In addition, many statutes in countries outside of the United States protect whistleblowers. About 50 countries have adopted national laws in one form or another to protect whistleblowers, including Australia, Canada, France, Japan, South Africa, and United Kingdom.[22] Almost no statutes outside of the United States provide for any bounties to whistleblowers, except in very limited situations in which the bounty is discretionary.[23]

Anti-retaliation statutes are much older than statutes that provide for a whistleblower bounty. Some public policy advocates view the anti-retaliation model for a statute to be much less effective than the bounty model. These advocates contend that the disincentives to whistleblowers (including subtle forms of retaliation) cannot be overcome by an anti-retaliation statute and that a bounty is necessary.[24]

An example of the anti-retaliation provisions against whistleblowers can be found in Section 922 of the Dodd-Frank Act. That section provides the following anti-retaliation protections:

(h) PROTECTION OF WHISTLEBLOWERS.—
    (A) IN GENERAL.—No employer may discharge, demote, suspend, threaten, harass, directly or indirectly, or in any other manner discriminate against, a whistleblower in the terms and conditions of employment because of any lawful act done by the whistleblower—
        (i)   in providing information to the Commission in accordance with this section;
        (ii) in initiating, testifying in, or assisting in any investigation or judicial or administrative action of the Commission based upon or related to such information; or
        (iii) in making disclosures that are required or protected under the Sarbanes-Oxley Act of 2002 (15 U.S.C. 7201 et seq.), the Securities Exchange Act of 1934 (15 U.S.C. 78a et seq.), including section 10A(m) of such Act

(15 U.S.C. 78f(m)), section 1513(e) of title 18, United States Code, and any other law, rule or regulation subject to the jurisdiction of the Commission.

(B) ENFORCEMENT.—

  (i)   CAUSE OF ACTION.— An individual who alleges discharge or other discrimination in violation of subparagraph (A) may bring an action under this subsection in the appropriate district court of the United States for the relief provided in subparagraph (C). . . .

  (ii) [Omitted.]

  (iii) STATUTE OF LIMITATIONS.—

    (I) IN GENERAL.— An action under this subsection may not be brought—

      (aa) more than 6 years after the date on which the violation of subparagraph (A) occurred; or

      (bb) more than 3 years after the date when facts material to the right of action are known or reasonably should have been known by the employee alleging a violation of subparagraph (A).

    (II) REQUIRED ACTION WITHIN 10 YEARS.— Notwithstanding subclause (I), an action under this subsection may not in any circumstance be brought more than 10 years after the date on which the violation occurs.

(C) RELIEF.—Relief for an individual prevailing in an action brought under subparagraph (B) shall include—

  (i)   reinstatement with the same seniority status that the individual would have had, but for the discrimination;

  (ii) 2 times the amount of back pay otherwise owed to the individual, with interest; and

  (iii) compensation for litigation costs, expert witness fees, and reasonable attorneys' fees.[25]

BARKER V. UBS

An interesting example of a whistleblower retaliation case brought under the Sarbanes-Oxley (SOX) anti-retaliation provisions can be found in the January 26, 2011, decision of the U.S. District Court for the District of Connecticut.[26]

Mary Barker was an employee in the Stamford, Connecticut, office of UBS AG and ABS Securities (collectively "UBS") for approximately ten years, from May 1998 until May 2008. When she began her employ-ment at UBS, she held the position of Administrative Assistant to Execu-tive Director Mark Bridges but was promoted to the position of Associate Director in 2004. In September 2005, UBS transferred Barker to a posi-tion in the Equities Americas Division, where she was responsible for providing support to the Equities Proprietary trading desk.

In December 2006, Barker was assigned the task of reconcil-ing UBS's existing exchange seat shares with former company records. This valuation was necessary because a recent merger of the New York Mercantile Exchange and the Commodity Exchange had resulted in a redistribution of UBS's holdings of exchange seat assets. During this reconciliation effort, Barker discovered that cer-tain of UBS's historical exchange seat holdings had been improperly accounted for, or not accounted for at all, on UBS's balance sheet. According to Barker, she went well beyond the scope of her original assignment to create and record an inventory of all UBS's exchange seat shares, including those that had never before been reported on the firm's balance sheet. Ultimately, UBS realized approximately $80 million from the sale of exchange seats that had previously been overlooked.

In February 2007, Barker informed her manager, Angela Sinni, of UBS's failure to disclose the seat holdings in accordance with fed-eral securities law. Sinni apparently did not address Barker's concerns or provide assistance, nor did she report Barker's findings to higher management. Frustrated at Sinni's silence, Barker then met with UBS Operational Risk officers, Eric Romstadt and Adam Rosenthal, on July 26, 2007, to present her findings and express concern that UBS might be subject to liability for its failure to properly report the exchange seat shares on the company's balance sheet. Romstadt and Rosenthal notified their supervisor, Clinton Mosley, in the global Chief Operating Officer's office, who in turn notified Sinni's supervisor and the head of Barker's group, Equities Americas, Gerald Hees.

According to Barker, Hees reprimanded her in early August 2007 for having allowed Mosley to learn of the accounting omissions and told her not to disclose or discuss the situation with anyone else outside their group. A few weeks later, in September 2007, Barker attended a meeting where Hees allegedly expressed concern about how to "spin" the exchange seat issue to UBS management. Soon after, Barker met the newly-appointed Chief Operating Officer for Equities Americas, John Ingrilli. However, on September 24, 2007, Barker was instructed by Hees not to discuss anything related to the exchange seat account-ing omission with Ingrilli.

According to Barker, Hees told her that reporting discrepancies was "not her place" and that she "should not go there" with Ingrilli. Barker reported this conversation to Mia Edwards, head of UBS's Compliance Department, who told her to disregard Hees' instructions and encouraged her to speak with Ingrilli about the exchange seat matter. Barker did so. For her work on the exchange seat project and the resulting profit to UBS, UBS management ultimately awarded Barker a "Thank You Award" on November 23, 2007.

Nonetheless, according to Barker, Hees began retaliating against her for her effort in reporting the exchange seat shares. Barker was given a poor performance rating at the end of 2007 and was denied a cost-of-living increase for 2008. According to Barker, she was passed over for an advanced position reporting to Hees and the job was instead awarded to a woman in her early twenties. In March 2008, Barker met with her direct supervisor to complain that she had been experiencing a pattern of adverse treatment, including being overlooked for project assignments and not receiving support comparable to that provided to her co-workers. According to Barker, these complaints went unheeded. Finally, in May 2008, Barker was notified that she was being terminated, as part of a general reduction in workforce affecting all of UBS. According to Barker, she was among the five oldest employees in the Equities Business Management section and was one of five individuals over the age of forty terminated, out of the eight total employees in her group who were discharged as a result of the reduction in force.

In August 2008, Barker filed a complaint with the Occupational Safety and Health Administration ("OSHA") claiming that her work reconciling the exchange seat shares was protected activity under the federal Sarbanes-Oxley Act, 18 U.S.C. § 1514A, and that her efforts on that project contributed to her termination. In September 2009, OSHA found that Barker's alleged protected activity was not a contributing factor to her discharge. Barker appealed this ruling, but later informed the Administrative Law Judge that she would rather proceed directly in federal court. On March 2, 2009, Barker also filed a discrimination charge with the Equal Employment Opportunity Commission and received a "right to sue" letter.[27]

The court denied UBS's motion to dismiss the SOX claim but denied Barker's age discrimination claim. The court stated:

The whistleblower provision of the Sarbanes-Oxley Act, 18 U.S.C. § 1514A, provides employees of publicly traded companies with whistleblower protection, prohibiting employers from terminating, or otherwise retaliating against, such employees when they report "potentially unlawful conduct" that has occurred or is in progress. See 18 U.S.C. § 1514A; *Welch v. Chao*, 536 F.3d 269, 275 (4th Cir. 2008). To state a prima facie case pursuant to this retaliation provision, a plaintiff must plead that "(1) [s]he engaged in protected activity; (2) the employer knew of the protected activity; (3) [s]he suffered an unfavorable personnel action; and (4) circumstances exist to suggest that the protected activity was a contributing factor to the unfavorable action." *O'Mahony v. Accenture Ltd.*, 537 F.Supp.2d 506, 510 (S.D.N.Y. 2008). UBS disputes only that Barker was engaged in protected activity and that such activity was a contributing factor in her discharge.

The first disputed element in this case involves the first prong of Barker's prima facie case, that is, whether Barker engaged in "protected activity" within the meaning of the Sarbanes-Oxley Act. Section 1514A defines protected activity as the providing of information regarding conduct the employee "reasonably believes constitutes" a violation: of 18 U.S.C. §§ 1341 [mail fraud], 1343 [wire fraud], 1344 [bank fraud], or 1348 [securities fraud], any rule or regulation of the Securities and Exchange Commission, or any provision of Federal law relating to fraud against shareholders. 18 U.S.C. § 1514A(a)(1). The plaintiff's "reasonable belief" is based on the knowledge available to her, taking into consideration the plaintiff's training and circumstances. See *Pardy v. Gray*, No. 07 Civ. 6324, 2008 WL 2756331, at *5 (S.D.N.Y. July 15, 2008). The plaintiff's belief contains both subjective and objective components, meaning that the plaintiff must show not only that she believed the conduct constituted a violation, but that a reasonable person in the plaintiff's position would have believed that the conduct constituted a violation. *Welch*, 536 F.3d at 277. Further, when determining the reasonableness of a plaintiff's belief that shareholder fraud may have occurred, the employee's belief must "at least approximate the basic elements of a claim for securities fraud." *Day v. Staples, Inc.*, 555 F.3d 42, 55 (1st Cir. 2009). Thus, Barker must plead an objectively reasonable belief that UBS intentionally misrepresented, or omitted, certain material facts to investors which led to the possibility of financial loss. See *id.* at 56.

Barker appears to have had both a subjective and objectively reasonable belief that UBS's failure to properly record the exchange seat shares could subject the company to federal liability. Barker's complaint indicates that she informed various individuals at UBS that she believed the failure to disclose the exchange seat assets on UBS's balance sheet was a significant problem. Indeed, after initial conversations with her supervisor, Sinni, produced no action, Barker continued to seek out other management employees to whom she could express her concern. As Barker is not a lawyer, nor does she appear to have any specialized knowledge of federal securities law, it seems objectively reasonable that she would imagine unreported assets valued subsequently at over $80 million substantial enough to trigger federal scrutiny.

Additionally, while certain employees at UBS did encourage Barker in her investigation, her complaint asserts valid reasons why she could still believe an intentional misrepresentation was occurring. A reasonable person could find that Barker's supervisors were attempting to cover up the incorrect reporting, based on the initial lack of response by Sinni, coupled with Hees's instructions to Barker that she was not to speak of the exchange seat discrepancy, as well as the fact that a meeting was held about how to "spin" the accounting error. That Barker felt obligated to approach Mia Edwards, head of UBS's Legal Compliance Division, for advice about disclosure indicates that she believed her supervisors were unlawfully encouraging her to conceal important information that had legal significance for shareholders.

UBS argued that Barker cannot adequately plead a Sarbanes-Oxley shareholder fraud claim because the discrepancy she unearthed was not material, a general requirement of shareholder fraud. . . . As such, the plaintiff does not need to prove the fraud was actually material, but rather only that she held an objectively reasonable belief that it was. Here, Barker asserts that she had discovered by September 2007, that a quarter of UBS's exchange seat shares were either incorrectly accounted for or not included at all on UBS's records. No matter the end value of these shares, the discrepancy could seem objectively serious enough to warrant shareholder concern. UBS's balance sheet was fundamentally inaccurate—a fact that could certainly affect stock price and value. See *Vodopia v. Koninklijke Philips Elecs., N.V.*, 09-4747-cv, 2010 WL 4186469, at *3 (2d Cir. Oct. 25, 2010) (noting that a plaintiff's Sarbanes-Oxley claim brought under a shareholder fraud theory would have been more persuasive had the plaintiff alleged that the misinformation he had reported would have been included in a public report that could have possibly misled investors).[28]

The court held that Barker's complaint pled a reasonably objective belief that UBS's conduct was in violation of federal law protecting shareholders and, as such, her activity can be considered protected activity. The court's decision merely rejected UBS's motion to dismiss the complaint and made no finding as to the merits of the allegations.

 ## OTHER STATUTORY WHISTLEBLOWER PROTECTIONS

The next case illustrates the effect of the federal and state whistleblower protections. On April 23, 2008, the California Department of Education settled a long-running lawsuit with a whistleblower, paying $4.25 million to James Lindberg, a former employee, who said he suffered retaliation after he reported corruption and fraud to the then superintendent of education.[29] The case centered on corruption in a program that handed out money to community-based organizations between 1995 and 2000 to teach English and citizenship to recent immigrants. Some of the schools that allegedly received grant money did not even exist. Lindberg, a 20-year state employee, alleged that when he and others reported $11 million in misappropriations to the superintendent, she ignored them. Then Lindberg allegedly was transferred to a job with no duties, leading to stress that he claimed triggered two heart attacks and put him in a wheelchair.

A patchwork of various federal and state laws protect government and other designated employees who call attention to violations, help with enforcement proceedings, or refuse to obey unlawful directions. These laws, for the most part, do not provide any bounty for the whistleblower.

The first U.S. law adopted specifically to protect whistleblowers was the Lloyd–La Follette Act of 1912. It guaranteed the right of federal employees to furnish information to the United States Congress. The first U.S. environmental law to include an employee protection was the Water Pollution Control Act of 1972, also called the Clean Water Act. Similar protections were incorporated into subsequent federal environmental laws, including:

- The Safe Drinking Water Act (1974)
- The Energy Reorganization Act of 1974 (through its 1978 amendment to protect nuclear whistleblowers)
- The Resource Conservation and Recovery Act (also called the Solid Waste Disposal Act) (1976)
- The Toxic Substances Control Act (1976)
- The Comprehensive Environmental Response, Compensation, and Liability Act (CERCLA, or the Superfund Law) (1980)
- The Clean Air Act (1990)[30]

Similar employee protections enforced through the Occupational Safety and Health Administration are included in the Surface Transportation Assistance Act (1982) to protect truck drivers, the Pipeline Safety Improvement Act of 2002, the Wendell H. Ford Aviation Investment and Reform Act for the 21st Century, the Sarbanes-Oxley Act of 2002, the Dodd-Frank Act enacted on July 21, 2010, and the U.S. Food and Drug Administration's Food Safety Modernization Act enacted on January 4, 2011.[31]

The Military Whistleblower Protection Act—Title 10 U.S.C. 1034, as amended—safeguards the rights of military members to make protected communications to members of Congress; inspectors general; members of the Department of Defense audit, inspection, investigation, or law enforcement organization; and other persons or organizations (including the chain of command) designated by regulation or administrative procedures. A protected communication is

> any lawful communication to a member of Congress or an Inspector General, as well as any communication made to a person or organization designated under competent regulations to receive such communications, which a member of the Armed Services reasonably believes reports, among other things, a violation of law or regulation (including sexual harassment, unlawful discrimination, mismanagement, a gross waste of funds or other resources, abuse of authority, or a substantial or specific danger to public health or safety).[32]

The Office of the Whistleblower Protection Program of the U.S. Department of Labor's Occupational Safety and Health Administration investigates retaliation against whistleblowers under 20 federal statutes.

Federal employees could also benefit from the Whistleblower Protection Act of 1989[33] and from the Notification and Federal Employee Antidiscrimination and Retaliation Act of 2002 (No FEAR Act), which made individual agencies directly responsible for the economic sanctions of unlawful retaliation.

Chapter 11 discusses the SEC bounty rules, adopted under Dodd-Frank, and contains a step-by-step guide to obtaining such a bounty.

 NOTES

1. "Ship Manager to Pay $4M for Oil-Pollution Repeat Offense," *Professional Mariner*, September 27, 2010. www.professionalmariner.com/ME2/dirmod .asp?sid=&nm=&type=news&mod=News&mid=9A02E3B96F2A415ABC72C B5F516B4C10&tier=3&nid=E87D5F74A2224068BE9D33CA1D2A3B29.

2. John Christoffersen, "Workers Rewarded for Cooperation in Oil Dump Case," Forbes.com, May 11, 2011. See also Department of Justice, "Tanker Company Fined $4.9 Million for Falsifying Records and Obstruction of Justice," December 14, 2007, www.usdoj.gov.
3. 33 U.S.C. § 1908.
4. 35 U.S.C. § 292.
5. 590 F.3d 1295 (Fed. Cir. 2009).
6. 35 U.S. C. § 292 (a).
7. *Solo Cup*, 2010 U.S. App. LEXIS 11820 at 6–7n. 1.
8. 19 U.S.C. § 1619.
9. www.phillipsandcohen.com/State-False-Claims-Statutes.
10. Carrick Mollenkamp, Lingling Wei, and Gregory Zuckerman, "States Widen Currency-Trade Probes," *Wall Street Journal*, February 3, 2011.
11. Ibid.
12. www.phillipsandcohen.com/State-False-Claims-Statutes.
13. See www.ag.ny.gov/media_center/2011/jan/jan18a_11.html.
14. www.taf.org/NY-FCA-law.htm.
15. www.phillipsandcohen.com/State-False-Claims-Statutes/California.shtml.
16. Ibid.
17. www.phillipsandcohen.com/State-False-Claims-Statutes.
18. Ibid.
19. Ibid.
20. Ibid.
21. Ibid.
22. Marie Chêne, "Good Practice in Whistleblowing Protection Legislation (WPL)," U4 Helpdesk, Transparency International, July 1, 2009. www .U4.no.
23. For example, the United Kingdom Public Interest Disclosure Act permits discretionary rewards to be given by public authorities, such as Revenue or Customs. See note 4 of "Rewarding Whistleblowers as Good Citizens—Response to the Home Office Consultation," *Public Concern at Work*, November 30, 2007. http://www.pcaw.co.uk/policy/policy_pdfs/rewardingwhistleblowers.pdf.
24. Jarod S. Gonzalez, "A Pot of Gold at the End of the Rainbow: An Economic Incentives-Based Approach to OSHA Whistleblowing," *Chicago-Kent College of Law, Employee Rights and Employment Policy Journal* 14 (2010); see also Richard Moberly, "Sarbanes-Oxley's Structural Model to Encourage Corporate Whistle-blowers," *Brigham Young University Law Review* (September 2006): 1107.
25. Public Law 111-203, Title IX, § 922(h).
26. *Mary J. Barker, Plaintiff, v. UBS AG and UBS Securities LLC, Defendants*, No. 3:09-cv-2084 (CFD), United States District Court, D. Connecticut, January 26, 2011.
27. http://employmentlawgroupblog.com/wp-content/Barker-v.-UBS-MTD.pdf.
28. Ibid.

29. John Hill, "California Department of Education Settles Whistle-Blower Suit for $4.25 Million," *Sacramento Bee*, April 23, 2008.

30. www.thewhistlebloweradvisor.com/whistleblower-protection.

31. www.huffingtonpost.com/2011/02/11/food-safety-law-protects-whistleblowers_n_821989.html.

32. Naval Inspector General, "Reprisal (Military Whistleblower Protection)." www.ig.navy.mil/complaints/Complaints%20%20(Reprisal%20Military%20 Whistleblower%20Protection).htm.

33. 5 U.S.C. § 1221(e); www.law.cornell.edu/uscode/5/1221/html.

A Step-by-Step Guide to SEC Whistleblower Awards under Dodd-Frank*

T HE ENORMOUS SCOPE OF the bounty provisions of the Dodd-Frank Act has been discussed extensively in Chapter 1 of this book. The Securities and Exchange Commission (SEC) has been inundated with whistleblower tips since the passage of Dodd-Frank. From July 21, 2010, the date of enactment of Dodd-Frank, until February 2011, the SEC received approximately 168 whistleblower tips.[1] According to the director of the SEC's Office of Market Intelligence, "his office was fielding one or two quality tips each day since the new law."[2]

On May 25, 2011, the SEC adopted its final whistleblower rules under Dodd-Frank, effective August 12, 2011. The rules define a "whistleblower" as an individual who, alone or jointly with others, provides the SEC with information relating to a possible violation of the federal securities laws (including any rules or regulations thereunder) that has occurred, is ongoing, or is about to occur. A whistleblower must be an individual. A company or another entity is not eligible to be a whistleblower.

A summary of the highlights of the rules follows. Please note that the SEC uses a number of defined terms in its bounty award rules whose meaning will

---

* This chapter was coauthored by Jeffrey M. Taylor, Esq.

be explored in this chapter. After the summary we present 10 simple steps for complying with the rules and further discuss certain provisions of the rules.

 SUMMARY

Subject to certain eligibility and other provisions, the SEC will pay an award or awards to one or more whistleblowers who meet these requirements:

- *Voluntarily* provide the SEC
- With *original information*
- That *leads to the successful enforcement* by the SEC of a federal court or administrative action
- In which the SEC obtains *monetary sanctions* totaling more than $1 million.

The SEC also will pay awards in certain *related actions* as defined in this chapter.

The terms "voluntarily," "original information," "leads to successful enforcement action," "monetary sanctions," and "related actions" are defined as described next.

Question: What does *voluntary* mean?

Answer: A submission is *voluntary* if the SEC is provided with the information before the whistleblower or anyone representing him or her (such as an attorney) receives any request, inquiry, or demand that relates to the subject matter of the submission (1) from the SEC; (2) in connection with a Public Company Accounting Oversight Board (PCAOB) or self-regulatory organization investigation, inspection, or examination; or (3) in connection with an investigation by Congress, any federal authority, or a state attorney general or securities regulatory authority (collectively, "covered authorities").

If any of these covered authorities direct such a request, inquiry, or demand to the whistleblower or his or her representative first, the submission will not be considered voluntary, even if the whistleblower is not required by law to respond. However, the submission will be considered voluntary if the whistleblower voluntarily provided the same information to one of these covered authorities prior to receiving a request, inquiry, or demand from the SEC. Furthermore, the submission will not be considered voluntary if the whistleblower is required to report the original information to the SEC as a result of a preexisting legal duty, a contractual duty that is owed to one of these covered authorities, or a duty that arises out of a court or administrative order.

Question: What is *original information?*

Answer: In order for the whistleblower's submission to be considered original information, it must be:

- Derived from *independent knowledge* or *independent analysis.*
- Not already known to the SEC from any other source, unless the whistle-blower is the *original source* of the information.
- Not exclusively derived from an allegation made in a judicial or administrative hearing; in a governmental report, hearing, audit, or investigation; or from the news media, unless the whistleblower is a source of the information.
- Provided to the SEC for the first time after July 21, 2010 (the date of enactment of Dodd-Frank).

Independent knowledge means factual information in the whistleblower's possession that is not derived from publicly available sources. The whistleblower may gain independent knowledge from his or her experiences, communications, and observations in business or social interaction.

Independent analysis generally means the whistleblower's own analysis, whether done alone or in combination with others. Analysis means the examination and evaluation of information that may be generally available, but that reveals information that is not generally known or available to the public. Independent analysis essentially requires the whistleblower to bring forth some additional evaluation assessment or insight.

The SEC will consider the whistleblower to be an *original source* of the same information that the SEC obtains from another source if the information is otherwise original information and the other source obtained the information from the whistleblower or his or her representative. In order to be considered an original source of information that the SEC receives from a covered authority (as defined below), the whistleblower must have voluntarily given the authority that information. Interestingly, two individuals may be deemed to be the original source of the same information. For example, if B submits whistleblower information based on what A told him, and A later submits a whistleblower claim, A would foremost be deemed to have been the original source of the information provided by B. B would not necessarily be left out in the cold, however, because B was the first to bring knowledge of the information to the

SEC based on his independent knowledge (i.e., what he learned from A). This of course does not necessarily imply that both B and A would be entitled to a whistleblower award; but if they otherwise met all of the requirements for an award, it would be allocated between them as provided under the whistleblower rules. The term *covered authority* refers to Congress, any other authority of the federal government, a state attorney general or securities regulatory authority, any self-regulatory authority, or the PCAOB.

Question: What does *leads to successful enforcement* mean?

Answer:

- The whistleblower's original information to the SEC is sufficiently specific, credible, and timely to cause the SEC staff to commence an examination, open an investigation, reopen an investigation that the SEC had previously closed, or inquire concerning different conduct as part of a current examination or investigation, and the SEC brings a successful judicial or administrative action based in whole or in part on conduct that was the subject of the whistleblower's original information.
- The whistleblower's original information to the SEC about conduct that is already under examination or investigation by the SEC or another covered authority (except in cases where the whistleblower is an original source of this information) significantly contributes to the success of the action.
- The whistleblower reports original information through an entity's internal whistleblower, legal, or compliance procedures for reporting allegations of possible violations of law before or at the same time the whistleblower reports them to the SEC, and
    - The entity later provides the information to the SEC or provides results of an audit or investigation initiated in whole or in part in response to information the whistleblower reported to the entity; and
    - The information otherwise leads to successful enforcement as defined earlier.

This information must be provided to the SEC within 120 days after the whistleblower provides it to the entity.

Question: What are *monetary sanctions?*

Answer: *Monetary sanctions* means any money, including penalties, disgorgement, and interest, ordered to be paid and any money deposited into a disgorgement fund or other fund pursuant to the Sarbanes-Oxley Act of 2002, as a result of an SEC action or a *related action*.

Question: What is a *related action* in which the SEC will also pay a reward?

Answer: A *related action* is a judicial or administrative action that is brought by the Attorney General of the United States, an appropriate regulatory agency, a self-regulatory organization, or a state attorney general in a criminal case, and is based on the same original information that the whistleblower voluntarily provided to the SEC and that led the SEC to successful enforcement of an action in which the SEC obtained monetary sanctions totaling more than $1 million.

Question: What is the amount of the reward?

Answer: The amount of the reward will be at least 10 percent and no more than 30 percent of the monetary sanctions that the SEC and the other authorities are able to collect. The percentage awarded in connection with an SEC action may differ from the percentage awarded in connection with a related action. The determination of the amount of the award is at the SEC's discretion.

Question: Are certain individuals disqualified from receiving SEC whistleblower awards?

Answer: No award is made to any of the following persons:

- Any whistleblower who is, or was at the time he or she acquired the original information submitted to the SEC, a member, officer, or employee of (1) certain regulatory agencies; (2) the Department of Justice; (3) a self-regulatory organization; (4) the PCAOB; (5) a law enforcement organization; (6) a foreign government or any political subdivision, department, agency, or instrumentality thereof; or (7) any other foreign financial regulatory authority (as defined in the Securities Exchange Act of 1934 (1934 Act))
- Any whistleblower who is convicted of a criminal violation related to the SEC action or to a related action for which the whistleblower otherwise could receive an award
- Any whistleblower who gains the information through the performance of an audit of financial statements and for whom such submission would be contrary to the requirements of Section 10A of the 1934 Act

- Any whistleblower who fails to submit information to the SEC in such form as the SEC may, by rule, require (subject to waiver at the SEC's discretion)
- Any whistleblower who is the spouse, parent, child, or sibling of an SEC member or employee, or who resides in the same household as an SEC member or employee
- Any whistleblower who acquired the information from a person who had obtained the information from an audit of a company's financial statements, where the submission would be contrary to the requirements of Section 10A of the 1934 Act, unless the information is not excluded from such other person's use or the whistleblower is providing the SEC with information about possible violations of that other person
- Any whistleblower who acquired the information with the intent to evade any provision of the whistleblower rules

In addition, a whistleblower is not entitled to an award if in his or her submission, other dealings with the SEC, or dealings with another authority in a related action, the whistleblower:

- Knowingly and willfully makes any false, fictitious, or fraudulent statement or representation; or
- Uses any false writing or document knowing the writing or document contains any false, fictitious, or fraudulent statement or entry with the intent to hinder or mislead the SEC or any other authority.

There is no requirement either in Dodd-Frank or the SEC rules that a whistleblower must be a U.S. citizen. This is particularly important in light of the fact that violations of federal securities laws include violations of the Foreign Corrupt Practices Act provisions of such laws, as discussed in Chapter 1.

 ## SEC INVESTOR PROTECTION FUND

All payments of awards are made from the SEC Investor Protection Fund. The SEC has created a fund containing approximately $452 million for payments of awards to whistleblowers.[3]

DOES THE WHISTLEBLOWER NEED AN ATTORNEY?

Dodd-Frank and SEC rules specifically provide that a whistleblower may be represented by an attorney in making a claim for an award. The statute also provides that any whistleblower who anonymously makes a claim for an award must be represented by an attorney.

Anyone who believes that they may have original information that might entitle them to a bounty under Dodd-Frank would do well to consider hiring a securities lawyer to assist them. Many securities lawyers will represent whistle-blowers on a contingent-fee basis. Their websites can be located by putting in the word "whistleblower" in a Google search. Many prominent law firms that perform this service do not advertise.

As can be seen from this chapter, seeking a bounty is not a simple process. The SEC rules are very detailed, and unsophisticated whistleblowers may have difficulty in complying with them.

More important, the SEC receives many whistleblower complaints and likely will not have sufficient staff to review all of them. The complaints that will likely receive the most attention are those submitted by prestigious law firms and other well-known whistleblower attorneys. For the SEC staff to pay any attention to the whistleblower's original information, the information will have to be presented in a cogent and compelling manner. That is exactly the skill that a securities lawyer brings to the table.

Although neither Dodd-Frank nor the SEC rules permit private qui tam actions, it may be important to actually provide a proposed draft complaint to the SEC to get its attention. The proposed draft complaint would reflect the SEC as the plaintiff and would contain detailed allegations based on the original information that the whistleblower has provided to the SEC. Assuming that the SEC Enforcement Staff is inundated with whistleblower tips, providing a proposed complaint could be helpful in getting staff attention, since the complaint, if properly prepared, eliminates some of their work. Obviously, the whistleblower will need a skilled securities attorney for this purpose.

The rest of this chapter is presented on the assumption that the whistleblower does not want to use a securities lawyer and will represent himself or herself.

The steps that the whistleblower should go through are presented next. After the step-by-step guide is an introduction to the SEC rules that apply to whistleblowers.

STEP-BY-STEP GUIDE

Once the whistleblower has determined that he or she is not disqualified from receiving an award, follow these 10 simple steps to determine qualification to receive an award.

Step 1: Determine Whether the Information Is Really Material to the SEC Enforcement Program

The passage of the Dodd-Frank Act has resulted in a number of tips to the SEC. For the whistleblower's information to obtain the attention of the SEC Enforcement Staff, it must be meaningful information that helps the SEC obtain monetary sanctions under the federal securities laws. The SEC is interested primarily in "high-quality tips," which are reliable and specific and have a meaningful connection to the SEC's ability to successfully complete its investigation and obtain a settlement or prevail in a litigated proceeding. If the information does not meet that requirement, it is likely to be put at the bottom of the pile.

Step 2: Determine Whether the Information Constitutes "Original Information"

There is no point in making a submission to the SEC for which the whistleblower expects a bounty if he or she is disqualified from receiving a bounty. The whistleblower cannot receive a bounty unless the information is, among other things, considered original information. To constitute original information, the information must, as previously discussed, meet four tests.

1. It must be derived from the whistleblower's independent knowledge or independent analysis.
2. It must not already be known to the SEC from any other source, unless the whistleblower is the original source of the information.
3. It must not be exclusively derived from an allegation made in a judicial or administrative hearing; in a governmental report, hearing, audit, or investigation; or from the news media unless the whistleblower is a source of the information.
4. It must be provided to the SEC for the first time after July 21, 2010.

Information is not considered derived from *independent knowledge or independent analysis* if the information was derived from any of these sources:

- Through a communication that was subject to the attorney-client privilege (unless disclosure of that information is otherwise permitted by SEC rules relating to permissive disclosure by attorneys), the applicable state attorney conduct rules, or otherwise
- In connection with the legal representation of a client on whose behalf the whistleblower or his or her employer or firm is providing services, and the whistleblower seeks to use the information to make a submission for his or her own benefit (unless disclosure of that information is otherwise permitted by SEC rules relating to permissive disclosures by attorneys, the applicable state attorney conduct rules, or otherwise)
- By a means or in a manner that violates applicable federal or state criminal law

Furthermore, information generally is not considered derived from *independent knowledge* or *independent analysis* if, in circumstances not covered by the attorney-client privilege or obtained through legal representation above, the whistleblower obtained the information because he or she was:

- An officer, director, trustee, or partner of an entity and another person informed the whistleblower of allegations of misconduct, or he or she learned the information in connection with the entity's processes for identifying, reporting, and addressing possible violations of law
- An employee whose principal duties involve compliance or internal audit responsibilities, or who was employed by or otherwise associated with a firm retained to perform compliance or internal audit functions for an entity
- Employed by or otherwise associated with a firm retained to conduct an inquiry or investigation into possible violations of law
- An employee of, or other person associated with, a public accounting firm, if the whistleblower obtained the information through the performance of an engagement required of an independent public accountant under the federal securities laws (other than an audit of a company's financial statements if a whistleblower submission would be contrary to the requirements of Section 10A of the 1934 Act), and that information related to a violation by the engagement client or the client's directors, officers, or other employees

These limitations are subject to a number of exceptions, including:

- There is reasonable basis to believe that disclosure of the information to the SEC is necessary to prevent the relevant entity from engaging in conduct that is likely to cause substantial injury to the financial interest or property of the entity or investors.

- There is a reasonable basis to believe that the relevant entity is engaging in conduct that will impede an investigation of the misconduct.
- At least 120 days have elapsed since the whistleblower provided the information to the relevant entity's audit committee, chief legal officer, chief compliance officer (or their equivalents), or his or her supervisor, or since the whistleblower received the information, if it was received under circumstances indicating that the entity's audit committee, chief legal officer, chief compliance officer (or their equivalents), or his or her supervisor was already aware of the information.

If the whistleblower obtains the information from any of the individuals previously described, it is not considered information derived from his or her independent knowledge or analysis. However, there is an exception if the information is not excluded from that person's use pursuant to the SEC rules, or the whistleblower is providing the SEC with information about possible violations involving that person, as noted above.

Step 3: Determine Whether the Submission of the Original Information Is Voluntary

The submission of original information must be made voluntarily under SEC rules. This means that the whistleblower must provide the SEC with the information before he or she or any representative (such as an attorney) receives any request, inquiry, or demand that relates to the subject matter of the submission (1) from the SEC; (2) in connection with a PCAOB or self-regulatory organization investigation, inspection, or examination; or (3) in connection with an investigation by Congress, any federal authority, or a state attorney general or securities regulatory authority.

If any of these covered authorities directs such a request, inquiry, or demand to the whistleblower or his or her representative first, the submission will not be considered voluntary, even if the whistleblower is not required by law to respond. However, the submission will be considered voluntary if the whistleblower voluntarily provided the same information to one of these covered authorities prior to receiving a request, inquiry, or demand from the SEC. Furthermore, the submission will not be considered voluntary if the whistleblower is required to report the original information to the SEC as a result of a preexisting legal duty, a contractual duty that is owed to one of these covered authorities, or a duty that arises out of a court or administrative order.

Step 4: Determine Whether the Whistleblower Is the Original Source of the Information

In order to constitute original information potentially entitling the whistleblower to a bounty, he or she must be the *original source* of that information. If the SEC obtains the same information from another source, and the other source obtained the information from the whistleblower or his or her representative, the whistleblower will still be deemed the original source.

If the SEC already knows some of the information about a matter from other sources at the time of the submission, the SEC will still consider the whistleblower an original source of the information provided that it is derived from the whistleblower's independent knowledge or analysis and that it materially adds to the information that the SEC already possesses. If the information is provided to a covered authority or to an entity's whistleblower's legal or compliance procedures, and the whistleblower, within 120 days, submits the same information to the SEC, the SEC will consider that the whistleblower provided the information as of the date of the original disclosure to the whistleblower's employer or other qualified entities.

Step 5: Consider Whether the Whistleblower Wishes to Submit the Original Information Anonymously

The whistleblower may submit original information to the SEC anonymously. To qualify for anonymous submission, he or she will need an attorney, and must provide the attorney with the completed and signed Form Tip, Complaint or Referral (TCR). In addition, the attorney must certify that he or she has verified the whistleblower's identity, has reviewed the form for completeness and accuracy, has obtained the whistleblower's nonwaivable consent to provide the Form TCR to the SEC, and will provide the signed original of the Form TCR upon request of the SEC within seven calendar days. Please note that if the whistleblower elects an anonymous submission, the whistleblower must disclose his or her identity when applying for the award.

Step 6: The Whistleblower Must Submit the Original Information in the Manner Required by the SEC

To qualify for an award, the whistleblower must complete Form TCR, which is contained in Appendix 2 of this book (or use the electronic alternative described). Carefully follow the instructions set forth in Appendix 2. The whistleblower can avoid submitting Form TCR only if he or she submits the information online through the SEC's Electronic Data Collection System. The whistleblower must also declare under penalty of perjury at the time the information is submitted that it is true and correct to the best of his or her knowledge.

If the information is submitted after July 21, 2010, but prior to the effective date of the SEC rules, the submission will be deemed to be sufficient to comply with the SEC's whistleblower rules. However, if the whistleblower was anonymous and submitted information before the effective date of the SEC rules, the whistleblower must provide his or her attorney with a completed and signed copy of Form TCR within 60 days of the effective date of these rules, and the attorney must provide of copy of the signed form to the SEC staff upon request prior to any payment of an award. The whistleblower must also follow the procedures and conditions for making a claim for an award described in the SEC's whistleblower rules.

Step 7: The Whistleblower Must Submit Form WB-APP on a Timely Basis

When an SEC action results in monetary sanctions totaling more than $1 million, the SEC Whistleblower Office will cause to be published on the SEC's website a "Notice of Covered Action." The whistleblower will have 90 calendar days from the date of the Notice of Covered Action to file a claim for an award based on that action, or the claim will be barred. To file a claim for an award, the whistleblower must file Form WB-APP (Application for Award for Original Information Provided Pursuant to Section 21F of the Securities Exchange Act of 1934), as set forth in Appendix 3 of this book. If the whistleblower provided the original information anonymously, he or she must disclose his or her identity on Form WB-APP; and the identity must be verified in a form and manner that is acceptable to the SEC Whistleblower Office prior to the payment of any award.

Step 8: The Whistleblower Must Provide Any Additional Eligibility Information upon Request of the SEC Whistleblower Office

Once the time for filing any appeals of the SEC's judicial or administrative action has expired or such an appeal has been concluded, the SEC Claims Review Staff designated by the SEC's director of the Division of Enforcement will evaluate all timely whistleblower claims. In connection with this process, the SEC Claims Review Staff may require that the whistleblower provide additional information relating to his or her eligibility for an award or satisfaction of any of the conditions for an award.

Step 9: If the Whistleblower Receives a Negative Preliminary Determination from the SEC Claims Review Staff, Comply with All Deadlines to Contest Such Preliminary Determination

Following an evaluation of the whistleblower's claim by the SEC Claims Review Staff, that office will send a Preliminary Determination setting forth a preliminary assessment as to whether the claim should be allowed or denied and, if allowed, setting forth the proposed award percentage amount. If the whistleblower is unhappy with the Preliminary Determination, he or she has a right to contest it through a written response in the form and substance required by the SEC Whistleblower Office setting forth the grounds for the objection to either the denial of an award or the proposed amount of an award (including supporting documentation). Before doing so, the whistleblower, within 30 calendar days of the determination, may request that the SEC Whistleblower Office make available for his or her review the materials that the determination was based on. The whistleblower may also, within the 30-calendar-day period, request a meeting with the SEC Whistleblower Office, although the office is not required to meet with the whistleblower. If the whistleblower decides to contest the Preliminary Determination, a written response and supporting materials must be submitted within 60 calendar days of the date of the Preliminary Determination, or, if a request to review materials has been made, then within 60 calendar days of the SEC Whistleblower Office making those materials available for review.

Step 10: The Whistleblower Must Timely Appeal to the Courts Any Adverse Award Determination by the SEC

If the whistleblower submitted a timely response, pursuant to Step 9, the Claims Review Staff will consider the issues, along with any supporting documentation, and make its Proposed Final Determination. The SEC Whistleblower Office will then notify the SEC Commissioners of the Proposed Final Determination. Any SEC Commissioner may request, within 30 calendar days, that the Proposed Final Determination be reviewed by all the SEC Commissioners. If no SEC Commissioner requests a review, the Proposed Final Determination becomes the Final Order of the SEC. If an SEC Commissioner requests such a review, the full SEC will review the record that the staff relied on in making its determinations. In either case, the whistleblower may appeal the Final Order of the SEC to the courts.

DETERMINING WHETHER THE OVER $1 MILLION THRESHOLD IS SATISFIED

To be eligible for an award, the SEC must collect monetary sanctions exceeding $1 million. Otherwise, the SEC action is not considered a "covered judicial or administrative action." The term "monetary sanctions" is defined to mean any money, including penalties, disgorgement, and interest, ordered to be paid and any money deposited into a disgorgement or other similar fund as a result of an SEC action or a related action.

An action generally means a single captioned judicial or administrative proceeding brought by the SEC. However, the SEC will treat as a single action two or more administrative or judicial proceedings brought by the SEC if these proceedings arise out of the same nucleus of operative facts. Also, the SEC will deem as part of the SEC action upon which an award is based any subsequent SEC proceeding that, individually, results in a monetary sanction of $1 million or less and that arises out of the same nucleus of operative facts. In determining whether two or more proceedings arise from the same nucleus of operative facts, the SEC will consider a number of factors, including whether the actions have the same or similar parties, factual allegations, alleged violations of the federal securities laws, or transactions or occurrences.

DETERMINING THE AMOUNT OF AN AWARD

The amount of the award will be at least 10 percent and no more than 30 percent of the monetary sanctions that the SEC and the other authorities in a related action are able to collect. The percentage awarded in connection with an SEC action may differ from the percentage awarded in connection with a related action.

If the SEC makes awards to more than one whistleblower in connection with the same action or related action, the SEC will determine an individual percentage award for each whistleblower, but in no event will the total amount awarded to all whistleblowers as a group be less than 10 percent or greater than 30 percent of the amount the SEC or the other authorities in any related action collect. Thus, for example, one whistleblower could receive an award of 25 percent of the collected sanctions, and another could receive an award of 5 percent, but they could not each receive an award of 30 percent.

In determining the amount of an award, Dodd-Frank requires the SEC to take into consideration:

- The significance of the information provided by a whistleblower to the success of the SEC action or related action
- The degree of assistance provided by the whistleblower and any legal representative of the whistleblower in the SEC action or related action
- The programmatic interest of the SEC in deterring violations of the securities laws by making awards to whistleblowers who provide information that leads to the successful enforcement of such laws
- Such additional relevant factors as the SEC may establish by rule or regulation

The SEC has stated that it will also consider the following factors, which are *not* listed in the order of importance and are not necessarily inclusive or applicable to any particular case:

- Whether, and to what extent, the whistleblower and his or her attorney participated in internal compliance systems
- The culpability of the whistleblower, including, among other things, the whistleblower's role in the violations; his or her education, training, or experience; whether the whistleblower acted with scienter (i.e., guilty knowledge); whether the whistleblower benefited financially from the violations; whether the whistleblower is a recidivist; the egregiousness of the underlying fraud committed by the whistleblower; and whether the whistleblower knowingly interfered with a relevant SEC investigation or enforcement action
- Whether the whistleblower delayed reporting the securities violations
- In cases where the whistleblower interacted with his or her entity's internal compliance or reporting system, whether the whistleblower undermined the integrity of such system, including whether the whistleblower made any false, fictitious, or fraudulent statements or provided any false writing or other document

The SEC is prohibited by Dodd-Frank from considering the balance of the fund in determining the amount of the award.

If the violation of the securities laws occurred before July 21, 2010, the date of enactment of Dodd-Frank, the whistleblower still may receive an award under Dodd-Frank provided the original information was given to the SEC after July 21, 2010.

MUST AN EMPLOYEE COMPLY WITH THE COMPANY'S INTERNAL COMPLIANCE PROGRAM?

One of the most controversial aspects of the SEC rules was the SEC's determination not to require initial compliance by an employee whistleblower with his or her company's internal compliance programs. Many organizations believed that permitting such noncompliance would undermine their internal compliance programs, since whistleblowers would immediately provide information to the SEC rather than permitting the company time to investigate the information themselves.

The SEC made it clear that reporting through the internal compliance system was not a requirement for an award above the 10 percent statutory minimum. The SEC also stated that whistleblowers would not be penalized if they did not avail themselves of the opportunity to report internally "for fear of retaliation or other legitimate reasons."

As a sop to these companies, the SEC decided to state that it would consider compliance with internal reporting systems as both positive and negative factors in determining the size of the award. The SEC also precluded certain persons with compliance-related responsibilities from being qualified whistleblowers. If the whistleblower provides information to a covered authority or to an entity's internal whistleblower, legal, or compliance procedures for reporting allegations of possible violations of law, and, within 120 days, submits the same information to the SEC under the whistleblower rules, then, for purposes of evaluating the whistleblower's claim to an award, the SEC will consider that the whistleblower provided information as of the date of his or her original disclosure, report, or submission to one of these covered authorities or other persons. The whistleblower must establish the effective date of any prior disclosure, report, or submission, to the SEC's satisfaction. The SEC may seek assistance and confirmation from the other authority or person in making this determination. This eliminates the risk to the whistleblower that, by delaying the submission to the SEC, some other whistleblower will be deemed the "original source" for the information and become entitled to the award.

Most important, the final rules would give credit to a whistleblower whose company passes the information along to the SEC, even if the whistleblower does not. According to the SEC chairman, "[T]his could create an opportunity for the whistleblower to obtain an award through internal reporting where the whistleblower might not otherwise have qualified for an award because the information was not sufficiently specific and credible."[4]

CONFIDENTIALITY

Subject to certain limited exceptions, the SEC and any officer or employee of the SEC must not disclose any information, including information provided by a whistleblower to the SEC that could reasonably be expected to reveal the identity of a whistleblower. The limited exceptions include:

- Disclosure in accordance with the Privacy Act of 1974
- Disclosure required to a defendant or respondent in a public proceeding instituted by the SEC or certain other regulatory or enforcement authorities to which the SEC is permitted to disclose the information

NONWAIVER OF WHISTLEBLOWER RIGHTS

Dodd-Frank provides that the rights and remedies of whistleblowers under the statute may not be waived by any agreement, policy form, or condition of employment, including by a predispute arbitration agreement. Moreover, no predispute arbitration agreement is valid or enforceable if the agreement requires arbitration of a dispute arising under the whistleblower bounty section of Dodd-Frank. SEC rules prohibit enforcing or threatening to enforce an employer confidentiality agreement to impede an individual from communicating with the SEC staff about a possible securities law violation.

APPEALS

Dodd-Frank gives the SEC discretion to determine whether there is an award, to whom the award was made, in what amount, and any other determination made in accordance with the law. Any such determination, except the amount of the award (assuming it was within the 10 to 30 percent parameter), is subject to appeal to the appropriate U.S. Court of Appeals. Any such appeal must be within 30 days after the SEC's determination is issued.

The detailed SEC Whistleblower Rules are contained in Appendix 4 of this book.

ANTI-RETALIATION PROVISION

Under the SEC rules, the whistleblower is protected by the SEC from retaliation if:

- He or she possesses a reasonable belief that the information that is provided relates to a possible securities law violation (or, where applicable, to a possible violation of certain other defined provisions) that has occurred, is ongoing, or is about to occur; and
- He or she provides that information in a manner described in the SEC rules (see Appendix 4).

The anti-retaliation protections apply whether or not the whistleblower satisfies the requirements, procedures, and conditions to qualify for an award.

 ## NOTES

1. Kaja Whitehouse, "SEC Whistleblower Call Draws Few Tipsters," *New York Post*, February 23, 2011.
2. Quoting Thomas Sporkin, Director, SEC's Office of Market Intelligence, *Just Anti-Corruption: Graft, The FCPA and Compliance*, dated February 23, 2011, http://www.mainjustice.com/justanticorruption/2011/02/23/tips-to-sec-whistleblower-program-reach-168.
3. "SEC Whistleblower Fund Is Juiced Up," *Wall Street Journal*, November 1, 2010; U.S. Securities and Exchange Commission, "Annual Report on Whistleblower Program, as Required by Section 21F(g)5 of the Securities Exchange Act of 1934," October 2010.
4. www.sec.gov/news/speech/2011/spch052511mls-item2.htm.

IRS Form 211

Copies of this form are available at www.irs.gov/pub/irs-pdf/f211.pdf.

Form 211 (Rev. December 2007)	Department of the Treasury - Internal Revenue Service **Application for Award for Original Information**	OMB No. 1545-0409
		Date Claim Received:
		Claim No. (completed by IRS)

1. Name of individual claimant	2. Claimant's Date of Birth Month Day Year	3. Claimant's SSN or ITIN
4. Name of spouse *(if applicable)*	5. Spouse's Date of Birth Month Day Year	6. Spouse's SSN or ITIN

7. Address of claimant, including zip code, and telephone number

8. Name & Title of IRS employee to whom violation was reported	9. Date violation reported:
10. Name of taxpayer (include aliases) and any related taxpayers who committed the violation:	11. Taxpayer Identification Number(s) (e.g., SSN, ITIN, or EIN):
12. Taxpayer's address, including zip code:	13. Taxpayer's date of birth or approximate age:

14. State the facts pertinent to the alleged violation. (Attach a detailed explanation and all supporting information in your possession and describe the availability and location of any additional supporting information not in your possession.) Explain why you believe the act described constitutes a violation of the tax laws.

15. Describe how you learned about and/or obtained the information that supports this claim and describe your present or former relationship to the alleged noncompliant taxpayer(s). (Attach sheet if needed.)

16. Describe the amount owed by the taxpayer(s). Please provide a summary of the information you have that supports your claim as to the amount owed. (Attach sheet if needed.)

Declaration under Penalty of Perjury
I declare under penalty of perjury that I have examined this application, my accompanying statement, and supporting documentation and aver that such application is true, correct, and complete, to the best of my knowledge.

17. Signature of Claimant	18. Date

MAIL THE COMPLETED FORM TO THE ADDRESS SHOWN ON THE BACK

Form **211** (Rev. 12-2007)   Catalog Number 16571S   publish.no.irs.gov   Department of the Treasury-**Internal Revenue Service**

General Information:
On December 20, 2006, Congress made provision for the establishment of a Whistleblower Office within the IRS. This office has responsibility for the administration of the informant award program under section 7623 of the Internal Revenue Code. Section 7623 authorizes the payment of awards from the proceeds of amounts the Government collects by reason of the information provided by the claimant. Payment of awards under 7623(a) is made at the discretion of the IRS. To be eligible for an award under Section 7623(b), the amount in dispute (including tax, penalties, interest, additions to tax, and additional amounts) must exceed $2,000,000.00; if the taxpayer is an individual, the individual's gross income must exceed $200,000.00 for any taxable year at issue.

Send completed form along with any supporting information to:

Internal Revenue Service
Whistleblower Office
SE: WO
1111 Constitution Ave., NW
Washington, DC 20224

Instructions for Completion of Form 211:
Questions 1 - 7
Information regarding Claimant (informant): Name, Date of Birth, Social Security Number (SSN) or Individual Taxpayer Identification Number (ITIN), address including zip code, and telephone number (telephone number is optional).

Questions 8 - 9
If you reported the violation to an IRS employee, provide the employee's name and title and the date the violation was reported.

Questions 10 - 13
Information about Taxpayer - Provide specific and credible information regarding the taxpayer or entities that you believe have failed to comply with tax laws and that will lead to the collection of unpaid taxes.

Question 14
Attach all supporting documentation (for example, books and records) to substantiate the claim. If documents or supporting evidence are not in your possession, describe these documents and their location.

Question 15
Describe how the information which forms the basis of the claim came to your attention, including the date(s) on which this information was acquired, and a complete description of your relationship to the taxpayer.

Question 16
Describe the facts supporting the amount you claim is owed by the taxpayer.

Question 17
Information provided in connection with a claim submitted under this provision of law must be made under an original signed Declaration under Penalty of Perjury. Joint claims must be signed by each claimant.

PRIVACY ACT AND PAPERWORK REDUCTION ACT NOTICE: We ask for the information on this form to carry out the internal revenue laws of the United States. Our authority to ask for this information is 26 USC 6109 and 7623. We collect this information for use in determining the correct amount of any award payable to you under 26 USC 7623. We may disclose this information as authorized by 26 USC 6103, including to the subject taxpayer(s) as needed in a tax compliance investigation and to the Department of Justice for civil and criminal litigation. You are not required to apply for an award. However, if you apply for an award you must provide as much of the requested information as possible. Failure to provide information may delay or prevent processing your request for an award; providing false information may subject you to penalties.

You are not required to provide the information requested on a form that is subject to the Paperwork Reduction Act unless the form displays a valid OMB control number. Books or records relating to a form or its instructions must be retained as long as their contents may become material in the administration of any internal revenue law. Generally, tax returns and return information are confidential, as required by 26 U.S.C. 6103.

The time needed to complete this form will vary depending on individual circumstances. The estimated average time is 35 minutes. If you have comments concerning the accuracy of these time estimates or suggestions for making this form simpler, we would be happy to hear from you. You can email us at *taxforms@irs.gov (please type "Forms Comment" on the subject line) or write to the Internal Revenue Service, Tax Forms Coordinating Committee, SE: W: CAR: MP: T: T: SP, 1111 Constitution Ave. NW, IR-6406, Washington, DC 20224.

Send the completed Form 211 to the above Washington address of the Whistleblower Office. Do NOT send the Form 211 to the Tax Forms Coordinating Committee.

Form **211** (Rev. 12-2007)   Catalog Number 16571S   publish.no.irs.gov   Department of the Treasury-**Internal Revenue Service**

2

SEC Form TCR—Tip, Complaint or Referral

Copies of this form are available at www.sec.gov/about/forms/formtcr.pdf.

UNITED STATES
SECURITIES AND EXCHANGE COMMISSION
Washington, DC 20549

FORM TCR
TIP, COMPLAINT OR REFERRAL

A. INFORMATION ABOUT YOU			
COMPLAINANT 1:			
1. Last Name		First	M.I.
2. Street Address			Apartment/ Unit #
City	State/ Province	ZIP/ Postal Code	Country
3. Telephone	Alt. Phone	E-mail Address	Preferred method of communication
4. Occupation			
COMPLAINANT 2:			
1. Last Name		First	M.I.
2. Street Address			Apartment/ Unit #
City	State/ Province	ZIP/ Postal Code	Country
3. Telephone	Alt. Phone	E-mail Address	Preferred method of communication
4. Occupation			

B. ATTORNEY'S INFORMATION (If Applicable - See Instructions)			
1. Attorney's Name			
2. Firm Name			
3. Street Address			
City	State/ Province	ZIP/ Postal Code	Country
4. Telephone	Fax	E-mail Address	

C. TELL US ABOUT THE INDIVIDUAL OR ENTITY YOU HAVE A COMPLAINT AGAINST

INDIVIDUAL/ENTITY 1:

If an individual, specify profession:

1. Type: ☐ Individual ☐ Entity

If an entity, specify type:

2. Name

3. Street Address			Apartment/ Unit #
City	State/ Province	ZIP/ Postal Code	Country
4. Phone	E-mail Address		Internet address

INDIVIDUAL/ENTITY 2:

If an individual, specify profession:

1. Type: ☐ Individual ☐ Entity

If an entity, specify type:

2. Name

3. Street Address			Apartment/ Unit #
City	State/ Province	ZIP/ Postal Code	Country
4. Phone	E-mail Address		Internet Address

D. TELL US ABOUT YOUR COMPLAINT

1. Occurrence Date (mm/dd/yyyy): / /   2. Nature of complaint:

3a. Has the complainant or counsel had any prior communication(s) with the SEC concerning this matter?   YES ☐   NO ☐

3b. If the answer to 3a is "Yes," name of SEC staff member with whom the complainant or counsel communicated

4a. Has the complainant or counsel provided the information to any other agency or organization, or has any other agency or organization requested the information or related information from you?   YES ☐   NO ☐

4b. If the answer to 4a is "Yes," please provide details. Use additional sheets if necessary.

4c. Name and contact information for point of contact at agency or organization, if known

5a. Does this complaint relate to an entity of which the complainant is or was an officer, director, counsel, employee, consultant or contractor?

YES ☐   NO ☐

5b. If the answer to question 5a is "yes," has the complainant reported this violation to his or her supervisor, compliance office, whistleblower hotline, ombudsman, or any other available mechanism at the entity for reporting violations?   YES ☐   NO ☐

5c. If the answer to question 5b is "yes," please provide details. Use additional sheets if necessary.

5d. Date on which the complainant took the action(s) described in question 5b (mm/dd/yyyy):   /   /

6a. Has the complainant taken any other action regarding your complaint?   YES ☐   NO ☐

6b. If the answer to question 6a is "yes," please provide details. Use additional sheets if necessary.

7a. Type of security or investment, if relevant

7b. Name of issuer or security, if relevant	7c. Security/ Ticker Symbol or CUSIP no.

8. State in detail all facts pertinent to the alleged violation. Explain why the complainant believes the acts described constitute a violation of the federal securities laws. Use additional sheets if necessary.

9. Describe all supporting materials in the complainant's possession and the availability and location of any additional supporting materials not in complainant's possession. Use additional sheets, if necessary.

10. Describe how and from whom the complainant obtained the information that supports this claim. If any information was obtained from an attorney or in a communication where an attorney was present, identify such information with as much particularity as possible. In addition, if any information was obtained from a public source, identify the source with as much particularity as possible. Attach additional sheets if necessary.

11. Identify with particularity any documents or other information in your submission that you believe could reasonably be expected to reveal your identity and explain the basis for your belief that your identity would be revealed if the documents were disclosed to a third party.

12. Provide any additional information you think may be relevant.

E. ELIGIBILITY REQUIREMENTS AND OTHER INFORMATION

1. Are you, or were you at the time you acquired the original information you are submitting to us, a member, officer or employee of the Department of Justice, the Securities and Exchange Commission, the Comptroller of the Currency, the Board of Governors of the Federal Reserve System, the Federal Deposit Insurance Corporation, the Office of Thrift Supervision; the Public Company Accounting Oversight Board; any law enforcement organization; or any national securities exchange, registered securities association, registered clearing agency, or the Municipal Securities Rulemaking Board?

YES ☐   NO ☐

2. Are you, or were you at the time you acquired the original information you are submitting to us, a member, officer or employee of a foreign government, any political subdivision, department, agency, or instrumentality of a foreign government, or any other foreign financial regulatory authority as that term is defined in Section 3(a)(52) of the Securities Exchange Act of 1934 (15 U.S.C. §78c(a)(52))?

YES ☐   NO ☐

3. Did you acquire the information being provided to us through the performance of an engagement required under the federal securities laws by an independent public accountant?

YES ☐   NO ☐

4. Are you providing this information pursuant to a cooperation agreement with the SEC or another agency or organization?

YES ☐   NO ☐

5. Are you a spouse, parent, child, or sibling of a member or employee of the SEC, or do you reside in the same household as a member or employee of the SEC?

YES ☐   NO ☐

6. Are you providing this information before you (or anyone representing you) received any request, inquiry or demand that relates to the subject matter of your submission (i) from the SEC, (ii) in connection with an investigation, inspection or examination by the Public Company Accounting Oversight Board, or any self-regulatory organization; or (iii) in connection with an investigation by the Congress, any other authority of the federal government, or a state Attorney General or securities regulatory authority?

YES ☐   NO ☐

7. Are you currently a subject or target of a criminal investigation, or have you been convicted of a criminal violation, in connection with the information you are submitting to the SEC?

YES ☐   NO ☐

8. Did you acquire the information being provided to us from any person described in questions E1 through E7?

YES ☐   NO ☐

9. Use this space to provide additional details relating to your responses to questions 1 through 8. Use additional sheets if necessary.

F. WHISTLEBLOWER'S DECLARATION

I declare under penalty of perjury under the laws of the United States that the information contained herein is true, correct and complete to the best of my knowledge, information and belief. I fully understand that I may be subject to prosecution and ineligible for a whistleblower award if, in my submission of information, my other dealings with the SEC, or my dealings with another authority in connection with a related action, I knowingly and willfully make any false, fictitious, or fraudulent statements or representations, or use any false writing or document knowing that the writing or document contains any false, fictitious, or fraudulent statement or entry.

Print name

Signature	Date

G. COUNSEL CERTIFICATION

I certify that I have reviewed this form for completeness and accuracy and that the information contained herein is true, correct and complete to the best of my knowledge, information and belief. I further certify that I have verified the identity of the whistleblower on whose behalf this form is being submitted by viewing the whistleblower's valid, unexpired government issued identification (e.g., driver's license, passport) and will retain an original, signed copy of this form, with Section F signed by the whistleblower, in my records. I further certify that I have obtained the whistleblower's non-waiveable consent to provide the Commission with his or her original signed Form TCR upon request in the event that the Commission requests it due to concerns that the whistleblower may have knowingly and willfully made false, fictitious, or fraudulent statements or representations, or used any false writing or document knowing that the writing or document contains any false fictitious or fraudulent statement or entry; and that I consent to be legally obligated to do so within 7 calendar days of receiving such a request from the Commission.

Signature	Date

Privacy Act Statement

This notice is given under the Privacy Act of 1974. This form may be used by anyone wishing to provide the SEC with information concerning a possible violation of the federal securities laws. We are authorized to request information from you by various laws: Sections 19 and 20 of the Securities Act of 1933, Sections 21 and 21F of the Securities Exchange Act of 1934, Section 321 of the Trust Indenture Act of 1939, Section 42 of the Investment Company Act of 1940, Section 209 of the Investment Advisers Act of 1940 and Title 17 of the Code of Federal Regulations, Section 202.5.

Our principal purpose in requesting information is to gather facts in order to determine whether any person has violated, is violating, or is about to violate any provision of the federal securities laws or rules for which we have enforcement authority. Facts developed may, however, constitute violations of other laws or rules. Further, if you are submitting information for the SEC's whistleblower award program pursuant to Section 21F of the Securities Exchange Act of 1934 (Exchange Act), the information provided will be used in connection with our evaluation of your or your client's eligibility and other factors relevant to our determination of whether to pay an award to you or your client.

The information provided may be used by SEC personnel for purposes of investigating possible violations of, or to conduct investigations authorized by, the federal securities law; in proceedings in which the federal securities laws are in issue or the SEC is a party; to coordinate law enforcement activities between the SEC and other federal, state, local or foreign law enforcement agencies, securities self-regulatory organizations, and foreign securities authorities; and pursuant to other routine uses as described in SEC-42 "Enforcement Files."

Furnishing the information requested herein is voluntary. However, a decision not to provide any of the requested information, or failure to provide complete information, may affect our evaluation of your submission. Further, if you are submitting this information for the SEC whistleblower program and you do not execute the Whistleblower Declaration or, if you are submitting information anonymously, identify the attorney representing you in this matter, you may not be considered for an award.

Questions concerning this form may be directed to the SEC Office of the Whistleblower, 100 F Street, NE, Washington, DC 20549, Tel. (202) 551-4790, Fax (703) 813-9322.

Submission Procedures

- After manually completing this Form TCR, please send it by mail or delivery to the SEC Office of the Whistleblower, 100 F. Street, NE, Washington, DC 20549, or by facsimile to (703) 813-9322.

- You have the right to submit information anonymously. If you are submitting anonymously and you want to be considered for a whistleblower award, however, you *must* be represented by an attorney in this matter and Section B of this form must be completed. Otherwise, you may, but are not required to, have an attorney. If you are not represented by an attorney in this matter, you may leave Section B blank.

- **If you are submitting information for the SEC's whistleblower award program, you *must* submit your information either using this Form TCR or electronically through the SEC's Electronic Data Collection System, available on the SEC website at [insert link].**

Instructions for Completing Form TCR:

Section A: Information about You

Questions 1–3: Please provide the following information about yourself:

- Last name, first name, and middle initial

- Complete address, including city, state and zip code

- Telephone number and, if available, an alternate number where you can be reached

- Your e-mail address (to facilitate communications, we strongly encourage you to provide your e-mail address),

- Your preferred method of communication; and

- Your occupation

Section B: Information about Your Attorney. Complete this section only if you are represented by an attorney in this matter. You must be represented by an attorney, and this section must be completed, if you are submitting your information anonymously and you want to be considered for the SEC's whistleblower award program.

Questions 1–4: Provide the following information about the attorney representing you in this matter:

- Attorney's name
- Firm name
- Complete address, including city, state and zip code
- Telephone number and fax number, and
- E-mail address

Section C: Tell Us about the Individual and/or Entity You Have a Complaint Against. If your complaint relates to more than two individuals and/or entities, you may attach additional sheets.

Question 1: Choose one of the following that best describes the individual or entity to which your complaint relates:

- **For Individuals**: accountant, analyst, attorney, auditor, broker, compliance officer, employee, executive officer or director, financial planner, fund manager, investment advisor representative, stock promoter, trustee, unknown, or other (specify).
- **For Entity**: bank, broker-dealer, clearing agency, day trading firm, exchange, Financial Industry Regulatory Authority, insurance company, investment advisor, investment advisor representative, investment company, Individual Retirement Account or 401(k) custodian/administrator, market maker, municipal securities dealers, mutual fund, newsletter company/investment publication company, on-line trading firm, private fund company (including hedge fund, private equity fund, venture capital fund, or real estate fund), private/closely held company, publicly held company, transfer agent/paying agent/registrar, underwriter, unknown, or other (specify).

Questions 2–4: For each subject, provide the following information, if known:

- Full name
- Complete address, including city, state and zip code
- Telephone number,
- E-mail address, and
- Internet address, if applicable

Section D: Tell Us about Your Complaint

Question 1: State the date (mm/dd/yyyy) that the alleged conduct began.

Question 2: Choose the option that you believe best describes the nature of your complaint. If you are alleging more than one violation, please list all that you believe may apply. Use additional sheets if necessary.

- Theft/misappropriation (advance fee fraud; lost or stolen securities; hacking of account)
- Misrepresentation/omission (false/misleading marketing/sales literature; inaccurate, misleading or non-disclosure by Broker-Dealer, Investment Adviser and Associated Person; false/material misstatements in firm research that were basis of transaction)
- Offering fraud (Ponzi/pyramid scheme; other offering fraud)
- Registration violations (unregistered securities offering)
- Trading (after hours trading; algorithmic trading; front-running; insider trading; manipulation of securities/prices; market timing; inaccurate quotes/pricing information; program trading; short selling; trading suspensions; volatility)
- Fees/mark-ups/commissions (excessive or unnecessary administrative fees; excessive commissions or sales fees; failure to disclose fees; insufficient notice of change in fees; negotiated fee problems; excessive mark-ups/markdowns; excessive or otherwise improper spreads)
- Corporate disclosure/reporting/other issuer matter (audit; corporate governance; conflicts of interest by management; executive compensation; failure to notify shareholders of corporate events; false/misleading financial statements, offering documents, press

releases, proxy materials; failure to file reports; financial fraud; Foreign Corrupt Practices Act violations; going private transactions; mergers and acquisitions; restrictive legends, including 144 issues; reverse stock splits; selective disclosure—Regulation FD, 17 CFR 243; shareholder proposals; stock options for employees; stock splits; tender offers)

- Sales and advisory practices (background information on past violations/integrity; breach of fiduciary duty/responsibility (IA); failure to disclose breakpoints; churning/excessive trading; cold calling; conflict of interest; abuse of authority in discretionary trading; failure to respond to investor; guarantee against loss/promise to buy back shares; high pressure sales techniques; instructions by client not followed; investment objectives not followed; margin; poor investment advice; Regulation E (Electronic Transfer Act); Regulation S-P, 17 CFR 248, (privacy issues); solicitation methods (non-cold calling; seminars); suitability; unauthorized transactions)

- Operational (bond call; bond default; difficulty buying/selling securities; confirmations/statements; proxy materials/prospectus; delivery of funds/proceeds; dividend and interest problems; exchanges/switches of mutual funds with fund family; margin (illegal extension of margin credit, Regulation T restrictions, unauthorized margin transactions); online issues (trading system operation); settlement (including T+1 or T=3 concerns); stock certificates; spam; tax reporting problems; titling securities (difficulty titling ownership); trade execution

- Customer accounts (abandoned or inactive accounts; account administration and processing; identity theft affecting account; IPOs: problems with IPO allocation or eligibility; inaccurate valuation of Net Asset Value; transfer of account)

- Comments/complaints about SEC, Self-Regulatory Organization, and Securities Investor Protection Corporation processes & programs (arbitration: bias by arbitrators/forum, failure to pay/comply with award, mandatory arbitration requirements, procedural problems or delays; SEC: complaints about enforcement actions, complaints about rulemaking, failure to act; Self-Regulatory Organization: failure to act; Investor Protection:

inadequacy of laws or rules; SIPC: customer protection, proceedings and Broker-Dealer liquidations

- Other (analyst complaints; market maker activities; employer/employee disputes; specify other).

Question 3a:	State whether you or your counsel have had any prior communications with the SEC concerning this matter.
Question 3b:	If the answer to question 3a is yes, provide the name of the SEC staff member with whom you or your counsel communicated.
Question 4a:	Indicate whether you or your counsel have provided the information you are providing to the SEC to any other agency or organization.
Question 4b:	If the answer to question 4a is yes, provide details.
Question 4c:	Provide the name and contact information of the point of contact at the other agency or organization, if known.
Question 5a:	Indicate whether your complaint relates to an entity of which you are, or were in the past, an officer, director, counsel, employee, consultant, or contractor.
Question 5b:	If the answer to question 5a is yes, state whether you have reported this violation to your supervisor, compliance office, whistleblower hotline, ombudsman, or any other available mechanism at the entity for reporting violations.
Question 5c:	If the answer to question 5b is yes, provide details.
Question 5d:	Provide the date on which you took the actions described in questions 5a and 5b.
Question 6a:	Indicate whether you have taken any other action regarding your complaint, including whether you complained to the SEC, another regulator, a law enforcement agency, or any other agency or organization; initiated legal action, mediation or arbitration, or initiated any other action.
Question 6b:	If you answered yes to question 6a, provide details, including the date on which you took the action(s) described, the name of the person or entity to whom you directed any report or complaint and contact information for the person or entity, if known, and the

complete case name, case number, and forum of any legal action you have taken. Use additional sheets if necessary.

Question 7a: Choose from the following the option that you believe best describes the type of security or investment at issue, if applicable:

- 1031 exchanges
- 529 plans
- American Depositary Receipts
- Annuities (equity-indexed annuities, fixed annuities, variable annuities)
- Asset-backed securities
- Auction rate securities
- Banking products (including credit cards)
- Certificates of deposit (CDs)
- Closed-end funds
- Coins and precious metals (gold, silver, etc.)
- Collateralized mortgage obligations (CMOs)
- Commercial paper
- Commodities (currency transactions, futures, stock index options)
- Convertible securities
- Debt (corporate, lower-rated or "junk," municipal)
- Equities (exchange-traded, foreign, Over-the-Counter, unregistered, linked notes)
- Exchange Traded Funds
- Franchises or business ventures
- Hedge funds
- Insurance contracts (not annuities)
- Money-market funds
- Mortgage-backed securities (mortgages, reverse mortgages)
- Mutual funds
- Options (commodity options, index options)

- Partnerships

- Preferred shares

- Prime bank securities/high yield programs

- Promissory notes

- Real estate (real estate investment trusts (REITs))

- Retirement plans (401(k), IRAs)

- Rights and warrants

- Structured note products

- Subprime issues

- Treasury securities

- U.S. government agency securities

- Unit investment trusts (UIT)

- Viaticals and life settlements

- Wrap accounts

- Separately Managed Accounts (SMAs)

- Unknown

- Other (specify)

Question 7b:	Provide the name of the issuer or security, if applicable.
Question 7c:	Provide the ticker symbol or CUSIP number of the security, if applicable.
Question 8:	State in detail all the facts pertinent to the alleged violation. Explain why you believe the facts described constitute a violation of the federal securities laws. Attach additional sheets if necessary.
Question 9:	Describe all supporting materials in your possession and the availability and location of additional supporting materials not in your possession. Attach additional sheets if necessary.
Question 10:	Describe how you obtained the information that supports your allegation. If any information was obtained from an attorney or in a communication where an attorney was present, identify such information with as much particularity as possible. In addition, if

any information was obtained from a public source, identify the source with as much

particularity as possible. Attach additional sheets if necessary.

Question 11:   You may use this space to identify any documents or other information in your

submission that you believe could reasonably be expected to reveal your identity.

Explain the basis for your belief that your identity would be revealed if the documents or

information were disclosed to a third party.

Question 12:   Provide any additional information you think may be relevant.

Section E: Eligibility Requirements

Question 1:   State whether you are currently, or were at the time you acquired the original information

that you are submitting to the SEC, a member, officer, or employee of the Department of

Justice; the Securities and Exchange Commission; the Comptroller of the Currency, the

Board of Governors of the Federal Reserve System, the Federal Deposit Insurance

Corporation, the Office of Thrift Supervision; the Public Company Accounting Oversight

Board; any law enforcement organization; or any national securities exchange, registered

securities association, registered clearing agency, the Municipal Securities Rulemaking

Board.

Question 2:   State whether you are, or were you at the time you acquired the original information you

are submitting to the SEC, a member, officer or employee of a foreign government, any

political subdivision, department, agency, or instrumentality of a foreign government, or

any other foreign financial regulatory authority as that term is defined in Section 3(a)(52)

of the Securities Exchange Act of 1934.

•   Section 3(a)(52) of the Exchange Act (15 U.S.C. §78c(a)(52)) currently defines

"foreign financial regulatory authority" as "any (A) foreign securities authority, (B)

other governmental body or foreign equivalent of a self-regulatory organization

empowered by a foreign government to administer or enforce its laws relating to

the regulation of fiduciaries, trusts, commercial lending, insurance, trading in

contracts of sale of a commodity for future delivery, or other instruments traded on or subject to the rules of a contract market, board of trade, or foreign equivalent, or (C) membership organization a function of which is to regulate participation of its members in activities listed above."

Question 3: State whether you acquired the information you are providing to the SEC through the performance of an engagement required under the securities laws by an independent public accountant.

Question 4: State whether you are providing the information pursuant to a cooperation agreement with the SEC or with any other agency or organization.

Question 5: State whether you are a spouse, parent, child or sibling of a member or employee of the SEC, or whether you reside in the same household as a member or employee of the SEC.

Question 6: State whether you acquired the information you are providing to the SEC from any individual described in questions 1 through 5 of this Section.

Question 7: If you answered "yes" to questions 1 through 6, please provide details.

Question 8a: State whether you are providing the information you are submitting to the SEC before you (or anyone representing you) received any request, inquiry or demand that relates to the subject matter of your submission in connection with: (i) an investigation, inspection or examination by the SEC, the Public Company Accounting Oversight Board, or any self-regulatory organization; or (ii) an investigation by Congress, or any other authority of the federal government, or a state Attorney General or securities regulatory authority.

Question 8b: If you answered "no" to question 8a, please provide details. Use additional sheets if necessary.

Question 9a: State whether you are the subject or target of a criminal investigation or have been convicted of a criminal violation in connection with the information you are submitting to the SEC.

Question 9b: If you answered "yes" to question 9a, please provide details, including the name of the agency or organization that conducted the investigation or initiated the action against you, the name and telephone number of your point of contact at the agency or organization, if available and the investigation/case name and number, if applicable. Use additional sheets, if necessary.

SECTION F: Whistleblower's Declaration.

You must sign this Declaration if you are submitting this information pursuant to the SEC whistleblower program and wish to be considered for an award. If you are submitting your information anonymously, you must still sign this Declaration, and you must provide your attorney with the original of this signed form.

If you are <u>not</u> submitting your information pursuant to the SEC whistleblower program, you do not need to sign this Declaration.

SECTION G: COUNSEL CERTIFICATION

If you are submitting this information pursuant to the SEC whistleblower program and are doing so anonymously, your attorney <u>must</u> sign the Counsel Certification section.

If you are represented in this matter but you are <u>not</u> submitting your information pursuant to the SEC whistleblower program, your attorney does not need to sign the Counsel Certification Section.

SEC Form WB-APP — Application for Award for Original Information Submitted Pursuant to Section 21F of the Securities Exchange Act of 1934

Copies of this form are available at www.sec.gov/about/forms/formwb-app.pdf.

UNITED STATES
SECURITIES AND EXCHANGE COMMISSION
Washington, DC 20549

FORM WB-APP

**APPLICATION FOR AWARD FOR ORIGINAL INFORMATION SUBMITTED
PURSUANT TO SECTION 21F OF THE SECURITIES EXCHANGE ACT OF 1934**

A. APPLICANT'S INFORMATION (REQUIRED FOR ALL SUBMISSIONS)				
1. Last Name	First		M.I.	Social Security No.
2. Street Address				Apartment/ Unit #
City	State/ Province	ZIP Code		Country
3. Telephone	Alt. Phone	E-mail Address		

B. ATTORNEY'S INFORMATION (IF APPLICABLE – SEE INSTRUCTIONS)				
1. Attorney's name				
2. Firm Name				
3. Street Address				
City	State/ Province	ZIP Code		Country
4. Telephone	Fax	E-mail Address		

C. TIP/COMPLAINT DETAILS

1. Manner in which original information was submitted to SEC: SEC website ☐ Mail ☐ Fax ☐ Other ☐	
2a. Tip, Complaint or Referral number	2b. Date TCR referred to in 2a submitted to SEC / /
2c. Subject(s) of the Tip, Complaint or Referral:	

D. NOTICE OF COVERED ACTION

1. Date of Notice of Covered Action to which claim relates: / /	2. Notice Number:
3a. Case Name	3b. Case Number

E. CLAIMS PERTAINING TO RELATED ACTIONS

1. Name of agency or organization to which you provided your information	
2. Name and contact information for point of contact at agency or organization, if known.	
3a. Date you provided your information / /	3b. Date action filed by agency/organization / /
4a. Case Name	4b. Case number

F. ELIGIBILITY REQUIREMENTS AND OTHER INFORMATION

1. Are you, or were you at the time you acquired the original information you submitted to us, a member, officer or employee of the Department of Justice, the Securities and Exchange Commission, the Comptroller of the Currency, the Board of Governors of the Federal Reserve System, the Federal Deposit Insurance Corporation, the Office of Thrift Supervision; the Public Company Accounting Oversight Board; any law enforcement organization; or any national securities exchange, registered securities association, registered clearing agency, the Municipal Securities Rulemaking Board?   YES ☐   NO ☐

2. Are you, or were you at the time you acquired the original information you submitted to us, a member, officer or employee of a foreign government, any political subdivision, department, agency, or instrumentality of a foreign government, or any other foreign financial regulatory authority as that term is defined in Section 3(a)(52) of the Securities Exchange Act of 1934 (15 U.S.C. §78c(a)(52))?
YES ☐　　　NO ☐

3. Did you obtain the information you are providing to us through the performance of an engagement required under the federal securities laws by an independent public accountant?
YES ☐　　　NO ☐

4. Did you provide the information identified in Section C above pursuant to a cooperation agreement with the SEC or another agency or organization?
YES ☐　　　NO ☐

5. Are you a spouse, parent, child, or sibling of a member or employee of the Commission, or do you reside in the same household as a member or employee of the Commission?
YES ☐　　　NO ☐

6. Did you acquire the information you are providing to us from any person described in questions F1 through F5?
YES ☐　　　NO ☐

7. If you answered "yes" to any of questions 1 through 6 above, please provide details. Use additional sheets if necessary.

8a. Did you provide the information identified in Section C above before you (or anyone representing you) received any request, inquiry or demand that relates to the subject matter of your submission (i) from the SEC, (ii) in connection with an investigation, inspection or examination by the Public Company Accounting Oversight Board, or any self-regulatory organization; or (iii) in connection with an investigation by the Congress, any other authority of the federal government, or a state Attorney General or securities regulatory authority?
YES ☐　　　NO ☐

8b. If you answered "yes" to question 8a, please provide details. Use additional sheets if necessary.

9a. Are you currently a subject or target of a criminal investigation, or have you been convicted of a criminal violation, in connection with the information upon which your application for an award is based?
YES ☐　　　NO ☐

9b. If you answered "Yes" to question 9a, please provide details. Use additional sheets if necessary.

G. ENTITLEMENT TO AWARD

Explain the basis for your belief that you are entitled to an award in connection with your submission of information to us, or to another agency in a related action. Provide any additional information you think may be relevant in light of the criteria for determining the amount of an award set forth in Rule 21F-6 under the Securities Exchange Act of 1934. Include any supporting documents in your possession or control, and attach additional sheets, if necessary.

H. DECLARATION

I declare under penalty of perjury under the laws of the United States that the information contained herein is true, correct and complete to the best of my knowledge, information and belief. I fully understand that I may be subject to prosecution and ineligible for a whistleblower award if, in my submission of information, my other dealings with the SEC, or my dealings with another authority in connection with a related action, I knowingly and willfully make any false, fictitious, or fraudulent statements or representations, or use any false writing or document knowing that the writing or document contains any false, fictitious, or fraudulent statement or entry.

Signature	Date

Privacy Act Statement

This notice is given under the Privacy Act of 1974. We are authorized to request information from you by Section 21F of the Securities Exchange Act of 1934. Our principal purpose in requesting this information is to assist in our evaluation of your eligibility and other factors relevant to our determination of whether to pay a whistleblower award to you under Section 21F of the Exchange Act.

However, the information provided may be used by SEC personnel for purposes of investigating possible violations of, or to conduct investigations authorized by, the federal securities law; in proceedings in which the federal securities laws are in issue or the SEC is a party; to coordinate law enforcement activities between the SEC and other federal, state, local or foreign law enforcement agencies, securities self-regulatory organizations, and foreign securities authorities; and pursuant to other routine uses as described in SEC-42 "Enforcement Files."

Furnishing this information is voluntary, but a decision not to do so, or failure to provide complete information, may result in our denying a whistleblower award to you, or may affect our evaluation of the appropriate amount of an award. Further, if you are submitting this information for the SEC whistleblower program and you do not execute the Declaration, you may not be considered for an award.

Questions concerning this form may be directed to the SEC Office of the Whistleblower, 100 F Street, NE, Washington, DC 20549-5631, Tel. (202) 551-4790, Fax (703) 813-9322.

General

- This form should be used by persons making a claim for a whistleblower award in connection with information provided to the SEC or to another agency in a related action. In order to be deemed eligible for an award, you must meet all the requirements set forth in Section 21F of the Securities Exchange Act of 1934 and the rules thereunder.

- You must sign the Form WB-APP as the claimant. If you provided your information to the SEC anonymously, you must now disclose your identity on this form and your identity must be verified in a form and manner that is acceptable to the Office of the Whistleblower prior to the payment of any award.

- o If you are filing your claim in connection with information that you provided to the SEC, then your Form WB-APP, and any attachments thereto, **must be received by the SEC Office of the Whistleblower within sixty (60) days of the date of the Notice of Covered Action to which the claim relates.**

- o If you are filing your claim in connection with information you provided to another agency in a related action, then your Form WB-APP, and any attachments thereto, must be received by the SEC Office of the Whistleblower as follows:
    - If a final order imposing monetary sanctions has been entered in a related action at the time you submit your claim for an award in connection with a Commission action, **you must submit your claim for an award in that related action on the same Form WB-APP that you use for the Commission action.**

    - If a final order imposing monetary sanctions in a related action has not been entered at the time you submit your claim for an award in connection with a Commission action, **you must submit your claim on Form WB-APP within sixty (60) days of the issuance of a final order imposing sanctions in the related action.**

- You must submit your Form WB-APP to us in one of the following two ways:
    - o By mailing or delivering the signed form to the SEC Office of the Whistleblower, 100 F Street NE, Washington, DC 20549-5631; or

    - o By faxing the signed form to (703) 813-9322.

<u>**Instructions for Completing Form WB-APP**</u>

Section A: Applicant's Information

Questions 1–3: Provide the following information about yourself:

- First and last name, and middle initial

- Complete address, including city, state and zip code

- Telephone number and, if available, an alternate number where you can be reached

- E-mail address

Section B: Attorney's Information. If you are represented by an attorney in this matter, provide the information requested. If you are not represented by an attorney in this matter, leave this Section blank.

Questions 1–4: Provide the following information about the attorney representing you in this matter:

- Attorney's name

- Firm name

- Complete address, including city, state and zip code

- Telephone number and fax number, and

- E-mail address.

Section C: Tip/Complaint Details

Question 1:   Indicate the manner in which your original information was submitted to the SEC.

Question 2a: Include the TCR (Tip, Complaint or Referral) number to which this claim relates.

Question 2b: Provide the date on which you submitted your information to the SEC.

Question 2c: Provide the name of the individual(s) or entity(s) to which your complaint related.

Section D: Notice of Covered Action

The process for making a claim for a whistleblower award begins with the publication of a "Notice of a Covered Action" on the Commission's website. This notice is published whenever a judicial or administrative action brought by the Commission results in the imposition of monetary sanctions exceeding $1,000,000. The Notice is published on the Commission's website subsequent to the entry of a final judgment or order in the action that by itself, or collectively with other judgments or orders previously entered in the action, exceeds the $1,000,000 threshold.

Question 1:   Provide the date of the Notice of Covered Action to which this claim relates.

Question 2:   Provide the notice number of the Notice of Covered Action.

Question 3a: Provide the case name referenced in Notice of Covered Action.

Question 3b: Provide the case number referenced in Notice of Covered Action.

Section E: Claims Pertaining to Related Actions

Question 1:   Provide the name of the agency or organization to which you provided your information.

Question 2:   Provide the name and contact information for your point of contact at the agency or organization, if known.

Question 3a: Provide the date on which you provided your information to the agency or organization referenced in question E1.

Question 3b: Provide the date on which the agency or organization referenced in question E1 filed the related action that was based upon the information you provided.

Question 4a: Provide the case name of the related action.

Question 4b: Provide the case number of the related action.

Section F: Eligibility Requirements

Question 1:   State whether you are currently, or were at the time you acquired the original information that you submitted to the SEC, a member, officer, or employee of the Department of Justice; the Securities and Exchange Commission; the Comptroller of the Currency, the Board of Governors of the Federal Reserve System, the Federal Deposit Insurance Corporation, the Office of Thrift Supervision; the Public Company Accounting Oversight Board; any law enforcement organization; or any national securities exchange, registered securities association, registered clearing agency, the Municipal Securities Rulemaking Board.

Question 2:   State whether you are, or were at the time you acquired the original information you submitted to the SEC, a member, officer or employee of a foreign government, any political subdivision, department, agency, or instrumentality of a foreign government, or any other foreign financial regulatory authority as that term is defined in Section 3(a)(52) of the Securities Exchange Act of 1934.

- Section 3(a)(52) of the Exchange Act (15 U.S.C. §78c(a)(52)) currently defines "foreign financial regulatory authority" as "any (A) foreign securities authority, (B) other governmental body or foreign equivalent of a self-regulatory organization empowered by a foreign government to administer or enforce its laws relating to the regulation of fiduciaries, trusts, commercial lending, insurance, trading in contracts of sale of a commodity for future delivery, or other instruments traded on or subject to the rules of a contract market, board of trade, or foreign equivalent, or other financial activities, or (C) membership organization a function of which is to regulate participation of its members in activities listed above."

Question 3:   Indicate whether you acquired the information you provided to the SEC through the performance of an engagement required under the securities laws by an independent public accountant.

Question 4:   State whether you provided the information submitted to the SEC pursuant to a cooperation agreement with the SEC or with any other agency or organization.

Question 5:   State whether you are a spouse, parent, child or sibling of a member or employee of the Commission, or whether you reside in the same household as a member or employee of the Commission.

Question 6:   State whether you acquired the information you are providing to the SEC from any individual described in questions 1 through 5 of this Section.

Question 7:   If you answered "yes" to questions 1 through 6, please provide details.

Question 8a: State whether you provided the information identified submitted to the SEC before you (or anyone representing you) received any request, inquiry or demand from the SEC,

Congress, or any other federal, state or local authority, or any self-regulatory
organization, or the Public Company Accounting Oversight Board about a matter to which
the information in your submission was relevant.

Question 8b: If you answered "no" to question 8a, please provide details. Use additional sheets if
necessary.

Question 9a: State whether you are the subject or target of a criminal investigation or have been
convicted of a criminal violation in connection with the information upon which your
application for award is based.

Question 9b: If you answered "yes" to question 9a, please provide details, including the name of the
agency or organization that conducted the investigation or initiated the action against
you, the name and telephone number of your point of contact at the agency or
organization, if available, and the investigation/case name and number, if applicable. Use
additional sheets, if necessary. If you previously provided this information on Form WB-
DEC, you may leave this question blank, unless your response has changed since the
time you submitted your Form WB-DEC.

Section G: Entitlement to Award

This section is optional. Use this section to explain the basis for your belief that you are
entitled to an award in connection with your submission of information to us or to another agency
in connection with a related action. Specifically address how you believe you voluntarily provided
the Commission with original information that led to the successful enforcement of a judicial or
administrative action filed by the Commission, or a related action. Refer to Rules 21F-3 and 21F-
4 under the Exchange Act for further information concerning the relevant award criteria. You may
attach additional sheets, if necessary.

Rule 21F-6 under the Exchange Act provides that in determining the amount of an award, the
Commission will evaluate the following factors: (a) the significance of the information provided by
a whistleblower to the success of the Commission action or related action; (b) the degree of
assistance provided by the whistleblower and any legal representative of the whistleblower in the

Commission action or related action; (c) the programmatic interest of the Commission in deterring violations of the securities laws by making awards to whistleblowers who provide information that leads to the successful enforcement of such laws; and (d) whether the award otherwise enhances the Commission's ability to enforce the federal securities laws, protect investors, and encourage the submission of high quality information from whistleblowers. Address these factors in your response as well.

Additional information about the criteria the Commission may consider in determining the amount of an award is available on the Commission's website at [insert WBO web page address]

Section H: Declaration

This section must be signed by the claimant.

SEC Whistleblower Rules

This appendix presents the detailed SEC whistleblower rules.

 ## § 240.21F-1 GENERAL

Section 21F of the Securities Exchange Act of 1934 ("Exchange Act") (15 U.S.C. 78u-6), entitled "Securities Whistleblower Incentives and Protection," requires the Securities and Exchange Commission ("Commission") to pay awards, subject to certain limitations and conditions, to whistleblowers who provide the Commission with original information about violations of the federal securities laws. These rules describe the whistleblower program that the Commission has established to implement the provisions of Section 21F, and explain the procedures you will need to follow in order to be eligible for an award. You should read these procedures carefully because the failure to take certain required steps within the time frames described in these rules may disqualify you from receiving an award for which you otherwise may be eligible. Unless expressly provided for in these rules, no person is authorized to make any offer or promise, or otherwise to bind the Commission with respect to the payment of any award or the amount thereof. The Securities and Exchange Commission's Office of the Whistleblower administers our whistleblower program. Questions about the program or these rules should be directed to the SEC Office of the Whistle-blower, 100 F Street, N.E., Washington, DC 20549-5631.

§ 240.21F-2 WHISTLEBLOWER STATUS AND RETALIATION PROTECTION

(a) <u>Definition of a whistleblower</u>. (1) You are a whistleblower if, alone or jointly with others, you provide the Commission with information pursuant to the procedures set forth in § 240.21F-9(a) of this chapter, and the information relates to a possible violation of the federal securities laws (including any rules or regulations thereunder) that has occurred, is ongoing, or is about to occur. A whistleblower must be an individual. A company or another entity is not eligible to be a whistleblower.

(2) To be eligible for an award, you must submit original information to the Commission in accordance with the procedures and conditions described in §§ 240.21F-4, 240.21F-8, and 240.21F-9 of this chapter.

(b) Prohibition against retaliation: (1) For purposes of the anti-retaliation protections afforded by Section 21F(h)(1) of the Exchange Act (15 U.S.C. 78u-6(h)(1)), you are a whistleblower if:

(i) You possess a reasonable belief that the information you are providing relates to a possible securities law violation (or, where applicable, to a possible violation of the provisions set forth in 18 U.S.C. 1514A(a)) that has occurred, is ongoing, or is about to occur, and;

(ii) You provide that information in a manner described in Section 21F(h)(1)(A) of the Exchange Act (15 U.S.C. 78u-6(h)(1)(A)).

(iii) The anti-retaliation protections apply whether or not you satisfy the requirements, procedures and conditions to qualify for an award.

(2) Section 21F(h)(1) of the Exchange Act (15 U.S.C. 78u-6(h)(1)), including any rules promulgated thereunder, shall be enforceable in an action or proceeding brought by the Commission.

§ 240.21F-3 PAYMENT OF AWARDS

(a) <u>Commission actions</u>: Subject to the eligibility requirements described in §§ 240.21F-2, 240.21F-8, and 240.21F-16 of this chapter, the Commission will pay an award or awards to one or more whistleblowers who:

(1) Voluntarily provide the Commission

(2) With original information

(3) That leads to the successful enforcement by the Commission of a federal court or administrative action

(4) In which the Commission obtains monetary sanctions totaling more than $1,000,000.

Note to paragraph (a): The terms voluntarily, original information, leads to successful enforcement, action, and monetary sanctions are defined in § 240.21F-4 of this chapter.

(b) Related actions: The Commission will also pay an award based on amounts collected in certain related actions.

(1) A related action is a judicial or administrative action that is brought by:

(i) The Attorney General of the United States;

(ii) An appropriate regulatory authority;

(iii) A self-regulatory organization; or

(iv) A state attorney general in a criminal case, and is based on the same original information that the whistleblower voluntarily provided to the Commission, and that led the Commission to obtain monetary sanctions totaling more than $1,000,000.

Note to paragraph (b): The terms appropriate regulatory authority and self-regulatory organization are defined in § 240.21F-4 of this chapter.

(2) In order for the Commission to make an award in connection with a related action, the Commission must determine that the same original information that the whistleblower gave to the Commission also led to the successful enforcement of the related action under the same criteria described in these rules for awards made in connection with Commission actions. The Commission may seek assistance and confirmation from the authority bringing the related action in making this determination. The Commission will deny an award in connection with the related action if:

(i) The Commission determines that the criteria for an award are not satisfied; or

(ii) The Commission is unable to make a determination because the Office of the Whistleblower could not obtain sufficient and reliable information that could be used as the basis for an award determination pursuant to § 240.21F-12(a) of this chapter. Additional procedures apply to the payment of awards in related actions. These procedures are described in §§ 240.21F-11 and 240.21F-14 of this chapter.

(3) The Commission will not make an award to you for a related action if you have already been granted an award by the Commodity Futures Trading

Commission ("CFTC") for that same action pursuant to its whistleblower award program under Section 23 of the Commodity Exchange Act (7 U.S.C. 26). Similarly, if the CFTC has previously denied an award to you in a related action, you will be precluded from relitigating any issues before the Commission that the CFTC resolved against you as part of the award denial.

§ 240.21F-4 OTHER DEFINITIONS

(a) <u>Voluntary submission of information</u>. (1) Your submission of information is made <u>voluntarily</u> within the meaning of §§ 240.21F-1 through 240.21F-17 of this chapter if you provide your submission before a request, inquiry, or demand that relates to the subject matter of your submission is directed to you or anyone representing you (such as an attorney):

(i) By the Commission;

(ii) In connection with an investigation, inspection, or examination by the Public Company Accounting Oversight Board, or any self-regulatory organization; or

(iii) In connection with an investigation by Congress, any other authority of the federal government, or a state Attorney General or securities regulatory authority.

(2) If the Commission or any of these other authorities direct a request, inquiry, or demand as described in paragraph (1) of this section to you or your representative first, your submission will not be considered voluntary, and you will not be eligible for an award, even if your response is not compelled by subpoena or other applicable law. However, your submission of information to the Commission will be considered voluntary if you voluntarily provided the same information to one of the other authorities identified above prior to receiving a request, inquiry, or demand from the Commission.

(3) In addition, your submission will not be considered voluntary if you are required to report your original information to the Commission as a result of a pre-existing legal duty, a contractual duty that is owed to the Commission or to one of the other authorities set forth in paragraph (1) of this section, or a duty that arises out of a judicial or administrative order.

(b) *Original information.* (1) In order for your whistleblower submission to be considered <u>original information</u>, it must be:

(i) Derived from your independent knowledge or independent analysis;

(ii) Not already known to the Commission from any other source, unless you are the original source of the information;

(iii) Not exclusively derived from an allegation made in a judicial or administrative hearing, in a governmental report, hearing, audit, or investigation, or from the news media, unless you are a source of the information; and

(iv) Provided to the Commission for the first time after July 21, 2010 (the date of enactment of the *Dodd-Frank Wall Street Reform and Consumer Protection Act*).

(2) Independent knowledge means factual information in your possession that is not derived from publicly available sources. You may gain independent knowledge from your experiences, communications and observations in your business or social interactions.

(3) Independent analysis means your own analysis, whether done alone or in combination with others. Analysis means your examination and evaluation of information that may be publicly available, but which reveals information that is not generally known or available to the public.

(4) The Commission will not consider information to be derived from your independent knowledge or independent analysis in any of the following circumstances:

(i) If you obtained the information through a communication that was subject to the attorney-client privilege, unless disclosure of that information would otherwise be permitted by an attorney pursuant to § 205.3(d)(2) of this chapter, the applicable state attorney conduct rules, or otherwise;

(ii) If you obtained the information in connection with the legal representation of a client on whose behalf you or your employer or firm are providing services, and you seek to use the information to make a whistleblower submission for your own benefit, unless disclosure would otherwise be permitted by an attorney pursuant to § 205.3(d)(2) of this chapter, the applicable state attorney conduct rules, or otherwise; or

(iii) In circumstances not covered by paragraphs (b)(4)(i) or (b)(4)(ii) of this section, if you obtained the information because you were:

(A) An officer, director, trustee, or partner of an entity and another person informed you of allegations of misconduct, or you learned the information in connection with the entity's processes for identifying, reporting, and addressing possible violations of law;

(B) An employee whose principal duties involve compliance or internal audit responsibilities, or you were employed by or otherwise associated with a firm retained to perform compliance or internal audit functions for an entity;

(C) Employed by or otherwise associated with a firm retained to conduct an inquiry or investigation into possible violations of law; or

(D) An employee of, or other person associated with, a public accounting firm, if you obtained the information through the performance of an

244 ■ Appendix Four

engagement required of an independent public accountant under the federal securities laws (other than an audit subject to § 240.21F-8(c)(4) of this chapter), and that information related to a violation by the engagement client or the client's directors, officers or other employees.

(iv) If you obtained the information by a means or in a manner that is determined by a United States court to violate applicable federal or state criminal law; or

(v) Exceptions. Paragraph (b)(4)(iii) of this section shall not apply if:

(A) You have a reasonable basis to believe that disclosure of the information to the Commission is necessary to prevent the relevant entity from engaging in conduct that is likely to cause substantial injury to the financial interest or property of the entity or investors;

(B) You have a reasonable basis to believe that the relevant entity is engaging in conduct that will impede an investigation of the misconduct; or

(C) At least 120 days have elapsed since you provided the information to the relevant entity's audit committee, chief legal officer, chief compliance officer (or their equivalents), or your supervisor, or since you received the information, if you received it under circumstances indicating that the entity's audit committee, chief legal officer, chief compliance officer (or their equivalents), or your supervisor was already aware of the information.

(vi) If you obtained the information from a person who is subject to this section, unless the information is not excluded from that person's use pursuant to this section, or you are providing the Commission with information about possible violations involving that person.

(5) The Commission will consider you to be an <u>original source</u> of the same information that we obtain from another source if the information satisfies the definition of original information and the other source obtained the information from you or your representative. In order to be considered an original source of information that the Commission receives from Congress, any other authority of the federal government, a state Attorney General or securities regulatory authority, any self-regulatory organization, or the Public Company Accounting Oversight Board, you must have voluntarily given such authorities the information within the meaning of these rules. You must establish your status as the original source of information to the Commission's satisfaction. In determining whether you are the original source of information, the Commission may seek assistance and confirmation from one of the other authorities described above, or from another entity (including your employer), in the event that you claim to be the original source of information that an authority or another entity provided to the Commission.

(6) If the Commission already knows some information about a matter from other sources at the time you make your submission, and you are not an original source of that information under paragraph (b)(5) of this section, the Commission will consider you an original source of any information you provide that is derived from your independent knowledge or analysis and that materially adds to the information that the Commission already possesses.

(7) If you provide information to the Congress, any other authority of the federal government, a state Attorney General or securities regulatory authority, any self-regulatory organization, or the Public Company Accounting Oversight Board, or to an entity's internal whistleblower, legal, or compliance procedures for reporting allegations of possible violations of law, and you, within 120 days, submit the same information to the Commission pursuant to § 240.21F-9 of this chapter, as you must do in order for you to be eligible to be considered for an award, then, for purposes of evaluating your claim to an award under §§ 240.21F-10 and 240.21F-11 of this chapter, the Commission will consider that you provided information as of the date of your original disclosure, report or submission to one of these other authorities or persons. You must establish the effective date of any prior disclosure, report, or submission, to the Commission's satisfaction. The Commission may seek assistance and confirmation from the other authority or person in making this determination.

(c) <u>Information that leads to successful enforcement</u>. The Commission will consider that you provided original information that led to the successful enforcement of a judicial or administrative action in any of the following circumstances:

(1) You gave the Commission original information that was sufficiently specific, credible, and timely to cause the staff to commence an examination, open an investigation, reopen an investigation that the Commission had closed, or to inquire concerning different conduct as part of a current examination or investigation, and the Commission brought a successful judicial or administrative action based in whole or in part on conduct that was the subject of your original information; or

(2) You gave the Commission original information about conduct that was already under examination or investigation by the Commission, the Congress, any other authority of the federal government, a state Attorney General or securities regulatory authority, any self-regulatory organization, or the PCAOB (except in cases where you were an original source of this information as defined in paragraph (b)(4) of this section), and your submission significantly contributed to the success of the action.

(3) You reported original information through an entity's internal whistleblower, legal, or compliance procedures for reporting allegations of possible violations of law before or at the same time you reported them to the Commission; the entity later provided your information to the Commission, or provided results of an audit or investigation initiated in whole or in part in response to information you reported to the entity; and the information the entity provided to the Commission satisfies either paragraph (c)(1) or (c)(2) of this section. Under this paragraph (c)(3), you must also submit the same information to the Commission in accordance with the procedures set forth in § 240.21F-9 within 120 days of providing it to the entity.

(d) An <u>action</u> generally means a single captioned judicial or administrative proceeding brought by the Commission. Notwithstanding the foregoing:

(1) For purposes of making an award under § 240.21F-10 of this chapter, the Commission will treat as a Commission action two or more administrative or judicial proceedings brought by the Commission if these proceedings arise out of the same nucleus of operative facts; or

(2) For purposes of determining the payment on an award under § 240.21F-14 of this chapter, the Commission will deem as part of the Commission action upon which the award was based any subsequent Commission proceeding that, individually, results in a monetary sanction of $1,000,000 or less, and that arises out of the same nucleus of operative facts.

(e) <u>Monetary sanctions</u> means any money, including penalties, disgorgement, and interest, ordered to be paid and any money deposited into a disgorgement fund or other fund pursuant to Section 308(b) of the Sarbanes-Oxley Act of 2002 (15 U.S.C. 7246(b)) as a result of a Commission action or a related action.

(f) <u>Appropriate regulatory agency</u> means the Commission, the Comptroller of the Currency, the Board of Governors of the Federal Reserve System, the Federal Deposit Insurance Corporation, the Office of Thrift Supervision, and any other agencies that may be defined as appropriate regulatory agencies under Section 3(a)(34) of the Exchange Act (15 U.S.C. 78c(a)(34)).

(g) <u>Appropriate regulatory authority</u> means an appropriate regulatory agency other than the Commission.

(h) <u>Self-regulatory organization</u> means any national securities exchange, registered securities association, registered clearing agency, the Municipal Securities Rulemaking Board, and any other organizations that may be defined as self-regulatory organizations under Section 3(a)(26) of the Exchange Act (15 U.S.C. 78c(a)(26)).

§ 240.21F-5 AMOUNT OF AWARD

(a) The determination of the amount of an award is in the discretion of the Commission.

(b) If all of the conditions are met for a whistleblower award in connection with a Commission action or a related action, the Commission will then decide the percentage amount of the award applying the criteria set forth in § 240.21F-6 of this chapter and pursuant to the procedures set forth in §§ 240.21F-10 and 240.21F-11 of this chapter. The amount will be at least 10 percent and no more than 30 percent of the monetary sanctions that the Commission and the other authorities are able to collect. The percentage awarded in connection with a Commission action may differ from the percentage awarded in connection with a related action.

(c) If the Commission makes awards to more than one whistleblower in connection with the same action or related action, the Commission will determine an individual percentage award for each whistleblower, but in no event will the total amount awarded to all whistleblowers in the aggregate be less than 10 percent or greater than 30 percent of the amount the Commission or the other authorities collect.

 ## § 240.21F-6 CRITERIA FOR DETERMINING AMOUNT OF AWARD

In exercising its discretion to determine the appropriate award percentage, the Commission may consider the following factors in relation to the unique facts and circumstances of each case, and may increase or decrease the award percentage based on its analysis of these factors. In the event that awards are determined for multiple whistleblowers in connection with an action, these factors will be used to determine the relative allocation of awards among the whistleblowers.

(a) <u>Factors that may increase the amount of a whistleblower's award</u>. In determining whether to increase the amount of an award, the Commission will consider the following factors, which are not listed in order of importance.

(1) <u>Significance of the information provided by the whistleblower</u>. The Commission will assess the significance of the information provided by a whistleblower to the success of the Commission action or related action. In considering this factor, the Commission may take into account, among other things:

(i) The nature of the information provided by the whistleblower and how it related to the successful enforcement action, including whether the reliability and completeness of the information provided to the Commission by the whistleblower resulted in the conservation of Commission resources;

(ii) The degree to which the information provided by the whistleblower supported one or more successful claims brought in the Commission or related action.

(2) <u>Assistance provided by the whistleblower</u>. The Commission will assess the degree of assistance provided by the whistleblower and any legal representative of the whistleblower in the Commission action or related action. In considering this factor, the Commission may take into account, among other things:

(i) Whether the whistleblower provided ongoing, extensive, and timely cooperation and assistance by, for example, helping to explain complex transactions, interpreting key evidence, or identifying new and productive lines of inquiry;

(ii) The timeliness of the whistleblower's initial report to the Commission or to an internal compliance or reporting system of business organizations committing, or impacted by, the securities violations, where appropriate;

(iii) The resources conserved as a result of the whistleblower's assistance;

(iv) Whether the whistleblower appropriately encouraged or authorized others to assist the staff of the Commission who might otherwise not have participated in the investigation or related action;

(v) The efforts undertaken by the whistleblower to remediate the harm caused by the violations, including assisting the authorities in the recovery of the fruits and instrumentalities of the violations; and

(vi) Any unique hardships experienced by the whistleblower as a result of his or her reporting and assisting in the enforcement action.

(3) <u>Law enforcement interest</u>. The Commission will assess its programmatic interest in deterring violations of the securities laws by making awards to whistleblowers who provide information that leads to the successful enforcement of such laws. In considering this factor, the Commission may take into account, among other things:

(i) The degree to which an award enhances the Commission's ability to enforce the federal securities laws and protect investors; and

(ii) The degree to which an award encourages the submission of high quality information from whistleblowers by appropriately rewarding whistleblowers' submission of significant information and assistance, even in cases where the monetary sanctions available for collection are limited or potential monetary sanctions were reduced or eliminated by the Commission because an entity self-reported a securities violation following the whistleblower's related internal disclosure, report, or submission.

(iii) Whether the subject matter of the action is a Commission priority, whether the reported misconduct involves regulated entities or fiduciaries, whether the whistleblower exposed an industry-wide practice, the type and severity of the securities violations, the age and duration of misconduct, the number of violations, and the isolated, repetitive, or ongoing nature of the violations; and

(iv) The dangers to investors or others presented by the underlying violations involved in the enforcement action, including the amount of harm or potential harm caused by the underlying violations, the type of harm resulting from or threatened by the underlying violations, and the number of individuals or entities harmed.

(4) <u>Participation in internal compliance systems</u>. The Commission will assess whether, and the extent to which, the whistleblower and any legal representative of the whistleblower participated in internal compliance systems. In considering this factor, the Commission may take into account, among other things:

(i) Whether, and the extent to which, a whistleblower reported the possible securities violations through internal whistleblower, legal or compliance procedures before, or at the same time as, reporting them to the Commission; and

(ii) Whether, and the extent to which, a whistleblower assisted any internal investigation or inquiry concerning the reported securities violations.

(b) <u>Factors that may decrease the amount of a whistleblower's award.</u> In determining whether to decrease the amount of an award, the Commission will consider the following factors, which are not listed in order of importance.

(1) <u>Culpability</u>. The Commission will assess the culpability or involvement of the whistleblower in matters associated with the Commission's action or related actions. In considering this factor, the Commission may take into account, among other things:

(i) The whistleblower's role in the securities violations;

(ii) The whistleblower's education, training, experience, and position of responsibility at the time the violations occurred;

(iii) Whether the whistleblower acted with scienter, both generally and in relation to others who participated in the violations;

(iv) Whether the whistleblower financially benefitted from the violations;

(v) Whether the whistleblower is a recidivist;

(vi) The egregiousness of the underlying fraud committed by the whistleblower; and

(vii) Whether the whistleblower knowingly interfered with the Commission's investigation of the violations or related enforcement actions.

(2) <u>Unreasonable reporting delay</u>. The Commission will assess whether the whistleblower unreasonably delayed reporting the securities violations. In considering this factor, the Commission may take into account, among other things:

(i) Whether the whistleblower was aware of the relevant facts but failed to take reasonable steps to report or prevent the violations from occurring or continuing;

(ii) Whether the whistleblower was aware of the relevant facts but only reported them after learning about a related inquiry, investigation, or enforcement action; and

(iii) Whether there was a legitimate reason for the whistleblower to delay reporting the violations.

(3) <u>Interference with internal compliance and reporting systems</u>. The Commission will assess, in cases where the whistleblower interacted with his or her entity's internal compliance or reporting system, whether the whistleblower undermined the integrity of such system. In considering this factor, the Commission will take into account whether there is evidence provided to the Commission that the whistleblower knowingly:

(i) Interfered with an entity's established legal, compliance, or audit procedures to prevent or delay detection of the reported securities violation;

(ii) Made any material false, fictitious, or fraudulent statements or representations that hindered an entity's efforts to detect, investigate, or remediate the reported securities violations; and

(iii) Provided any false writing or document knowing the writing or document contained any false, fictitious or fraudulent statements or entries that hindered an entity's efforts to detect, investigate, or remediate the reported securities violations.

§ 240.21F-7 CONFIDENTIALITY OF SUBMISSIONS

(a) Section 21F(h)(2) of the Exchange Act (15 U.S.C. 78u-6(h)(2)) requires that the Commission not disclose information that could reasonably be expected to reveal the identity of a whistleblower, except that the Commission may disclose such information in the following circumstances:

(1) When disclosure is required to a defendant or respondent in connection with a federal court or administrative action that the Commission files or in another public action or proceeding that is filed by an authority to which we provide the information, as described below:

(2) When the Commission determines that it is necessary to accomplish the purposes of the Exchange Act (15 U.S.C. 78a) and to protect investors, it may provide your information to the Department of Justice, an appropriate regulatory authority, a self-regulatory organization, a state attorney general in connection with a criminal investigation, any appropriate state regulatory authority, the Public Company Accounting Oversight Board, or foreign securities and law enforcement authorities. Each of these entities other than foreign securities and law enforcement authorities is subject to the confidentiality requirements set forth in Section 21F(h) of the Exchange Act (15 U.S.C. 78u-6(h)). The Commission will determine what assurances of confidentiality it deems appropriate in providing such information to foreign securities and law enforcement authorities.

(3) The Commission may make disclosures in accordance with the Privacy Act of 1974 (5 U.S.C. 552a).

(b) You may submit information to the Commission anonymously. If you do so, however, you must also do the following:

(1) You must have an attorney represent you in connection with both your submission of information and your claim for an award, and your attorney's name and contact information must be provided to the Commission at the time you submit your information;

(2) You and your attorney must follow the procedures set forth in § 240.21F-9 of this chapter for submitting original information anonymously; and

(3) Before the Commission will pay any award to you, you must disclose your identity to the Commission and your identity must be verified by the Commission as set forth in § 240.21F-10 of this chapter.

 ## § 240.21F-8 ELIGIBILITY

(a) To be eligible for a whistleblower award, you must give the Commission information in the form and manner that the Commission requires. The procedures for submitting information and making a claim for an award are described in § 240.21F-9 through § 240.21F-11 of this chapter. You should read these procedures carefully because you need to follow them in order to be eligible for an award, except that the Commission may, in its sole discretion, waive any of these procedures based upon a showing of extraordinary circumstances.

(b) In addition to any forms required by these rules, the Commission may also require that you provide certain additional information. You may be required to:

(1) Provide explanations and other assistance in order that the staff may evaluate and use the information that you submitted;

(2) Provide all additional information in your possession that is related to the subject matter of your submission in a complete and truthful manner, through follow-up meetings, or in other forms that our staff may agree to;

(3) Provide testimony or other evidence acceptable to the staff relating to whether you are eligible, or otherwise satisfy any of the conditions, for an award; and

(4) Enter into a confidentiality agreement in a form acceptable to the Office of the Whistleblower, covering any non-public information that the Commission provides to you, and including a provision that a violation of the agreement may lead to your ineligibility to receive an award.

(c) You are not eligible to be considered for an award if you do not satisfy the requirements of paragraphs (a) and (b) of this section. In addition, you are not eligible if:

(1) You are, or were at the time you acquired the original information provided to the Commission, a member, officer, or employee of the Commission, the Department of Justice, an appropriate regulatory agency, a self-regulatory organization, the Public Company Accounting Oversight Board, or any law enforcement organization;

(2) You are, or were at the time you acquired the original information provided to the Commission, a member, officer, or employee of a foreign government, any political subdivision, department, agency, or instrumentality of a foreign government, or any other foreign financial regulatory authority as that term is defined in Section 3(a)(52) of the Exchange Act (15 U.S.C. 78c(a)(52));

(3) You are convicted of a criminal violation that is related to the Commission action or to a related action (as defined in § 240.21F-4 of this chapter) for which you otherwise could receive an award;

(4) You obtained the original information that you gave the Commission through an audit of a company's financial statements, and making a whistleblower submission would be contrary to requirements of Section 10A of the Exchange Act (15 U.S.C. 78j-a).

(5) You are the spouse, parent, child, or sibling of a member or employee of the Commission, or you reside in the same household as a member or employee of the Commission;

(6) You acquired the original information you gave the Commission from a person:

(i) Who is subject to paragraph (c)(4) of this section, unless the information is not excluded from that person's use, or you are providing the Commission with information about possible violations involving that person; or

(ii) With the intent to evade any provision of these rules; or

(7) In your whistleblower submission, your other dealings with the Commission, or your dealings with another authority in connection with a related action, you knowingly and willfully make any false, fictitious, or fraudulent statement or representation, or use any false writing or document knowing that it contains any false, fictitious, or fraudulent statement or entry with intent to mislead or otherwise hinder the Commission or another authority.

§ 240.21F-9 PROCEDURES FOR SUBMITTING ORIGINAL INFORMATION

(a) To be considered a whistleblower under Section 21F of the Exchange Act (15 U.S.C. 78u-6(h)), you must submit your information about a possible securities law violation by either of these methods:

(1) Online, through the Commission's website located at www.sec.gov; or

(2) By mailing or faxing a Form TCR (Tip, Complaint or Referral) (referenced in § 249.1800 of this chapter) to the SEC Office of the Whistleblower, 100 F Street NE, Washington, DC 20549-5631, Fax (703) 813-9322.

(b) Further, to be eligible for an award, you must declare under penalty of perjury at the time you submit your information pursuant to paragraph (a) (1) or (2) of this section that your information is true and correct to the best of your knowledge and belief.

(c) Notwithstanding paragraphs (a) and (b) of this section, if you are providing your original information to the Commission anonymously, then your attorney must submit your information on your behalf pursuant to the procedures specified in paragraph (a) of this section. Prior to your attorney's submission, you must provide your attorney with a completed Form TCR (referenced in § 249.1800 of this chapter) that you have signed under penalty of perjury. When your attorney makes his or her submission on your behalf, your attorney will be required to certify that he or she:

(1) Has verified your identity;

(2) Has reviewed your completed and signed Form TCR (referenced in § 249.1800 of this chapter) for completeness and accuracy and that

the information contained therein is true, correct and complete to the best of the attorney's knowledge, information and belief;

(3) Has obtained your non-waivable consent to provide the Commission with your original completed and signed Form TCR (referenced in § 249.1800 of this chapter) in the event that the Commission requests it due to concerns that you may have knowingly and willfully made false, fictitious, or fraudulent statements or representations, or used any false writing or document knowing that the writing or document contains any false, fictitious or fraudulent statement or entry; and

(4) Consents to be legally obligated to provide the signed Form TCR (referenced in § 249.1800 of this chapter) within seven (7) calendar days of receiving such request from the Commission.

(d) If you submitted original information in writing to the Commission after July 21, 2010 (the date of enactment of the Dodd-Frank Wall Street Reform and Consumer Protection Act) but before the effective date of these rules, your submission will be deemed to satisfy the requirements set forth in paragraphs (a) and (b) of this section. If you were an anonymous whistleblower, however, you must provide your attorney with a completed and signed copy of Form TCR (referenced in § 249.1800 of this chapter) within 60 days of the effective date of these rules, your attorney must retain the signed form in his or her records, and you must provide of copy of the signed form to the Commission staff upon request by Commission staff prior to any payment of an award to you in connection with your submission. Notwithstanding the foregoing, you must follow the procedures and conditions for making a claim for a whistleblower award described in §§ 240.21F-10 and 240.21F-11 of this chapter.

§ 240.21F-10 PROCEDURES FOR MAKING A CLAIM FOR A WHISTLEBLOWER AWARD IN SEC ACTIONS THAT RESULT IN MONETARY SANCTIONS IN EXCESS OF $1,000,000

(a) Whenever a Commission action results in monetary sanctions totaling more than $1,000,000, the Office of the Whistleblower will cause to be published on the Commission's website a "Notice of Covered Action." Such Notice will be published subsequent to the entry of a final judgment or order that alone, or collectively with other judgments or orders previously entered in the Commission action, exceeds $1,000,000; or, in the absence of such judgment or order subsequent to the deposit of monetary sanctions exceeding $1,000,000 into a disgorgement or other fund pursuant to Section 308(b) of the Sarbanes-Oxley Act of 2002. A claimant will have ninety (90) days from the date of the Notice of Covered Action to file a claim for an award based on that action, or the claim will be barred.

(b) To file a claim for a whistleblower award, you must file Form WB-APP, *Application for Award for Original Information Provided Pursuant to Section 21F of the Securities Exchange Act of 1934* (referenced in § 249.1801 of this chapter). You must sign this form as the claimant and submit it to the Office of the Whistleblower by mail or fax. All claim forms, including any attachments, must be received by the Office of the Whistleblower within ninety (90) calendar days of the date of the Notice of Covered Action in order to be considered for an award.

(c) If you provided your original information to the Commission anonymously, you must disclose your identity on the Form WB-APP (referenced in § 249.1801 of this chapter), and your identity must be verified in a form and manner that is acceptable to the Office of the Whistleblower prior to the payment of any award.

(d) Once the time for filing any appeals of the Commission's judicial or administrative action has expired, or where an appeal has been filed, after all appeals in the action have been concluded, the staff designated by the Director of the Division of Enforcement ("Claims Review Staff") will evaluate all timely whistleblower award claims submitted on Form WB-APP (referenced in § 249.1801 of this chapter) in accordance with the criteria set forth in these rules. In connection with this process, the Office of the Whistleblower may require that you provide additional information relating to your eligibility for an award or satisfaction of any of the conditions for an award, as set forth in § 240.21F-(8)(b) of this chapter. Following that evaluation, the Office of the Whistleblower will send you a Preliminary Determination setting forth a preliminary assessment as to whether the claim should be allowed or denied and, if allowed, setting forth the proposed award percentage amount.

(e) You may contest the Preliminary Determination made by the Claims Review Staff by submitting a written response to the Office of the Whistleblower setting forth the grounds for your objection to either the denial of an award or the proposed amount of an award. The response must be in the form and manner that the Office of the Whistleblower shall require. You may also include documentation or other evidentiary support for the grounds advanced in your response.

(1) Before determining whether to contest a Preliminary Determination, you may:

(i) Within thirty (30) days of the date of the Preliminary Determination, request that the Office of the Whistleblower make available for your review the materials from among those set forth in § 240.21F-12(a) of this chapter that formed the basis of the Claims Review Staff's Preliminary Determination.

(ii) Within thirty (30) calendar days of the date of the Preliminary Determination, request a meeting with the Office of the Whistleblower; however, such meetings are not required and the office may in its sole discretion decline the request.

(2) If you decide to contest the Preliminary Determination, you must submit your written response and supporting materials within sixty (60) calendar days of the date of the Preliminary Determination, or if a request to review materials is made pursuant to paragraph (e)(1) of this section, then within sixty (60) calendar days of the Office of the Whistleblower making those materials available for your review.

(f) If you fail to submit a timely response pursuant to paragraph (e) of this section, then the Preliminary Determination will become the Final Order of the Commission (except where the Preliminary Determination recommended an award, in which case the Preliminary Determination will be deemed a Proposed Final Determination for purposes of paragraph (h) of this section). Your failure to submit a timely response contesting a Preliminary Determination will constitute a failure to exhaust administrative remedies, and you will be prohibited from pursuing an appeal pursuant to § 240.21F-13 of this chapter.

(g) If you submit a timely response pursuant to paragraph (e) of this section, then the Claims Review Staff will consider the issues and grounds advanced in your response, along with any supporting documentation you provided, and will make its Proposed Final Determination.

(h) The Office of the Whistleblower will then notify the Commission of each Proposed Final Determination. Within thirty (30) days thereafter, any Commissioner may request that the Proposed Final Determination be reviewed by the Commission. If no Commissioner requests such a review within the 30-day period, then the Proposed Final Determination will become the Final Order of the Commission. In the event a Commissioner requests a review, the Commission will review the record that the staff relied upon in making its determinations, including your previous submissions to the Office of the Whistleblower, and issue its Final Order.

(i) The Office of the Whistleblower will provide you with the Final Order of the Commission.

§ 240.21F-11 PROCEDURES FOR DETERMINING AWARDS BASED UPON A RELATED ACTION

(a) If you are eligible to receive an award following a Commission action that results in monetary sanctions totaling more than $1,000,000, you also may be eligible to receive an award based on the monetary sanctions that are collected from a related action (as defined in § 240.21F-3 of this chapter).

(b) You must also use Form WB-APP (referenced in § 249.1801 of this chapter) to submit a claim for an award in a related action. You must sign this form as the claimant and submit it to the Office of the Whistleblower by mail or fax as follows:

(1) If a final order imposing monetary sanctions has been entered in a related action at the time you submit your claim for an award in connection with a Commission action, you must submit your claim for an award in that related action on the same Form WB-APP (referenced in § 249.1801 of this chapter) that you use for the Commission action.

(2) If a final order imposing monetary sanctions in a related action has not been entered at the time you submit your claim for an award in connection with a Commission action, you must submit your claim on Form WB-APP (referenced in § 249.1801 of this chapter) within ninety (90) days of the issuance of a final order imposing sanctions in the related action.

(c) The Office of the Whistleblower may request additional information from you in connection with your claim for an award in a related action to demonstrate that you directly (or through the Commission) voluntarily provided the governmental agency, regulatory authority or self-regulatory organization the same original information that led to the Commission's successful covered action, and that this information led to the successful enforcement of the related action. The Office of the Whistleblower may, in its discretion, seek assistance and confirmation from the other agency in making this determination.

(d) Once the time for filing any appeals of the final judgment or order in a related action has expired, or if an appeal has been filed, after all appeals in the action have been concluded, the Claims Review Staff will evaluate all timely whistleblower award claims submitted on Form WB-APP (referenced in § 249.1801 of this chapter) in connection with the related action. The evaluation will be undertaken pursuant to the criteria set forth in these rules. In connection with this process, the Office of the Whistleblower may require that you provide additional information relating to your eligibility for an award or satisfaction of any of the conditions for an award, as set forth in § 240.21F-(8)(b) of this chapter. Following this evaluation, the Office of the Whistleblower will send you a Preliminary Determination setting forth a preliminary assessment as to whether the claim should be allowed or denied and, if allowed, setting forth the proposed award percentage amount.

(e) You may contest the Preliminary Determination made by the Claims Review Staff by submitting a written response to the Office of the Whistleblower setting forth the grounds for your objection to either the denial of an award or the proposed amount of an award. The response must be in the form and manner that the Office of the Whistleblower shall require. You may also include documentation or other evidentiary support for the grounds advanced in your response.

(1) Before determining whether to contest a Preliminary Determination, you may:

(i) Within thirty (30) days of the date of the Preliminary Determination, request that the Office of the Whistleblower make available for your review the materials from among those set forth in § 240.21F-12(a) of this chapter that formed the basis of the Claims Review Staff's Preliminary Determination.

(ii) Within thirty (30) days of the date of the Preliminary Determination, request a meeting with the Office of the Whistleblower; however, such meetings are not required and the office may in its sole discretion decline the request.

(2) If you decide to contest the Preliminary Determination, you must submit your written response and supporting materials within sixty (60) calendar days of the date of the Preliminary Determination, or if a request to review materials is made pursuant to paragraph (e)(1)(i) of this section, then within sixty (60) calendar days of the Office of the Whistleblower making those materials available for your review.

(f) If you fail to submit a timely response pursuant to paragraph (e) of this section, then the Preliminary Determination will become the Final Order of the Commission (except where the Preliminary Determination recommended an award, in which case the Preliminary Determination will be deemed a Proposed Final Determination for purposes of paragraph (h) of this section). Your failure to submit a timely response contesting a Preliminary Determination will constitute a failure to exhaust administrative remedies, and you will be prohibited from pursuing an appeal pursuant to § 240.21F-13 of this chapter.

(g) If you submit a timely response pursuant to paragraph (e) of this section, then the Claims Review Staff will consider the issues and grounds that you advanced in your response, along with any supporting documentation you provided, and will make its Proposed Final Determination.

(h) The Office of the Whistleblower will notify the Commission of each Proposed Final Determination. Within thirty (30) days thereafter, any

Commissioner may request that the Proposed Final Determination be reviewed by the Commission. If no Commissioner requests such a review within the 30-day period, then the Proposed Final Determination will become the Final Order of the Commission. In the event a Commissioner requests a review, the Commission will review the record that the staff relied upon in making its determinations, including your previous submissions to the Office of the Whistleblower, and issue its Final Order.

(i) The Office of the Whistleblower will provide you with the Final Order of the Commission.

§ 240.21F-12 MATERIALS THAT MAY FORM THE BASIS OF AN AWARD DETERMINATION AND THAT MAY COMPRISE THE RECORD ON APPEAL

(a) The following items constitute the materials that the Commission and the Claims Review Staff may rely upon to make an award determination pursuant to §§ 240.21F-10 and 240.21F-11 of this chapter:

(1) Any publicly available materials from the covered action or related action, including:

(i) The complaint, notice of hearing, answers and any amendments thereto;

(ii) The final judgment, consent order, or final administrative order;

(iii) Any transcripts of the proceedings, including any exhibits;

(iv) Any items that appear on the docket; and

(v) Any appellate decisions or orders.

(2) The whistleblower's Form TCR (referenced in § 249.1800 of this chapter), including attachments, and other related materials provided by the whistleblower to assist the Commission with the investigation or examination;

(3) The whistleblower's Form WB-APP (referenced in § 249.1800 of this chapter), including attachments, and any other filings or submissions from the whistleblower in support of the award application;

(4) Sworn declarations (including attachments) from the Commission staff regarding any matters relevant to the award determination;

(5) With respect to an award claim involving a related action, any statements or other information that the entity provides or identifies in connection with an award determination, provided the entity has authorized the Commission to share the information with the claimant. (Neither the Commission nor the Claims Review Staff may rely upon information that the entity has not authorized the Commission to share with the claimant); and

(6) Any other documents or materials including sworn declarations from third-parties that are received or obtained by the Office of the Whistleblower to assist the Commission resolve the claimant's award application, including information related to the claimant's eligibility. (Neither the Commission nor the Claims Review Staff may rely upon information that the entity has not authorized the Commission to share with the claimant).

(b) These rules do not entitle claimants to obtain from the Commission any materials (including any pre-decisional or internal deliberative process materials that are prepared exclusively to assist the Commission in deciding the claim) other than those listed in paragraph (a) of this section. Moreover, the Office of the Whistleblower may make redactions as necessary to comply with any statutory restrictions, to protect the Commission's law enforcement and regulatory functions, and to comply with requests for confidential treatment from other law enforcement and regulatory authorities. The Office of the Whistleblower may also require you to sign a confidentiality agreement, as set forth in § 240.21F-(8)(b)(4) of this chapter, before providing these materials.

§ 240.21F-13 APPEALS

(a) Section 21F of the Exchange Act (15 U.S.C. 78u-6) commits determinations of whether, to whom, and in what amount to make awards to the Commission's discretion. A determination of whether or to whom to make an award may be appealed within 30 days after the Commission issues its final decision to the United States Court of Appeals for the District of Columbia Circuit, or to the circuit where the aggrieved person resides or has his principal place of business. Where the Commission makes an award based on the factors set forth in § 240.21F-6 of this chapter of not less than 10 percent and not more than 30 percent of the monetary sanctions collected in the Commission or related action, the Commission's determination regarding the amount of an award (including the allocation of an award as between multiple whistleblowers, and any factual findings, legal conclusions, policy judgments, or discretionary assessments involving the Commission's consideration of the factors in § 240.21F-6 of this chapter) is not appealable.

(b) The record on appeal shall consist of the Preliminary Determination, the Final Order of the Commission, and any other items from those set forth in § 240.21F-12(a) of this chapter that either the claimant or the Commission identifies for inclusion in the record. The record on appeal shall not include any pre-decisional or internal deliberative process materials that are prepared exclusively to assist the Commission in deciding the claim (including the staff's Draft Final Determination in the event that the Commissioners reviewed the claim and issued the Final Order).

§ 240.21F-14 PROCEDURES APPLICABLE TO THE PAYMENT OF AWARDS

(a) Any award made pursuant to these rules will be paid from the Securities and Exchange Commission Investor Protection Fund (the "Fund").

(b) A recipient of a whistleblower award is entitled to payment on the award only to the extent that a monetary sanction is collected in the Commission action or in a related action upon which the award is based.

(c) Payment of a whistleblower award for a monetary sanction collected in a Commission action or related action shall be made following the later of:

(1) The date on which the monetary sanction is collected; or

(2) The completion of the appeals process for all whistleblower award claims arising from:

(i) The Notice of Covered Action, in the case of any payment of an award for a monetary sanction collected in a Commission action; or

(ii) The related action, in the case of any payment of an award for a monetary sanction collected in a related action.

(d) If there are insufficient amounts available in the Fund to pay the entire amount of an award payment within a reasonable period of time from the time for payment specified by paragraph (c) of this section, then subject to the following terms, the balance of the payment shall be paid when amounts become available in the Fund, as follows:

(1) Where multiple whistleblowers are owed payments from the Fund based on awards that do not arise from the same Notice of Covered Action (or related action), priority in making these payments will be determined based upon the date that the collections for which the whistleblowers are owed payments occurred. If two or more of these collections occur on the same date, those whistleblowers owed payments based on these collections will be paid on a pro rata basis until sufficient amounts become available in the Fund to pay their entire payments.

(2) Where multiple whistleblowers are owed payments from the Fund based on awards that arise from the same Notice of Covered Action (or related action), they will share the same payment priority and will be paid on a pro rata basis until sufficient amounts become available in the Fund to pay their entire payments.

§ 240.21F-15 NO AMNESTY

The Securities Whistleblower Incentives and Protection provisions do not provide amnesty to individuals who provide information to the Commission. The fact that you may become a whistleblower and assist in Commission investigations and enforcement actions does not preclude the Commission from bringing an action against you based upon your own conduct in connection with violations of the federal securities laws. If such an action is determined to be appropriate, however, the Commission will take your cooperation into consideration in accordance with its Policy Statement Concerning Cooperation by Individuals in Investigations and Related Enforcement Actions (17 CFR § 202.12).

§ 240.21F-16 AWARDS TO WHISTLEBLOWERS WHO ENGAGE IN CULPABLE CONDUCT

In determining whether the required $1,000,000 threshold has been satisfied (this threshold is further explained in § 240.21F-10 of this chapter) for purposes of making any award, the Commission will not take into account any monetary sanctions that the whistleblower is ordered to pay, or that are ordered against any entity whose liability is based substantially on conduct that the whistleblower directed, planned, or initiated. Similarly, if the Commission determines that a whistleblower is eligible for an award, any amounts that the whistleblower or such an entity pays in sanctions as a result of the action or related actions will not be included within the calculation of the amounts collected for purposes of making payments.

§ 240.21F-17 STAFF COMMUNICATIONS WITH INDIVIDUALS REPORTING POSSIBLE SECURITIES LAW VIOLATIONS

(a) No person may take any action to impede an individual from communicating directly with the Commission staff about a possible securities law violation, including enforcing, or threatening to enforce, a confidentiality agreement (other than agreements dealing with information covered by § 240.21F-4(b)(4)(i) and § 240.21F-4(b)(4)(ii) of this chapter related to the legal representation of a client) with respect to such communications.

(b) If you are a director, officer, member, agent, or employee of an entity that has counsel, and you have initiated communication with the Commission relating to a possible securities law violation, the staff is authorized to communicate directly with you regarding the possible securities law violation without seeking the consent of the entity's counsel.

About the Author

FREDERICK D. LIPMAN is a senior partner with the international law firm of Blank Rome LLP and also the president of the Association of Audit Committee Members, Inc., a nonprofit organization devoted to developing best practices for audit committees. He was a lecturer in the MBA program at the Wharton School of Business and at the University of Pennsylvania Law School. A graduate of Harvard Law School, he has more than 50 years' experience in corporate governance, mergers and acquisitions, and initial public offerings. Mr. Lipman is the author of 13 other books, including *Executive Compensation Best Practices* (John Wiley & Sons, 2008), *Corporate Governance Best Practices* (John Wiley & Sons, 2006), and *Audit Committees* (Bureau of National Affairs, Inc., 2010). He has appeared on television programs on CNBC, CNN, Bloomberg, and Chinese television as a national commentator on business topics and has lectured internationally in China, India, and Thailand. He has been quoted in the *Wall Street Journal*, the *New York Times*, *USA Today*, *Forbes*, and other business publications. Mr. Lipman is located in the Philadelphia, PA, office of Blank Rome LLP.

Index